The Future of Economics

The Future of Economics

Edited by

John D. Hey

BLACKWELL
Oxford UK & Cambridge USA

Copyright © Royal Economic Society 1992

First published 1992

Blackwell Publishers
108 Cowley Road
Oxford OX4 1JF
UK

3 Cambridge Center
Cambridge, Massachusetts 02142
USA

British Library Cataloguing in Publication Data

A CIP catalogue record for this book is available from
the British Library.

Library of Congress Cataloging-in-Publication Data

ISBN 0–631–18493–7   ISBN 0–631–18487–2 (pbk)

Typeset in 10½ on 12½pt Baskerville
by Cambridge University Press
Printed in Great Britain by Biddles Ltd, Guildford

This book is printed on acid-free paper

CONTENTS

CONTRIBUTORS

William J. Baumol is Professor of Economics at Princeton and New York Universities.

Jagdish Bhagwati is Arthur Lehman Professor of Economics, Columbia University in the City of New York.

James M. Buchanan is Advisory General Director, Harris University Professor, and Nobel Laureate in Economics, 1986, Center for Study of Public Choice, George Mason University.

Partha Dasgupta is Professor of Economics and Philosophy, Stanford University and Professor of Economics, University of Cambridge.

Peter C. Fishburn is Distinguished Member of the Technical Staff, AT & T Bell Laboratories, Murray Hill, New Jersey.

Milton Friedman is Professor Emeritus of Economics, University of Chicago, and Senior Research Fellow, Hoover Institution, Stanford University.

John K. Galbraith is Paul M. Warburg Professor of Economics, Emeritus, Harvard University. Past President of the American Economic Association and American Academy and Institute of Arts and Letters.

Frank Hahn is Professor of Economics in the University of Cambridge and Fellow of Churchill College, Cambridge.

Jack Johnston is Professor of Econometrics, University of California, Irvine and Fellow of the Econometric Society.

John A. Kay is Chairman of London Economics, a group providing specialist economic consulting services to businesses. He is also Professor of Economics at the London Business School and a Fellow of St John's College, Oxford.

E. E. Malinvaud is Professor au College de France.

Michio Morishima is Professor Emeritus, University of London and formerly Sir John Hicks Professor of Economics, London School of Economics.

Andrew J. Oswald is Senior Research Fellow, Centre for Economic Performance, London School of Economics.

John Pencavel is Professor of Economics, Stanford University and Editor of the *Journal of Economic Literature*.

Charles R. Plott is the Edward S. Harkness Professor of Economics and Political Science, Division of Humanities and Social Sciences, California Institute of Technology.

Austin Robinson is Emeritus Professor of Economics, Cambridge University.

Alvin E. Roth is the Andrew Mellon Professor of Economics at the University of Pittsburgh.

Richard Schmalensee is Gordon Y. Billard Professor of Economics and Management at the Massachusetts Institute of Technology, and Director of MIT's Center for Energy Policy Research. Member of the President's Council of Economic Advisers from 1989 through to 1991.

Nicholas Stern is the Sir John Hicks Professor of Economics at the London School of Economics and Political Science and Chairman of the Suntory–Toyota International Centre for Economics and Related Disciplines.

Joseph E. Stiglitz is Professor of Economics, Stanford University.

Stephen J. Turnovsky is Professor of Economics at the University of Washington, Seattle and Research Associate of the National Bureau of Economic Research, Cambridge, Massachusetts.

Jack Wiseman 1919–1991, late Professor Emeritus, University of York.

PREFACE

The first issue of volume 101 of the ECONOMIC JOURNAL, published in January 1991, was special not only because it was the first issue of the second century of the JOURNAL's existence and the first issue of the first 6-issues-a-year volume, but also because it was specially commissioned. It was specially commissioned to look forward to the economics of the coming century. The invited authors were all distinguished economists who, at one time or another, had published in the ECONOMIC JOURNAL in its first century. I put no constraints on their response (except length) and invited them to respond freely to the question 'The Next 100 Years?' Of the economists whom I invited, some declined (some on the grounds that economists were not particularly good at forecasting the future); others accepted but did not deliver; while others accepted and delivered. This volume is the result.

Although a little like the curate's egg, the issue as a whole makes interesting and provocative reading. While some authors have returned to well-trodden fields, others have taken the opportunity to cast caution to the wind – secure in the knowledge that they will not be around when their predictions come home to roost! The visions most writers paint of their predicted futures are constructive ones; if all their predictions come to pass, the next one hundred years will be exciting and fruitful for economists and economics.

We shall see.

John D. Hey

BUCKINGHAM PALACE

19th February, 1990.

Dear Mr Hey.

    I am commanded by The Queen to thank you
for your kind and loyal message of greetings,
sent on the occasion of the Centenary of "The
Economic Journal".

    As Patron of the Society, Her Majesty
received this message with much pleasure and
sends you her best wishes for an enjoyable
and successful start to the second century.

Yours sincerely,

Kenneth Scott

(KENNETH SCOTT)

John Hey, Esq.

TOWARD A NEWER ECONOMICS: THE FUTURE LIES AHEAD!

*William J. Baumol**

My title is about as far as I have ever been willing to go in the way of prognostication. Surely, the mind-boggling political events of 1989 in eastern Europe, with their equally mind-boggling implications, should have tempered any urge to engage in long-term prediction (and perhaps for shorter-run use of the crystal ball as well). Despite the comforting reassurance offered to the authors here that they will certainly be dead long before their forecasts can possibly be tested against reality, I feel obliged to confess that I can offer with any degree of confidence only one prediction – that the future will surprise me.[1]

So, rather than attempting to suggest what I believe the future will bring to our discipline, this note will offer a wish list of what this author *hopes* the next hundred years will provide, without implying any confidence that it will actually do so. Four subjects will be discussed: research methods, teaching matter, subjects for relatively pure research and topics for applied economics.

I. ON RESEARCH METHOD[2]

A. The Role of Mathematics

We superannuated practitioners of our discipline can still remember the time when those who made use of mathematical analysis in their theoretical work

* The author is grateful to the C. V. Starr Center for Applied Economics for its support in the preparation of this paper. For the second half of the title he is indebted to Mort Sahl.

[1] I know of only one exception – of something that one *can* predict for the longer run with some degree of confidence. If I may be permitted a bit of self indulgence, I refer to what has come to be called 'the cost disease of the stagnant services', that is, the difficulty of achieving continuing increases in productivity in services such as teaching, health care, postal services, legal services and the performing arts. Nearly a quarter century ago W. G. Bowen and I proposed that this would lead to real price increases for these items that would be persistent and cumulative, and that if relative outputs of these items did not fall, they must absorb increasing shares of the economy's labour force and its GNP. Subsequent developments have borne all this out, and have also borne out the implications for quality of such activities as elementary education, postal service and urban street cleaning that the early discussions raised. Despite all this and the seriousness of the prospects raised by the cost disease I doubt whether economists will in the future engage in a great deal of research on the subject because it does not seem to lend itself to esoteric theoretical constructs, and the analysis of the pertinent data seems fairly straightforward and unambiguous in its results.

[2] The title of this section is a calculated attempt to defend the English language (shades of Fritz Machlup!). Writers, these days, are all too prone to use the term 'methodology' for the purpose, presumably because it has an aura of profundity. But the dictionary reminds us that 'methodology' is the discipline whose focus is the study of method. Clearly, the topic here is the latter, and certainly cannot pretend to be a contribution to the branch of formal logic that deals with methodology.

[1]

were expected to begin with a few words of apology, arguing, or at least asserting, that employment of this tool did not necessarily make the resulting work less 'realistic' or less relevant. Even so, it was customary for the algebra to be relegated to an appendix where it would not disturb the sensibilities of the normal reader. As one of those who worked with some determination to change this state of affairs and to introduce some grounding in mathematics as a standard part of the postgraduate curriculum in several universities, it may be pardonable for me to suggest that things may have gone a bit far in the opposite direction.

In saying this I should not be interpreted as arguing that the *Journal of Economic Theory* would best be abolished, or that other fields should be plowed by those of our colleagues or students whose awesome mastery of mathematics elicits our admiration and despair. There surely is no philosopher's stone in economic method – no one approach whose unqualified success and power mean that it deserves to replace all (or even any) of its rivals. *Every* method used in the social sciences has its glaring shortcomings which one can only hope to ameliorate by recourse, as a supplement, to other approaches. Here, if anywhere, there is need to let a thousand flowers bloom, and there is, consequently, no reason to impede or discourage the work of even the most abstraction-minded and esoteric of mathematical economists. In short, I believe their work should be afforded all possible protection and support, within suitable limits imposed by availability of resources.

But, surely, the problem is not that mathematical economists are in need of protection from others; rather, the peril is the reverse. These days few specialised students are allowed to proceed without devoting a very considerable portion of their time to the acquisition of mathematical tools, and they often come away feeling that any piece of writing they produce will automatically be rejected as unworthy if it is not liberally sprinkled with an array of algebraic symbols.

There are at least two grounds on which such a state of affairs is to be deplored – its preclusion of other promising lines of attack, and its consequences for those students whose talents are for approaches other than the mathematical.

There can hardly be any argument with the proposition that the use of mathematical methods has not solved all problems in economic analysis, and that some problems lend themselves more readily to statistical, experimental, historical or other lines of attack. While formal mathematical theory has made invaluable contributions in fields where its success might have caused considerable surprise in an earlier day – fields such as public finance and industrial organisation – each of these areas surely still leaves considerable scope for other research procedures. And there are still other areas, for example, labour economics, in which this is probably even truer. The trouble is that if individuals are not respected for the pursuit of alternative approaches, if only those whose writings are pockmarked by algebraic symbols receive kudos, one can expect a misallocation of resources like that which always results from a distortion of relative prices.

The second consequence follows from the first; not only can we expect more than the optimal amount of study and publication to be based on mathematical methods, but we can expect people to be induced to adopt this approach even though they are relatively poorly endowed with the requisite talents. Graduate programmes, for example, will be burdened with a spate of dissertations that qualify primarily as mathematical (or econometric) exercises whose sole *raison d'etre* seems to be the opportunity they afford to their authors to display whatever facility they can muster in manipulation of the tools of abstraction. Even the most mathematically-oriented of our colleagues will undoubtedly agree that this is what has already happened.

B. The Short-Run Orientation of Macroeconomics

When Keynes led the way for macroeconomics to become a major branch of our discipline, part of his legacy to future specialists in this field was a preoccupation with the short run. Given the critical and immediate economic problems facing society at the time the *General Theory* was written Keynes' orientation was entirely understandable – it was the right thing to do. There is no reason to consider unemployment and depression to be problems of the long run, and there can be no question that in 1936 these were the subjects to which highest priority had to be given. Nor has the short run lost its importance since that time, as is demonstrated by today's very appropriate preoccupation with balance of payments problems, the threat of inflation and governmental budget deficits. But recognition of the significance of short-run issues does not justify inattention to those of the longer run.

Things were not always thus. The classical and neo-classical economists were prone to concern themselves largely with the long run – with equilibria that one could only expect to be approximated eventually – and they paid limited attention to the nature of the transition paths along which movement toward such an equilibrium might proceed.

There are at least two major grounds for encouragement of increased attention to the longer run by academic economists. First, of course, is the inherent importance of developments for which substantial periods of time are required. This is particularly true of topics such as productivity growth, where compounding plays a critical role. Changes in productivity growth rates that fall within any plausible range are unlikely to produce any substantial consequences for the economy in a matter of a few months or several years. Yet, in the course of, say, five decades they are apt to compound dramatically. For this reason it would seem that growth in productivity and other macroeconomic aggregates is a subject particularly suited for study in long-run rather than short-run terms. And it is at least arguable that there are few if any areas more important than growth for the wealth of nations, that is, for the topic that was at least at one time considered the prime preoccupation of our discipline.

The second reason it is incumbent upon academic economists to devote some attention to the longer run is that there probably is no one else available to do it. Business persons, politicians and civil servants all too often find themselves forced to work from crisis to crisis, and to struggle incessantly to bring today's and tomorrow's problems under control. This sort of obligation is hardly conducive to reasoned consideration of the requisites for effective long-run policy. Yet, failure to consider well in advance the needs of the distant future can contribute or exacerbate the crises of the day after tomorrow that will in their turn monopolise the attention of the practising decision makers. If academic economists also are prone to devote little effort to the analysis of long-run issues, it is all too likely that this critical task will be neglected altogether.

II. DESIDERATA FOR FUTURE RESEARCH ORIENTATION

The comments of the two preceding sections telegraph my wish list for tomorrow's research orientation. Clearly, I am hoping for some changes in the degree of reliance upon mathematical tools and some modification of the predilection of macro economists for concern with the short run. In saying this I must make it clear that I am not seeking any reduction either in the work which is at the cutting edge of new mathematical economics, or for neglect of the important short-run subjects to which macroeconomic analysis has addressed itself far more successfully than it is nowadays fashionable to admit. But from others whose comparative advantage does not assign them unambiguously to analysis at the highest level of abstraction or to exclusive concern with the shorter-run side of economic issues I seek considerably more eclecticism and even for some increase in the number of those who choose to specialise elsewhere. In sum, I hope that current fashions in economics, like fashion in other fields, will wane after a time. But I look for them only to wane – to give up their undisputed position at the summit of the hierarchy – not to vanish or to remain only as minor vestiges, because both abstract analysis and short-run macroeconomics have already contributed a great deal and still have much to contribute.

This is the obvious general conclusion which follows from my previous discussion. However, there are additional and more-specific implications for curriculum and for the orientation of pure and applied research. Let me, then, consider each of these topics in turn.

III. ON FUTURE CURRICULUM

The modification in curriculum to which I look forward is in some degree a return to the past – but not entirely. For undergraduates I would advocate a greater emphasis on econometrics, stressing its techniques, practice in its use and avoidance of its pitfalls. I would hope for some of this to penetrate even first-year courses which are taken by students who may never have another course in economics. Since an increase in the time spent on this subject presumably requires an offsetting reduction in some other area, it would seem to me that some of the more-abstract portion of the microeconomics curriculum is a prime candidate for omission or compression. It is hardly plausible that a student who will not specialise in economics will get much out of indifference maps and Slutsky theorems, and one can be reasonably confident that anything the student learns on such matters will be forgotten rapidly (and with some enthusiasm) once the final course examination has been taken. On the other hand, most students are likely at some time or other to be faced with tasks entailing empirical analysis or at least readings that contain such materials. Here a little bit of teaching time can help to arm the student against naivete and shoddy reasoning.

For the graduate student I would also urge emphasis on training in the tools of econometrics; but this is already rather common, so there is probably little need for change here. The change I do hope for is the reintroduction of emphasis on the teaching of economic history, with some effort to induce it to be taken by all students who are not expecting to specialise in pure theory. It seems to me that many institutional areas lend themselves to study via historical materials, and in some it may not even be possible to carry out effective research without them. Besides, for those whose forte is not a high level of abstraction, history is apt to prove a very good source of ideas and is apt to contribute considerably to general understanding. It should also provide vital practice in the empirical analysis of messy and complicated problems of which economic history has an endless supply.

In addition, I should hope that every student who does not specialise in pure theory will be expected in the future to master several institutional areas, to carry out some research in at least two of them, and to write reports on the results which meet professional standards of exposition. This would serve several purposes which, to me, are matters of high priority: it will increase the student's grasp of the workings of some element of the economy as it operates in reality, it will offer the student practice in research techniques before the doctoral dissertation is begun and it will end the current tendency to neglect professional writing techniques which sends the students out from the universities unprepared in the use of the one tool that is likely to play a critical role in the future of virtually every one of them.

It might be suspected from my advocacy of a revival of widespread study of economic history that I take a similar view about a course in the history of economic ideas. Yet, though I have taught such a course for many years, I am much more skeptical about any attempt to inveigle more students in that direction. It is my belief that much attention is paid to the work of the past only in fields where there is currently little progress at the frontier. In rapidly-evolving disciplines such as physics, history of thought is not unknown as a field of study, but the high opportunity cost of the time that it requires drives most students elsewhere. Undoubtedly, an understanding of the history of economic analysis has some value for every student and may prevent the waste of effort entailed in rediscovery of what was already known. Still, there are undoubtedly matters of greater urgency demanding the student's very scarce time, and so it is my predisposition to leave the area to those who are attracted to it (or to any other specialised research area) by what Veblen described as 'idle curiosity'.

IV. ON SUBJECTS FOR TOMORROW'S BASIC RESEARCH

It should by now be obvious that I am hoping that the future will bring some decrease in the display of technique for its own sake, with models constructed so as to increase what they tell us about the workings of the economy rather than just displaying the properties of some analytical procedure. This is not repetition of the ancient and tired demand for enhancement of the 'realism' of our models, for it is perfectly clear that there is a trade off between the analytic tractability of a model and the degree to which it incorporates the complex minutiae of reality, and that this trade off often does not favour the latter. The desire for economic pertinence of our constructs is *not* tantamount to a wish for unworkable complication. The contrary is apt to be closer to the truth.

An illustration of what that hope for the future does entail is provided by the current research in behavioural economics. A group of able economists and psychologists has, for some time, sought experimental and other types of empirical evidence on the ways that economic agents actually behave, and they have shown that in at least some arenas this behaviour deviates substantially and systematically from what the formal rationality premise leads us to believe. For example, there is ample evidence that sunk outlays do matter in ways that they should not to a 'rational consumer', and that changes in apparently irrelevant ancillary circumstances that constitute the decision-making environment can alter systematically the outcome of the decision process even if they do not affect the nature of the 'optimal' decision.

Behavioural economists have been disappointed by the quiet reception that has greeted their findings, and the fact that there has been little effort to incorporate those results in the central corpus of mainstream analysis. I believe one reason those results have tended to be ignored is that there has been too little analytic work examining whether and, if so, where, and to what extent, such behavioural anomalies can be expected to affect the behaviour and performance of markets. There are clearly some circumstances in which 'irrational behaviour' serves only to create the opportunity for profitable arbitrage that can be relied upon to undo its effects in short order. For example, if such behaviour affects the exchange rates of the currencies of three countries in such a way that it is cheaper to use currency A to buy B and then to exchange B for C, instead of trading A for C directly, it is clear that a quick and substantial profit can be made in the process of bringing the exchange rates into line. However, one can think of other circumstances in which incompleteness of markets, high transaction costs or other impediments prevent or inhibit such arbitrage. One should hope that the future will provide a more general theory that investigates more clearly where such behavioural considerations can be expected to make a significant difference for market behaviour and which indicates the nature of the difference it is likely to make.

The case of behavioural economics is meant only to be illustrative, suggesting the sorts of direction pure economics will have to take if it is to pursue the goal of greater pertinence. I hope that the future will bring forth effort on this and other parallel lines, and that in the process models pertinent to such matters will emerge which retain their analytical tractability, and while continuing to provide a rich flow of theorems of the sort that has trditionally given substance to the economic literature.

V. ON SUBJECTS FOR APPLIED ECONOMICS

It is, perhaps, easier to offer a more concrete menu of wishes for applied rather than basic economics, starting from the desire for a return to the wealth of nations as a leading focus for the economist's research. This is, obviously, particularly critical for the LDCs, with their great stake in our ability to learn which measures promise to be sufficient to offer them rates of growth in their *per capita* incomes that bring them progressively closer to the living standards of the industrial countries. The pertinent theory still has a long way to go, and much remains to be learned from the experience of the LDCs that have managed to break away from poverty and achieve the status of 'miracle economies' in recent decades.

The urgency of this subject for the world's poorest countries, and, indirectly, for the interests of the wealthy nations is clear enough. But the past decade has shown that understanding of means that promise to achieve relatively rapid increases in productivity and *per capita* income are critical not only for the LDCs. Recent events in eastern Europe and the somewhat more-extended experience of Latin American countries have demonstrated dramatically the threat of political turmoil both within the countries immediately concerned and in their relations to other nations that failure to achieve viable growth rates entails.

We have also seen the importance of the subject even for the industrialised economies when their performance threatens to be surpassed by that of other nations. Great Britain and the United States have, in turn, encountered grounds for concern even though their absolute growth rates have continued to exceed anything ever experienced before the 19th century. The fact that others have come from behind and achieved growth rates greater than theirs has also drawn attention to our limited knowledge of means that can effectively stimulate growth.

Attention to this subject will undoubtedly require more intensive use of standard analytic techniques and exploration of some of the obvious topics. However, it will also require intensive examination of topics such as the economics of education which have largely escaped the attention of mainstream economists. Not only concern with the LDCs requires us to understand more fully just what education contributes to growth, what types of education are critical for the purpose, and what allocation of educational expenditure can be most effective in facilitating growth. In several other countries, notably the United States, the growing proportion in the labour force of groups traditionally associated with inferior education constitutes a threat not only to themselves but also to the remainder of the society.

There is, then, a good deal to be learned about subjects such as this and there is little reason to think that these topics will become less urgent in the foreseeable future. I therefore hope, and even expect, that applied economic research will address itself to such subjects with greater intensity in the decades before us, and that our discipline will thereby enhance its contribution to the general welfare.

VI. CONCLUDING COMMENT

I remain skeptical about our ability to foresee the future – certainly about the future extending a century ahead. One need only imagine a similar game being played in 1890 to recognise how wide of the mark any prognosticative effort would surely have landed. Research is by its nature peculiarly resistant to foresight, if only because one of the investigator's most valued goals is to surprise his audience. If I could foresee tomorrow's discovery I would no doubt be tempted to begin work on it at once; what better way to achieve priority!

Here I have, consequently, adopted a more-modest stance, describing my wishes rather than my expectations. Yet, if there is an element of rationality in the investigator's choice of topics the two may not prove entirely unrelated. At least so one would hope.

Princeton University and New York University

ECONOMICS BEYOND THE HORIZON

Jagdish Bhagwati

The next 100 years! Foretelling the course of our science over the coming century is to gaze into the stars, but without a telescope. If the past is any guide, the future will elude the best of us. Where astrology fails, we can fare no better.

And yet, how can economists, doomed to maximisation subject to frustrating constraints, pass up the opportunity to speculate, unfettered by constraints? So, I walk, in tandem with several adventurers banded together by the distinguished Editors of this JOURNAL, down the path of prophecy.

The leap into the unknown must be from where one stands. What then does the present tell us? Is Economics moving in directions that suggest, not a passing fancy or a vanishing blip, but the gathering strength of a trend? I believe it is.

The two significant trends that shape and enrich economic analysis today have little in common but nonetheless share the characteristic that they reflect integrating forces that are breaking down older distinctions.

The first, and foremost, is the reversal of the longstanding fragmentation of the social sciences that took Economics out of the realm of moral philosophy and gave it the uniqueness that it has enjoyed for nearly two centuries. Economics is spreading out to embrace questions that, until only recently, were left to Politics, Psychology, Sociology and Philosophy. The phenomenon is often considered to be a product of unrequited outreach by Economics; but this 'imperialist' viewpoint ignores the fact that there is definite mutuality of knowhow in the unfolding process of integration.

The other trend reflects, not a shift in the intellectual perception of the true domain of Economics, but rather the growing integration of the world economy as trade, investments, portfolio capital flows and people move increasingly across national borders, creating a veritable 'spider's web' defining the modern world economy. This is leading to a dramatic shift in the nature of the questions posed and consequently in the content of Economics as we have traditionally defined. Let me then consider each trend, in turn.

I

The intellectual broadening of the scope of Economics is indeed remarkable.[1] It is partly a 'supply' side phenomenon insofar as it reflects the scholarly ambitions of pioneering economists: e.g. Gary Becker who has systematically extended Economics to embrace Sociology, seeking to explain institutions such

[1] This is evident from the growth of new journals such as *Economics & Politics, Economics and Philosophy* on the interface of Economics and other disciplines, but also from the increasing appearance of articles on subjects such as political economy in the traditional journals such as the *American Economic Review*.

as marriage, divorce and suicide with the conventional tools of Economics in a display of the extraordinary explanatory power of our discipline. But Economics has also developed traditionally in response to 'demand': and dissatisfaction with the illumination that Economics provides in understanding even the phenomena that are conventionally considered within the province of Economics, and in guiding policy, has also been a major source of change.

This is nowhere more manifest than in the growing interaction between Economics and Politics. Economic theorists have generally considered the political process as outside their purview.[2] This has translated equally into the theory of economic policy where the government plays no functional role: it is only a 'black box' of goodwilled mandarins to whom economists supply the menu of policies, descending from the first-best optimal to successively inferior second-best instruments, expecting the government then to choose the best feasible ones.[3] I have christened this the 'puppet government' view: the government is simply to implement what the puppeteer economist figures out for it to do.[4]

But this will not do. There is no way to explain what governments actually do concerning policy, and therefore what actually happens to the economic variables or phenomena that one seeks to explain and predict, without dropping the strict puppet-government assumption. Economic theorists have attempted to do this in various ways. Some theorists have modelled a 'clearinghouse' government where mutually-opposed rival lobbies determine the government's choice of policy: but the government is only a battleground where the lobbies slug it out, and the government has no will or life of its own. It is much like weather in agricultural production functions. The more sophisticated models explicitly endow governments, however, with an objective function of their own, opening up a rich menu of modelling possibilities: governments disaggregated into executive and legislature, each (with or without political Parties) with its own objectives and constraints reflecting electoral prospects, campaign contributions *et al*.

The effect of these developments, and they are manifold, is almost revolutionary in scope. It is essentially twofold. First, by endogenising government, in one or more of many forms, the economic analysis begins to get us closer to predicting what happens when parametric variations occur. E.g. the traditional analysis of the effects an exogenous improvement in the terms of trade (or, in more familiar language, intensified import competition) would

---

[2] I refer to the mainstream thinking, of course, and to the policy approach in the writings of James Meade, Jan Tinbergen etc. The 'public choice' economists, such as James Buchanan and Gordon Tullock, evidently do not belong here.

[3] What *should* be recommended belongs, of course, in part to the theory of welfare economics and therefore takes us into the other interface, between Economics and Philosophy. Here too, as in Economics and Politics as argued in the text below, there are significant developments, especially in relation to the reexamination of the conventional dependence on the utilitarian criterion. In this context, perhaps I should mention, as an international economist, that international economists were in the vanguard in the late 1950s and 1960s, in incorporating nonutilitarian ('noneconomic') objectives into their policy-theoretic analyses: the major contributors being Max Corden, Harry Johnson, Bhagwati and Srinivasan, and their pupils. Oddly, the philosophers writing in this area in recent years are wholly ignorant of this important branch of the literature on the theory of economic policy.

[4] Cf. Bhagwati (1990).

take the trade policy as given exogenously and then choose one of many possible models (say, the popular 2×2 Heckscher–Ohlin model or the Samuelson $m \times n$ model or the Ricardo–Viner specific-factors model or the Komiya model with nontraded goods) to analyse the problem at hand. But, with endogenous governments, the exogenous terms-of-trade change will trigger, depending on the precise political modelling chosen, a change in the trade policy itself: initial free trade may be replaced by an $x\%$ tariff in the new equilibrium that follows.

To be sure, the policy itself is determined within the augmented economic-political model. But, generally speaking, this implies that one loses the degree of freedom to vary policies and to rank-order them according to an accepted welfare criterion. This 'determinacy paradox' strikes then at the heart of the policy-ranking approach that is so centrally embedded in the conventional welfare-theoretic analysis of economic policy: policy now is what economists get, not what they choose.[5] I have recently suggested that not all is lost, that the drastic shift to modelling endogenous governments implies that we undertake an equally drastic reformulation of the theory of economic policy. This can be done, not by asking inconsistently how alternative exogenously-imposed policies compare in a model where policies are endogenously determined, but by asking *variational* welfare-theoretic questions. E.g. if terms of trade improve exogenously, and a new equilibrium (including induced policy change) is established, how will welfare have *changed*?[6]

Evidently, as Economics continues getting into bed with other disciplines, such dramatic rethinking of its inherited ways should occur, altering our thinking in fundamental ways.

II

But the integration of the world economy also is pushing economic analysis forcefully into new areas and, in turn, accelerating the broadening of Economics that I just sketched.

'Interdependence' among nation states has increased dramatically in the last two decades. This has happened in regard to trade-to-GNP ratios, in terms of a variety of indices that suggest closer integration of capital markets among the OECD countries, and in several important instances even in the increased flows of human beings (often illegally and as 'refugees') across nation states.

These phenomena reflect a combination of 'market forces' and policy changes. Thus, the growth of world trade has long dominated the growth of world income, leading to even doubling of the trade-to-GNP ratios within a decade for some nations. This has followed both the increased openness of the world's markets (despite the protectionist bark, and lesser bite, of the 1980s) and the ongoing globalisation of world production through direct foreign

[5] The 'determinacy paradox' and its implications are discussed at greater length in Bhagwati, Brecher and Srinivasan (1986).

[6] Questions concerning alternative ways of writing constitutions that could constrain and change the political component of one's model are yet another type of analysis that opens up once politics is allowed to endogenise policy. These issues have been discussed in the pioneering contributions by Buchanan and Tullock and by other public-choice economists.

investment. Both phenomena, in turn, have been stimulated by policy efforts at liberalising the rules governing trade and investment and by market forces that prompt multinationals to seek out better factor costs and conditions to site their locations.

The strength of the market forces in driving the increasing integration of the world economy is particularly manifest in regard to portfolio capital flows and human movements. With modern technological change in the information sector, huge capital flows occur almost instantaneously; and few consider it possible any more that we could control these flows by some version of the Tobin–Triffin tax proposal, even if we decided that it was in the national or international interest to do so. The flow of people is equally constrained by the inability to enforce sanctions, either at the border or once the illegals are inside your nation: ethics and our civil liberties traditions combine to prevent draconian ways of dealing with this influx, driven as it is by a combination of economic and noneconomic factors.

Then again, interdependence has been accentuated by the deeper integration, by fiat and on schedule, that is being implemented by Europe 1992, which should generate over the European Community, and foreseeably over Eastern Europe in turn, the significant mobility of capital and people that is feasible, and often occurs, within nation states. What will all this do to Economics as it responds, inevitably, to the problems that we economists must now confront in consequence?

1. It is evident that Economics must rapidly revert to the broader international framework, with trade and factor flows across nation states brought frontally into the analysis, that the classical economists since David Ricardo faced in their time of outward British and European expansion and confronted through their analysis of the effects, for instance, of cheaper corn from the Colonies, and exports of capital and labour to them, on the approach of the Stationary State.

Economic theory necessarily abstracts. But the 'closed economy' models of economic theory are increasingly abstractions that can be fatal in the messages that they provide to the policymaker, and will rapidly be seen to be so.

This is manifest, for instance, from the dramatic impact that the introduction of capital mobility, by Egon Sohmen and Robert Mundell, made to the conventional comparison of the efficacy of fixed and flexible exchange rate regimes on the ability of a country to insulate itself from external shocks. Correspondingly, a quick check of current courses at most, and indeed at the best, universities would show that the 'openness' of the economy is now routinely explored even in regular macroeconomic courses instead of being banished as before to the specialised 'international economics' field.

2. But the deeper integration of nation states through links such as capital and labour flows also raises fundamental questions that can only reinforce the broadening trend integrating Economics with other disciplines.

Thus, for example, if people move across nations, several questions arise. In particular, over which set of people should one define the 'national' (or social) utility function that we seek to maximise to arrive at our policy recommendations? The (legal) migrants from Mexico to the United States may be counted as part of Mexican, or American, or both, or neither country's welfare, depending entirely on how one interprets, sociologically and politically, the nature of the migration and how it is perceived in the two countries. The economist cannot proceed by simply treating, as has usually been the case in the theoretical analysis of immigration, the immigrants as necessarily outside of the group over which the country of immigration defines its welfare or, in the theoretical analysis of emigration, by treating the emigrés as exclusively outside the group over which the country of emigration defines its welfare.[7]

In turn, those fundamental questions open up yet other issues of theoretical and policy significance. To take one telling example, if people move across borders so that citizens reside elsewhere, which country should exercise income tax jurisdiction over them? Historically, the United States has taxed on the basis of citizenship – an American citizen may be on the moon but must bear the burden of American income taxes – but the European tax systems have gone by residence – the pub-crawling Englishman in Paris may be rich but owes no taxes to the United Kingdom if he resides in France, while his poor compatriots in the East End of London carry the burden of income taxation. The different tax systems are historical accidents, though political-economy explanations may be advanced. In any event, they have been regarded conventionally as matters that lie outside the purview of economic theory and concerns. Not so any longer.[8] The growing phenomenon of migration or international personal mobility has now elevated the analysis of the appropriate exercise of income tax jurisdiction over internationally mobile citizens to centre stage in public finance theory. And, as should now be evident, the analysis is sensitive precisely to the broader questions such as 'who should be counted where' for social welfare evaluations.

Countless such examples can be produced of the unceasing way in which theoretical questions are being reshaped, and simultaneously being extended to a broader framework requiring explicit attention to political, sociological and moral-philosophical considerations for adequate treatment, by the growing integration of the world economy. E.g. with illegal immigration inevitable, since it is impossible to enforce restrictions and penalties in a draconian fashion because of ethical and political constraints, can one use aid and investment as policy instruments to reduce the numbers seeking entry and hence the numbers that get in? Again, if one can, there are possible tradeoffs between using one's resources thus to reduce illegal immigration and deriving 'noneconomic' welfare from this result, and the loss of conventional welfare from using resources thus and diverting them from producing goods and services. In turn, if some illegal immigration will persist, no matter what we can do, should one treat the illegal immigrants decently, assuring them civil and other rights, or should one feel free to go after them with the full strength of the state apparatus

---

[7] See the analysis in Bhagwati and Rodriguez (1975) and Bhagwati and Wilson (1989, chapter 1).

[8] See the extensive theoretical analysis of the question in Bhagwati (1976), Bhagwati and Partington (1976) and, most importantly, the contributions of James Mirrlees, William Baumol et al. in Bhagwati and Wilson (1989).

in shape of roundups, raids at workplace, deportations, denial of educational access to their children etc?

These are the kinds of issues that are shaping up as our century ends and the next unfolds. They will necessarily force economists into broader analytical frameworks, challenging and changing our discipline in fundamental ways.

Columbia University

REFERENCES

Bhagwati, Jagdish (ed.) (1976). *The Brain Drain and Taxation*, vol. ii. Amsterdam: North Holland.
—— (1990). 'The theory of political economy, economic policy, and foreign investment policy.' In *Public Policy and Economic Development: Essays in Honour of Ian Little* (ed. Deepak Lal and Maurice Scott). Oxford: Clarendon.
—— and Partington, Martin (eds) (1976). *Taxing the Brain Drain: A Proposal*, vol. i. Amsterdam: North Holland.
—— and Rodriguez, Carlos (1975). 'Welfare-theoretic analyses of the brain drain.' *Journal of Development Economics*, vol. 2, no. 3, pp. 195–221.
—— and Wilson, John (eds) (1989). *International Taxation and Personal Mobility*. Cambridge, Mass: MIT Press.
—— Brecher, Richard A. and Srinivasan, T. N. (1984). 'DUP activities and economic theory.' In *Neoclassical Political Economy: The Analysis of Rent-Seeking and DUP Activities* (ed. David C. Colander). Cambridge: Ballinger.

ECONOMICS IN THE POST-SOCIALIST CENTURY*

James M. Buchanan

My title specifically suggests that the focus of scientific inquiry in our discipline is not independent of history. Nor are the events of history independent of developments in economics. Both in our roles as citizens (public choosers) and as economic analysts, we have learned from this century's experiments in politicised direction of economic activity, and this learning must, itself, affect both socio-political processes and the shape of further scientific inquiry. In both of these symbiotically related capacities, we simultaneously learn from and make our history.

The verb 'make' deserves emphasis, because it points to the basic difference between the subject matter of the social and the natural sciences. There is no set of relationships among persons that we can label to be 'natural' in the definitional sense of independence from human agency. The political economy is *artifactual*; it has been constructed by human choices, whether or not these have been purposeful in any structural sense. And the political economy that exists is acknowledged to be subject to 'unnatural' change. As the great experiments of this century demonstrate, attempts can be made to *reform* social structures, in the proper meaning of the term. By comparison and by contrast, it would be misleading to use the word 'reform' with reference to the natural world even with the dramatic advances in our scientific understandings. From the artifactual quality of that which is the subject of inquiry in economics, we infer, firstly, the necessary interdependence between science and history and, secondly, the relatively more direct linkage between science and purposive design.

In Section I, I shall argue that the post-socialist century will be marked by a convergence of scientific understanding among those who profess to be economists. This convergence will contrast starkly with the sometime acrimonious controversy that described discourse in the century past. This relatively clear difference in the economics of the two centuries will, itself, prompt inquiry into the sources of the earlier conflict. Section II previews the possible re-evaluative enterprise that may take place in ensuing decades and introduces the suggestion that in such an enterprise, profound methodological transformation may be accomplished. The convergence of understanding will also modify the relevance of the positive-normative distinction that became familiar only in this century. Section III elaborates the argument, and here I suggest that the political economy of the next century will indeed become more normative in the now conventional meaning of this term. But the normative focus will necessarily be quite different from that which seemed appropriate in

* I am indebted to Geoffrey Brennan, Hartmut Kliemt, Robert Tollison, Viktor Vanberg and Karen Vaughn for helpful suggestions.

the setting where all economies, to greater or lesser degrees, were subjected to politicised direction and control. The revised normative focus will be on the constraints within which economic actors, individually or corporately, make choices among alternatives. And the accompanying, and indeed prior, positive analysis will involve comparisons among alternative sets of constraints, or rules. As Section V suggests, 'constitutional economics' will command increasing scientific attention in the upcoming century, whether or not the relevant research programmes are explicitly classified under this particular rubric. Section VI adds a postscript.

I. TOWARD A SCIENTIFIC CONSENSUS

Consider the following statement by a widely respected observer:

> They (the diverse parties in Eastern Europe in 1990) are also saying – and for the left this is perhaps the most important statement – there is no 'socialist economics,' there is only economics. And economics means not a socialist market economy, but a social market economy.
>
> Timothy Garton Ash, 'Eastern Europe: the year of truth',
> *New York Review of Books*, vol. 37, No. 2 (15 February 1990), p. 21.

In 1990 few, who profess to call themselves economists in East or West, will challenge the elementary proposition to the effect that economies that are described by individual (private) ownership of the means of production work better than economies where individual ownership is absent. And there exists widespread agreement on what is meant by the descriptive predicate 'work better'. More goods and services are produced, with 'more' being measured in terms of the values placed on such goods and services by individual participants. This convergence of scientific judgment within economics has already been evident for three decades. Since the 1960s, there have been relatively few claims advanced by economists concerning the superiority of centrally planned economies. And, indeed, few modern economists are either old enough or honest enough to recall the frequency of such claims during the middle decades of the century. This still-emerging consensus on the relative efficiency of market and socialist systems of economic order will characterise the first several decades of this JOURNAL's second century.

Since the emergence of economics as an independent discipline, there has been near-unanimity in analysis of the effects of particularised constraints on voluntary exchange. The destruction of potential value generated by tariffs, price floors or ceilings, or prohibitions on entry and exit – the demonstration of this result has remained a central emphasis over two centuries and can be predicted to remain in place over a third. But scientific advances have been made in understanding why collectivities impose such value-reducing constraints, and, in addition, economists can now measure the opportunity losses more accurately. Differences will continue as analysis comes to be applied and especially if policy alternatives are presented in piecemeal fashion. But emerging scientific consensus will be indicated by the crossing of the intellectual-analytical bridge between the acknowledged failure of socialist organisation in the large and the inefficacy of politicisation in the small (market by market).

Predictions of convergence seem more dicey when attention shifts to macroeconomics, the domain of inquiry opened by the Keynesian revolution. Market organisation works but within what set of parameters? And how detailed need political direction be in determining the values of the relevant parameters here? Controversy rather than consensus describes the state of play in the early 1990s. What might be projected for the 2000s?

Convergence here will occur in what might seem a reverse order. Economists will attain broad consensus on choices among policy options *before* observed agreement on underlying analytical models of macroeconomic interaction. The lasting Keynesian contribution will be the emphasis on the dominance of man's 'animal spirits' in the subjectively-derived definitions of the expectational environment within which entrepreneurs, in particular, make future-oriented choices. The attempted extension of rational choice models to intertemporal and interdependent choices within an equilibrating adjustment framework will, ultimately, be deemed a failure. Both strands of inquiry here will converge early in application to policy. Those economists who stress expectational instability will move toward recognition that only structural reform can serve the implied macroeconomic purpose. And those who extended rationality precepts have already restricted reform efficacy to structural parameters.

Ultimately, this convergence on policy norms will be matched by broader consensus in the underlying analytical exercise. And here the Keynesian heritage will win the day even if, in yet another sense, the implied results may seem non-Keynesian. The limits on man's capacity to choose rationally in any operationally meaningful way must, finally, be reckoned with and the scope for subjectively determined choice behaviour acknowledged. At the same time, however, those and additional limits on the choice behaviour of political agents, and the interaction of these agents within the institutions of politics, will be incorporated into the whole macro-analysis.

II. RE-EVALUATION OF THE ECONOMICS OF THE SOCIALIST CENTURY

If my central prediction proves accurate, economists must, increasingly, begin to raise – and try to answer – the following set of questions: Why did economists share in the 'fatal conceit' (Hayek, 1989) that socialism represented? How were economists, who claimed scientific competence in analysis of human choice behaviour and the interdependent interactions of choices within institutional structures, duped or lulled into the neglect of elementary principles? Why did economists, who model man as *homo economicus* in analysing markets, fail to recognise that incentives remain relevant in all choice settings? Why did economists forget so completely the simple Aristotelian defence of private property? Why did so many economists overlook the psychology of value, which locates evaluation in persons not in goods? Why did so many professionals in choice analysis fail to recognise the informational requirements of a centrally controlled economy in both the logical and empirical dimensions? Why was there the near total failure to incorporate the creative potential of human choice in models of economic interaction?

These and similar questions will occupy many man-years of effort in the century ahead. In the examination of the flaws in economics over the socialist century, the perspective of the discipline itself will be challenged and perhaps changed in dramatic fashion. Economists may come to recognise, finally, that the dominance of the implicitly collectivist allocationist paradigm, elaborated in a setting characterised by developing mathematical sophistication, lies at the root of much of the intellectual confusion. The alternative perspective that conceives of the economy as an *order* of social interaction (see my essay in Sichel, 1989) should gradually gain adherents. The accompanying mathematical representations will shift, and game theory's search for solutions to complex interactions under complex sets of rules will surely replace extensions of general equilibrium analysis at the frontiers of formalism.

The shift toward emergent order as a central perspective will be paralleled by a corollary, even if not necessary, reduction of emphasis on equilibrium models. The properties of systems in dynamic disequilibrium will come to centre stage, and especially as economics incorporates influences of the post-Prigogine developments in the theory of self-organising systems of spontaneous order, developments that can be integrated much more readily into the catallactic than into the maximising perspective.

III. A RECOVERY IN NORMATIVE RELEVANCE

A predictable by-product of the ideologically-driven controversy that character-ised the socialist century was concerted effort to separate positive from normative elements of the economists' enterprise. Methodologists variously reiterated the is-ought and fact-value distinctions. With controversy receding, we can predict some increase in reasoned discourse in defence of normative standards. Such a return to respectability of normative argument applying economic analysis can serve to re-invigorate the discipline for aspiring young scholars who have been turned away by the antiseptic aridity of a science without heat. A bit of the excitement that described the zeniths of both classical political economy and early Keynesian macroeconomics seems well within the possible.

No direct challenge to the logic of the naturalistic fallacy need be invoked in the recognition that the very definition of the 'is', which itself depends critically on the perspective adopted in looking at the subject matter, will influence the shape of the 'ought', which emerges when a value ordering is applied to the analysis of the 'is'. The possible 'deconversion' of economists away from the allocationist-maximisation-equilibrium paradigm and toward some vision of the economic process in subjectivist-catallactic-disequilibrium terms must, in itself, have implications for the sort of institutional change that *any* ultimate value stance might suggest as appropriate. The complementary shift in the perspective on politics and political process, a shift that has already occurred, will force normative evaluation to incorporate comparisons among institutional alternatives that remain within the possible. From this evaluation there must emerge, even at the level of practical proposals for reform, a much wider range of agreement among economists than that which described the past century.

IV. TOWARD A REVISED NORMATIVE FOCUS ON INSTITUTIONAL CONSTRAINTS: THE EMERGENCE OF 'CONSTITUTIONAL POLITICAL ECONOMY'

The predicted convergence of attitudes among economists at the level of normative evaluation will only take place within, and in part because of, a dramatically revised focus of the whole of the enterprise. A century ago, Knut Wicksell warned his fellow economists against the proffering of normative policy advice to government implicitly modelled as a benevolent despot (Wicksell, 1896). He suggested that improvements in policy results could emerge only from changes in the structure of political decision making. The normative attention of the economists must be shifted from choices among alternative policy options within given sets of rules to choices among alternative sets of rules.

As we know, Wicksell's advice was totally ignored during the first two-thirds of this JOURNAL's first century. Only since the middle of this century have economists increasingly come to appreciate the force of Wicksell's message. In several research programmes, economists have commenced to turn some of their attention to *choices among constraints* and away from the exclusive focus on the familiar *choices within constraints*. At the level of individual behaviour, the economics of self-control has emerged as a viable research programme on its own. And at the much more important level of collective action, constitutional economics or political economy has come to command increasing scientific interest, especially in the 1970s and 1980s. These research programmes, along with the closely related programmes in the 'new institutional economics', broadly defined, seem almost certain to become more dominant in the next century.

The extension in the range of possible agreement on the ranking of alternatives, whether treated at the level of the analysts' normative discourse or at the level of direct choices by participating and affected persons, is a logical consequence of the shift of focus away from in-period, or within-rules, choices to choices among constraints or sets of rules. The necessary increase in uncertainty over the predicted sequences of outcomes generated by the workings of differing rules will force any rational chooser to adopt more generalisable criteria for choices among rules than for choices among outcomes. Any attenuation of identifiable interest produces this convergence effect; the conceptual model need not extend to the limits of the familiar Rawlsian veil of ignorance.

Wicksell was the most important precursor of the public choice 'revolution' in the analysis of politics and political process. His call for attention to structure, to constitutional rules, reflected an early recognition of interest-motivated choice behaviour in politics that might be incompatible with ideally preferred results. By contrast, the normative economics of both the classical and the ordinal utilitarians incorporated comparisons between imperfect markets and idealised politics. Almost in tandem with the development of public choice, which in its positive analysis simply extends the behavioural models of economics to persons in varying roles as public choosers, the events of history during the last decades of the century have offered observers demonstrable evidence of the failure of politicised direction of economic activity.

As this JOURNAL enters its second century, economists in their normative capacities must, by necessity, compare institutional alternatives on a pragmatic basis, as informed by an understanding of organisational principles in the large. They will be unable to rely on the crutch of an idealised political order which seemed to make the task of their predecessors, the theoretical welfare economists, so easy and, in consequence, made their arguments so damaging to the standards of discourse. As they enter the second century of publication of this JOURNAL, the economists will find, because of the emerging consensus in both positive and normative elements of their task and in both micro and macro applications, a greater role to play in political dialogue.

Economists, almost alone, understand the notion of choice itself, and the simple intrusion of opportunity cost logic into continuing debates provides, on its own, sufficient *raison d'être* for the profession's existence. And, having got their intellectual house in order after the internal confusion that described almost the whole of the first century, with a renewed inner-disciplinary confidence economists can expose the arguments of the intellectuals who discuss policy alternative as if there are no limits on the possible.

V. POSTSCRIPT

I acknowledge that my predictions are tinged with hope. I sense some moral obligation to believe that preferred developments remain within the set of possibles. Little would be gained by speculation about worse-case scenarios, especially when I do not consider myself to be issuing precautionary warnings.

One caveat: I have limited discussion to possible developments that retain at least some relevance to economic reality. I have not speculated about the intellectualised irrelevancies that will continue to command some 'economists' attention so long as the discipline's ultimate *raison d'être* fails to exert positive feedbacks on the structure of inquiry.

A more significant qualification to projections here, and to those advanced by my peers, stems from the necessary limits imposed by temporal constraints. We can, perhaps, speculate meaningfully about developments in research programmes that have emerged or are emerging, and we may offer up descriptive narratives that extend over three or possibly four decades. But even to imagine developments over a full century must reckon on the emergence of research programmes that remain now within the unthinkable.

An instructive exercise is one in which we imagine ourselves to be time-transported to 1890, and to suppose that we were then asked to speculate about developments in economics over the century, 1890–1990. The record would tend to confirm the hypothesis set out earlier; the subject matter of our discipline was, indeed, influenced strongly by the events of history, and, to some much lesser extent, these events were themselves influenced by the scientific inquiry of economists. But history, inclusively considered, also embodies technological change. And who could question the critical importance of the information processing revolution in shaping the very questions that economists ask and attempt to answer? The veritable rage for empirical falsifiability of the ordinary sort may be near to running its course. But the still-developing technological frontier has enhanced economists' ability to simulate interactive behavioural results in complex institutional arrangements. Experimental economics, and especially as applied to imaginative game-like settings, seems to be a research programme in its ascendancy.

As an end note, let me suggest that prediction, in any strict sense, is impossible. Rational expectations models have reemphasised the point that all information we can have about the future is contained in the data that we now observe. Any prediction will, therefore, be nothing more than an articulation of that which already exists. But, if 'the future', as embodied in such predictions, exists 'now', we are frozen in the time-space of the present. If we accept real time, we must acknowledge that the real future remains unknowable for the simple reason that it does not yet exist, (Shackle, 1972).

George Mason University

REFERENCES

Hayek, F. A. (1989). *The Fatal Conceit*, Chicago: University of Chicago Press.
Shackle, G. L. S. (1972). *Epistemics and Economics*, Cambridge: Cambridge University Press.
Sichel, Werner, ed. (1989). *The State of Economic Science: Views of Six Novel Laureates*, Kalamazoo: Upjohn Institute.
Wicksell, Knut. (1896). *Finanztheoretische Untersuchungen*, Jena: Gustav Fischer.

NUTRITION, NON-CONVEXITIES AND REDISTRIBUTIVE POLICIES

*Partha Dasgupta**

Of the varying motivations underlying research in economics, forecasting has proved to be the most discomfiting. It is not so much that economists are not good at it; it is more that we do not have any firm idea if we are bad at it. We do not yet have a consensus on how to judge the matter. What I shall therefore do in this note is avoid even trying to make a prediction of which way we will be moving in economics research. Instead, I will outline the kind of work I would like to see come to fruition in the field in which my current research interest lies; namely, the economics of destitution. We need a redirection in how we go about our research in this area. My motivation here springs from an unease I have over methodological matters in current studies of poverty in poor countries. In what follows, I will first present in abstract terms how I think we are going wrong. I will then exemplify this with a key example.

I. THE GENERAL METHODOLOGICAL WEAKNESS

We wish to study characteristic U of a social system. We have a rudimentary theory of what U amounts to, and how we would expect it to be related to other characteristics of the social system. We have thereby accumulated a good deal of data on the matter. We know the incidence of U among the population, and we have regressed U with other characteristics of the system. U is a ghastly property, and so we are eager to fashion public policy in such ways as to reduce it; possibly even to eliminate it. But we cannot do this unless we have a model of the social system in which a policy is put into effect. The point, as always, is that if we do not have a good model, we will not know what are the possible outcomes of any given policy; we will not know how to choose among contending policies. We have therefore now reached a stage in our work where we should be eager to move beyond the rudimentary theory in which to put various hypothetical policies to work.

In fact we do not display any such eagerness. What we do instead is to make perfunctory use of a sophisticated theory of social systems in which U does not appear at all. By this I mean that the sophisticated theory, as it stands, does not have a *vocabulary* for U in it. What it does have is a vocabulary for a not-unrelated property, P. However, P misses an essential feature of U, and so it makes the sophisticated theory even circuitously unsuitable for analysing U; most especially, if we wish to come to acquire a quantitative grip on the matter. More generally, we cannot begin to ask questions that hinge on that feature of U which is not contained in P, a feature of critical importance.

* I am most grateful to Julie Anderson for her comments.

Clearly, this will not do. Nevertheless, we do not show any concern about the fact that P misses a vital aspect of U. What we do instead is to say that U is caused by a resource allocation failure, a failure which public policy needs to fashion itself against. We then use the existing sophisticated theory, and identify general policies which reduce P. From this we claim that we have identified policies which go to confront U.

Stated in such bald terms, the methodological weakness is patently transparent to anyone. But within the context of the example I have in mind, it is evidently not transparent to most of us. So I turn to the actual example. It concerns our reluctance to make use in a non-trivial manner of what we should by now have learnt from nutrition science and epidemiology in the modelling of consumption possibilities, and thereby the modelling of resource allocation mechanisms.

II. UNDERNOURISHMENT AND ITS MODELLING CONSEQUENCES

Modern economics has made enormous progress in incorporating in it the continually shifting technology of commodity production. We have today as a result a sophisticated apparatus for thinking about resource allocation in a world in which commodities and services can be transformed into further commodities and services by means of technological knowledge. The same progress has not, however, been made on the 'consumption' side. Modern resource allocation theory in the main does not explicitly recognise that nutrition and health care, among other things, are an essential input for the production of *labour power* (more broadly, the ability of persons to perform tasks), which in turn is an essential input in the production of goods and services. For the most part (namely, general competitive analysis), it takes these abilities as given.

Now it is tempting to argue that this is not any serious weakness, that the essential insights of modern resource allocation theory would be retained were we to model such bio-medical production processes as are involved in the conversion of food and fuel and health care into labour inputs. More specifically, it can be argued that the economics of human capital can be re-interpreted in such a way as to get resource allocation theory to do exactly what I am seeking it to do here.

But such a move will not do either. From our perspective, the central weakness in modern consumer theory is that it is totally oblivious of minimal physiological truths. It takes no account, for example, of the fact there is a *fixed cost*, measured by what is called the *resting metabolic rate* in the bio-medical literature, which each person must cover before he or she can do anything else over the medium and long run.[1] Admittedly, recent work shows that this fixed

---

[1] The resting metabolic rate (RMR) of a healthy person is his daily calorie requirement when he is engaged in the most minimal of activities, such as eating and maintaining essential hygiene. Energy requirements for work and play and for preparing food are *not* included. It is the level which maintains a totally inactive, dependent person. To provide the reader with an order of magnitude, the RMR of an average male in Bangladesh is judged to be about 1,550 kcal. per day, which is about 70% of the daily needs of a typical subsistence farmer. See FAO (1985, p. 120). (Assessments of energy *requirements*, such as this, have

cost is not solely a genetically determined parameter. There is scope for physiological adaptation to low energy intake; in the short run through, for example, changes in metabolic efficiency (see especially Prentice, 1984), and in the long run through, for example, retardation in early growth (see, for example, Martorell and Habicht, 1986).[2] But there are bounds on the extent of such adaptation, and so the impact of fixed costs on feasible resource allocation mechanisms remains, despite the possibility of adaptation.[3]

Now these 'fixed' costs, and their implied non-convexities, are person-specific, but occur in the same region of the consumption space for everyone. From the point of view of resource allocation theory what counts, therefore, is that people are nutritionally similar, *not* that they are different. To put it another way, these non-convexities cannot be made to disappear in 'large' economies. We simply have to incorporate them in our models.

To be sure, it has been noted before that consumer theory is vulnerable to this charge.[4] But very little has been done to rectify it. To be sure also, it is possible that in many circumstances (for example if the economy under review is rich in assets) modern resource allocation theory is not at risk from this fixed cost. But this needs to be proved, it cannot merely be assumed.[5]

The matter is of course a great deal more awkward for development economics. It is to me a very curious fact that a large, and often impressive literature should have been erected on the concept of absolute poverty (I should now reveal that this is what I was referring to earlier as P), have it then related to the phenomenon of undernourishment, and the literature should nevertheless not have felt the need to provide an analytical construct which makes essential use of the physiological phenomenon of undernourishment (what I was earlier referring to as U). Thus, the concept of malnutrition has made repeated appearances in recent development economics (e.g. Reutlinger and Pellekaan, 1986; Berg, 1987; UNICEF, 1987; Dreze and Sen, 1989; UNDP, 1990; World Bank, 1990), but it has found little to no operational room in it. By this I mean that the underlying models on the basis of which these authors derive policies concerning undernourishment do not have undernourishment as a phenomenon in them. It is true that the poverty line is often drawn at an income level which, given other essential expenditures, enables a household to be able just barely to purchase 'nutritional requirements'. But that is about the only formal connection to be seen in the literature between absolute poverty and undernourishment. Operationally,

been much criticised in recent years, for reasons I go into below in the text. But these criticisms have possible force only when people estimate the magnitude of undernourishment in a population: they have no bite for the analytical point I am making in the text.)

[2] I will ignore here the question whether such adaptation can be regarded costless. On this, see Dasgupta and Ray (1990).

[3] No amount of adaptation is going to allow the resting metabolic rate to go to zero.

[4] See the penetrating diagnosis of the analytical problem in Bliss and Stern (1978). The formal point is that modern resource allocation theory assumes for the most part that each person's consumption possibility set is convex, and in particular that each person can survive even if he or she were not to engage in any transactions with others in the social system in question. Koopmans (1957) provides an early discussion of the role of this assumption in general competitive analysis.

[5] See Dasgupta and Ray (1986) for confirmation of this in a simple class of models accommodating such non-convexities.

poverty even when thus defined does not pick up the underlying non-convexity associated with undernourishment. Replace 'poverty' by 'low income' or 'low welfare', and we will not detect any change in the analysis. Modern resource allocation theory is at home with each of these concepts, what it is not familiar with is the concept of undernourishment.

I want to argue that all this has serious implications. The methodological weakness is behind the ambivalence poverty studies display towards policy. One implication is that the lacuna has prevented policy-makers and academic economists from asking in clear contexts whether there is a necessary trade-off between growth in average well-being, as caught, say, in *per-capita* national income estimates, and redistribution in well-being among contemporaries. To put it in different words, it has prevented them from asking the related question whether 'trickle down' (or 'pulling up', to use Bhagwati's recent expression; see Bhagwati, 1988), is the most appropriate route to take for the elimination of poverty. That there need not be a trade-off between growth and redistribution if redistributive policies are judiciously chosen is a point which has, of course, on occasion been made, mostly notably by Adelman (1979) and Streeten *et al.* (1981). (See also Chenery *et al.*, 1974; Hicks, 1979.) But they were not provided with formal constructions built on adequate physiological foundations in which to undertake such inquiries, and so they were unable to discuss the issue in any quantitative manner *through* the use of such a construct. For this reason their claims are ultimately not convincing. If quantitative planning models glide over the phenomenon of undernourishment, as for example current computable general equilibrium models do, they are perforce incapable of addressing the issue of possible productivity growth through redistributive policies. Such claims remain an act of faith, backed only by an unquantified intuition. Until we are provided with quantitative models we will have to be content with recommendations such as the one offered by Reutlinger and Pellekaan (1986, p. 6) in their influential monograph: '...long run economic growth is often slowed by widespread chronic food insecurity. People who lack energy are ill-equipped to take advantage of opportunities for increasing their productivity and output. That is why policymakers in some countries may want to consider interventions that speed up food security for the groups worst affected without waiting for the general effect of long-run growth.'

It is in all probability *because* such claims do not as yet have either an analytical or a numerical grounding that economists are also led to advocate policies based upon an opposite causal mechanism, such as, for example, the one in the otherwise excellent report of the World Bank (1986, p. 7): 'The best policies for alleviating malnutrition and poverty are those which increase growth and the competitiveness of the economy, for a growing and competitive economy facilitates a more even distribution of human capital and other assets and ensures higher incomes for the poor. Progress in the battle against malnutrition and poverty can be sustained if, and only if, there is a satisfactory economic growth.'

There does not appear to me to be a conflict in values in the quotations here.

It reads much more as though there is disagreement about the most effective means for eliminating destitution. Such disagreements are bound to prevail if quantitative models are not adapted to incorporate the very phenomenon they are designed to study. Methodologically, this state of affairs in poverty analyses is inexplicable. A consequence of prevailing practice is that what passes for explanation is more often than not merely a description. As a result, the gap between research intention and its execution is large in this field. As it happens, the lacuna matters when we come to count lives and deaths. There is much to be done.

Stanford University, Cambridge University and World Institute for Development Economics Research

REFERENCES

Adelman, I. (1979). *Redistribution Before Growth.* University of Leiden.
Berg, A. (1987). *Malnutrition: What Can be Done?* Baltimore: Johns Hopkins University Press.
Bhagwati, J. (1988). 'Poverty and public policy.' *World Development*, vol. 16.
Bliss, C. and Stern, N. (1978). 'Productivity, wages and nutrition, 1: the theory.' *Journal of Development Economics*, vol. 5.
Chenery, H. *et al.* (1975). *Redistribution With Growth.* New York: Oxford University Press.
Dasgupta, P. and Ray, D. (1986). 'Inequality as a determinant of malnutrition and unemployment: theory.' ECONOMIC JOURNAL, vol. 96.
—— and —— (1990). 'Adapting to undernourishment: the clinical evidence and its implications.' Forthcoming in *Poverty and Hunger: The Poorest Billion* (ed. J. Dreze and A. Sen). Oxford: Oxford University Press.
Dreze, J. and Sen, A. (1989). *Hunger and Public Action.* Oxford: Clarendon Press.
FAO (1985). *Fifth World Food Survey.* Rome: Food and Agricultural Organisation.
Hicks, N. (1979). 'Growth vs. basic needs: is there a trade-off.' *World Development*, vol. 7.
Koopmans, T. C. (1957). 'The price system and the allocation of resources.' In *Three Essays in the State of Economic Science.* New York: McGraw Hill.
Martorell, R. and Habicht, J.-P. (1986). 'Growth in early childhood in developing countries.' In *Human Growth: A Comprehensive Treatise*, 2nd ed., vol. 3 (ed. F. Faulkner and J. M. Tanner). New York: Plenum Press.
Prentice, A. M. (1984). 'Adaptations to long-term low energy intake.' In *Energy Intake and Activity* (ed. E. Pollitt and P. Amante). New York: Alan R. Liss.
Reutlinger, S. and Pellekaan, H. (1986). *Poverty and Hunger: Issues and Options for Food Security in Developing Countries.* Washington, DC: World Bank Publications.
Streeten, P. *et al.* (1981). *First Things First: Meeting Basic Needs in Developing Countries.* Oxford: Oxford University Press.
UNICEF (1987). *The State of the World's Children.* New York: Oxford University Press.
UNDP (1990). *Human Development Report.* New York: United Nations Development Programme.
World Bank (1986, 1990). *World Development Report.* New York: Oxford University Press.

DECISION THEORY: THE NEXT 100 YEARS?*

Peter C. Fishburn

Decision theory includes theories of preference, utility and value, subjective probability and ambiguity, decision under risk or uncertainty, Bayesian decision analysis, probabilistic choice, social choice, and elections. To divine its future we begin with historical episodes and mention trends from the past half-century.

I. HISTORICAL EPISODES

Advances in decision theory have often been driven by paradoxes. Early in the eighteenth century, Daniel Bernoulli and others wrestled with why prudent individuals often violate the principle of maximising expected return. They were fascinated by the paradox of people paying at most a few pounds to engage in an infinite expectation game that returns 2^n shillings if the first 'heads' in a succession of coin tosses occurs at toss n. Later in the same century, the Marquis de Condorcet was intrigued by the paradox of cyclical majorities for multicandidate elections in which there is no majority candidate who could defeat or tie every other candidate under simple majority comparisons based on voter preference rankings.

Bernoulli's (1738) resolution of the prudent people paradox was an early version of expected utility theory in which one's utility for money increases at a decreasing rate. His legacy is evident in later expected utility theories as well as the principle of diminishing marginal utility of wealth that was so popular in nineteenth-century economics (Stigler, 1950). Condorcet (1785) resolved his voters' paradox by probabilistic reasoning intended to reveal the most deserving candidate in elections that lack a majority candidate. *His* legacy is evident in many nineteenth-century publications (a prime example is Nanson, 1883) and a vast number in the present century.

II. THE PAST 50 YEARS

Facilitated by Enlightenment rationalism and the turn-of-the-century rise of the axiomatic method in mathematics, decision theory reached a new plateau of sophistication in the midst of the twentieth century. The books by John von Neumann and Oskar Morgenstern (1944), Kenneth Arrow (1951), and Leonard J. Savage (1954) led the way.

Von Neumann and Morgenstern's monumental treatise on the theory of games not only established that subject as an important subdiscipline but also propelled expected utility into the mainstream of economic thought through an

* Prepared in celebration of the Joint Centenary of the Royal Economic Society and the ECONOMIC JOURNAL.

axiomatisation based solely on simple preference comparisons between risky prospects (Fishburn, 1989). Savage followed a decade later with his axiomatisation of subjective expected utility in which subjective or personal probabilities for uncertain events as well as von Neumann–Morgenstern utilities are derived from preferences between uncertain prospects. His theory, which bears similarities to Frank P. Ramsey's (1931) outline and set Bayesian statistical decision theory on a firm foundation, owes much to Bruno de Finetti's pioneering work on subjective probability.

In the interval between von Neumann–Morgenstern and Savage, Arrow (1951) discovered that general conditions for preference aggregation do not overcome problems first uncovered by Condorcet. The challenge for social choice theory posed by Arrow remains alive today.

The story of decision theory since mid-century revolves around the themes established by these people. Cryptic reminders of subjects developed since then must suffice to indicate the magnitude of their influence. We expand on some of these in the next section:

- expected utility extensions/generalisations (Fishburn, 1981, 1982)
- Bayesian decision theory (Raiffa and Schlaifer, 1961; Lindley, 1990)
- risk attitudes (Markowitz, 1959; Pratt, 1964; Arrow, 1965)
- stochastic dominance (Quirk and Saposnik, 1962; Fishburn, 1964; Whitmore and Findlay, 1978)
- experiments that refute expected utility's ability to describe actual behaviour: von Neumann–Morgenstern independence (Allais, 1953; Kahneman and Tversky, 1979); Savage's substitution principle (Ellsberg, 1961; MacCrimmon and Larsson, 1979); preference reversal (Slovic and Lichtenstein, 1983; Tversky et al. 1990)
- experiments that challenge transitivity (May, 1954; Tversky, 1969; MacCrimmon and Larsson, 1979)
- distinctions between descriptive and normative decision theories (Savage, 1954; Tversky and Kahneman, 1986; Fishburn and LaValle, 1989)
- non-linear alternatives to expected utility (Allais, 1953; Machina, 1982; Chew, 1983; Fishburn, 1988)
- non-transitive alternatives to expected utility (Loomes and Sugden, 1982; Fishburn, 1988)
- alternatives to subjective expected utility that accommodate ambiguity (Schmeidler, 1989; Hogarth, 1989)
- multiattribute preferences (Debreu, 1960; Krantz et al. 1971; Wakker, 1989); in expected utility (Fishburn, 1964; Keeney and Raiffa, 1976)
- non-transitive multiattribute preferences (Sonnenschein, 1971; Vind, 1990; Fishburn, 1990)
- probabilistic choice theory (Luce, 1959; Tversky, 1972; Suppes et al. 1989; Marley, 1990)
- time preferences (Koopmans, 1960; Hammond, 1976; Kreps and Porteus, 1979; Fishburn and Rubinstein, 1982)
- voting paradoxes (Fishburn, 1974; Niemi and Riker, 1976; Fishburn and Brams, 1983; Saari, 1987)

- social choice impossibility theorems (Kelly, 1978; Fishburn, 1987); non-strategy-proof theorems (Gibbard, 1973; Satterthwaite, 1975)
- alternative voting systems (Fishburn, 1973; Brams and Fishburn, 1983; Nurmi, 1987; Merrill, 1988)

The pervasive use of computers in applications should also be recognised.

III. THE NEXT 100 YEARS?

Computers will play an increasingly important role in applications during the next century. Along with routine tasks of data compression and high speed analysis, computers will have ever more sophisticated programs to ferret out interactively the most salient features of decision problems and structure problems accordingly. A few well-directed questions about values, acceptable risks and probabilities will yield a proposed solution or menu of solutions. Programs will discern the most likely directions for improvements and determine their promise by means of challenge questions. Sensitivity analyses that account for vagueness in preferences and probability judgements, and tend to discount marginal improvements, will be standard.

I continue with speculations for the next 100 years on some of the theoretical items noted earlier.

The twentieth century in decision theory will come to be known as the age of axiomatisation. Researchers will continue to axiomatise new models to reveal their basic assumptions, potentials for assessment and application, and experiential vulnerabilities, but the status of axiomatising will diminish. At the same time, experimental research on decision behaviour in laboratory and field will flourish. A much better understanding of risk typology, attitudes toward ambiguity, and the effects of time on preferences will emerge.

The distinction between descriptive or actual decision behaviour and normative or idealised decision making will persist, with refined boundaries. However, a confluence of the two that might be called holistic decision theory will become the main paradigm for microeconomic analysis. Holistic theory will retain vestiges of expected utility, but will be more flexible as regards traditional assumptions like independence and transitivity, and will embrace dynamic phenomena that are presently invisible or only dimly perceived.

The sanctity of transitivity as a bulwark of rationality and order will gradually erode, but this will take time. As it happens, more attention will be devoted to flexible, interdependent and quasi-chaotic preference structures. Dynamical systems of preference and choice will occupy a central place in decision theory by the middle of the twenty-first century.

It was mentioned earlier that alternatives to expected utility that accommodate non-linearities, intransitivity and/or ambiguity already exist. A great deal more work on these and related models, both axiomatic and practice oriented, will occur in the next twenty to thirty years. Special importance will be attached to ambiguity, or imprecise/insecure judgments of subjective probabilities, which is not yet well understood. In a similar vein, the modest beginnings in non-transitive multiattribute preference theory in the classical realm of decision under certainty as well as decision under risk or uncertainty will give rise to substantial new developments during the same period.

The great paradoxes of the past in decision theory focus on social choice and expected utility: Condorcet's paradox, Arrow's impossibility theorem, Allais's paradox, Ellsberg's paradox. The presently nameless paradoxes of the next century will focus on enigmas of preference and time. Although my files on this topic alone contain over 150 papers, we have barely scratched its surface. And past disregard for our planet's health as well as its impending overcrowding and population catastrophes can only heighten sensitivities to time in decision making. It is impossible to foresee clear directions, but there is little doubt that the dynamics of time and timing will be a vital part of the decision theory of the future.

I conclude with a few words on social choice and elections. As Arrow's discovery was being absorbed into the fabric of social choice theory, it encouraged a new focus on practical aspects of elections and the design of good voting systems. The aspects include nomination processes, ease and accuracy of voter responses, vulnerability to strategic voting, propensity to elect a majority candidate when one exists, fairness to voters, candidates, and parties, costs, and effects on institutions. Such concerns have produced the simple but effective method of approval voting for multicandidate elections, fostered extensive comparisons of alternative voting systems, and motivated a new look at systems of proportional representation for parliamentary democracies. Recent events in Eastern Europe and parts of Asia highlight the importance of the last item.

The emphasis on the design of good voting systems will continue well into the next century. Approval voting, which is presently used in several professional societies, will increase in popularity and become the standard method in large-scale elections in which one candidate is to be elected from a number of nominees. And new methods for proportional representation in multiparty systems will be devised and put into place in several countries. Because there is usually strong opposition to major changes in election procedures, shifts to new systems may be slow in coming but will occur nevertheless.

AT&T Bell Laboratories, New Jersey

REFERENCES

Allais, M. (1953). 'Fondements d'une théorie positive des choix comportant un risque et critique des postulats et axiomes de l'école américaine.' *Colloque International CNRS, Econométrie*, vol. 40, pp. 257–332. English translation with additions in *Expected Utility Hypotheses and the Allais Paradox* (ed. M. Allais and O. Hagen), pp. 27–145. Dordrecht: Reidel, 1979.

Arrow, K. J. (1951). *Social Choice and Individual Values*. New York: Wiley.

—— (1965). *Aspects of the Theory of Risk-Bearing*. Helsinki: Yrjö Jahnssonin Säätiö.

Bernoulli, D. (1738). 'Specimen theoriae novae de mensura sortis.' *Commentarii Academiae Scientiarum Imperialis Petropolitanae*, vol. 5, pp. 175–92. English translation by L. Sommer, *Econometrica*, vol. 22 (January), 1954, pp. 23–36.

Brams, S. J. and Fishburn, P. C. (1983). *Approval Voting*. Boston: Birkhaüser.

Chew, S. H. (1983). 'A generalization of the quasilinear mean with applications to the measurement of income inequality and decision theory resolving the Allais paradox.' *Econometrica*, vol. 51 (July), pp. 1065–92.

Condorcet, Marquis de (1785). *Essai sur l'application de l'analyse à la probabilité des décisions rendues à la pluralité des voix*. Paris.

Debreu, G. (1960). 'Topological methods in cardinal utility theory.' In *Mathematical Methods in the Social Sciences 1959* (ed. K. J. Arrow, S. Karlin and P. Suppes), pp. 16–26. Stanford: Stanford University Press.

Ellsberg, D. (1961). 'Risk, ambiguity and the Savage axioms.' *Quarterly Journal of Economics*, vol. 75 (November), pp. 643–69.

Fishburn, P. C. (1964). *Decision and Value Theory*. New York: Wiley.

—— (1973). *The Theory of Social Choice*. Princeton: Princeton University Press.

—— (1974). 'Paradoxes of voting.' *American Political Science Review*, vol. 68 (June), pp. 537–46.

—— (1981). 'Subjective expected utility: a review of normative theories.' *Theory and Decision*, vol. 13 (June), pp. 139–99.

—— (1982). *The Foundations of Expected Utility*. Dordrecht: Reidel.

—— (1987). *Interprofile Conditions and Impossibility*. Chur, Switzerland: Harwood Academic.

—— (1988). *Nonlinear Preference and Utility Theory*. Baltimore: Johns Hopkins University Press.

—— (1989). 'Retrospective on the utility theory of von Neumann and Morgenstern.' *Journal of Risk and Uncertainty*, vol. 2 (June), pp. 127–58.

—— (1990). 'Nontransitive additive conjoint measurement.' *Journal of Mathematical Psychology* (in press).

—— and Brams, S. J. (1983). 'Paradoxes of preferential voting.' *Mathematics Magazine*, vol. 56 (September), pp. 207–14.

—— and LaValle, I. H. (eds. 1989). *Choice under Uncertainty*. Basel: Baltzer.

—— and Rubinstein, A. (1982). 'Time preference.' *International Economic Review*, vol. 23 (October), pp. 677–94.

Gibbard, A. (1973). 'Manipulation of voting schemes: a general result.' *Econometrica*, vol. 41 (July), pp. 587–601.

Hammond, P. J. (1976). 'Changing tastes and coherent dynamic choice.' *Review of Economic Studies*, vol. 43 (February), pp. 159–73.

Hogarth, R. M. (1989). 'Ambiguity and competitive decision making: some implications and tests.' *Annals of Operations Research*, vol. 19, pp. 31–50.

Kahneman, D. and Tversky, A. (1979). 'Prospect theory: an analysis of decision under risk.' *Econometrica*, vol. 47 (March), pp. 263–91.

Keeney, R. L. and Raiffa, H. (1976). *Decision with Multiple Objectives: Preferences and Value Tradeoffs*. New York: Wiley.

Kelly, J. S. (1978). *Arrow Impossibility Theorems*. New York: Academic Press.

Koopmans, T. C. (1960). 'Stationary ordinal utility and impatience.' *Econometrica*, vol. 28 (April), pp. 287–309.

Krantz, D. H., Luce, R. D., Suppes, P. and Tversky, A. (1971). *Foundations of Measurement*, vol. I. New York: Academic Press.

Kreps, D. M. and Porteus, E. L. (1979). 'Temporal von Neumann–Morgenstern and induced preferences.' *Journal of Economic Theory*, vol. 20 (February), pp. 81–109.

Lindley, D. V. (1990). 'The 1988 Wald memorial lectures: the present position in Bayesian statistics.' *Statistical Science*, vol. 5 (February), pp. 44–65.

Loomes, G. and Sugden, R. (1982). 'Regret theory: an alternative theory of rational choice under uncertainty.' ECONOMIC JOURNAL, vol. 92 (December), pp. 805–24.

Luce, R. D. (1959). *Individual Choice Behavior: a Theoretical Analysis*. New York: Wiley.

MacCrimmon, K. R. and Larsson, S. (1979). 'Utility theory: axioms versus "paradoxes".' In *Expected Utility Hypotheses and the Allais Paradox* (ed. M. Allais and O. Hagen), pp. 333–409. Dordrecht: Reidel.

Machina, M. J. (1982). '"Expected utility" analysis without the independence axiom.' *Econometrica*, vol. 50 (March), pp. 277–323.

Markowitz, H. M. (1959). *Portfolio Selection: Efficient Diversification of Investments*. New York: Wiley.

Marley, A. A. J. (1990). 'A historical and contemporary perspective on random scale representations of choice probabilities and reaction times in the context of Cohen and Falmagne's (1990, *Journal of Mathematical Psychology*, **34**) results.' *Journal of Mathematical Psychology*, vol. 34 (March), pp. 81–7.

May, K. O. (1954). 'Intransitivity, utility, and the aggregation of preference patterns.' *Econometrica*, vol. 22 (January), pp. 1–13.

Merrill, S. (1988). *Making Multicandidate Elections more Democratic*. Princeton: Princeton University Press.

Nanson, E. J. (1883). 'Methods of elections.' *Transactions and Proceedings of the Royal Society of Victoria*, vol. 19 (May), pp. 197–240.

Niemi, R. G. and Riker, W. H. (1976). 'The choice of voting system.' *Scientific American*, vol. 234 (June), pp. 21–7.

Nurmi, H. (1987). *Comparing Voting Systems*. Dordrecht: Reidel.

Pratt, J. W. (1964). 'Risk aversion in the small and in the large.' *Econometrica*, vol. 32 (January–April), pp. 122–36.

Quirk, J. P. and Saposnik, R. (1962). 'Admissibility and measurable utility functions.' *Review of Economic Studies*, vol. 29 (February), pp. 140–6.

Raiffa, H. and Schlaifer, R. (1961). *Applied Statistical Decision Theory*. Boston: Harvard Graduate School of Business Administration.

Ramsey, F. P. (1931). 'Truth and probability.' In *The Foundations of Mathematical and Other Logical Essays* (ed. R. B. Braithwaite), pp. 156–98. London: Routledge and Kegan Paul.

Saari, D. G. (1987). 'The source of some paradoxes from social choice and probability.' *Journal of Economic Theory*, vol. 41 (February), pp. 1–22.

Satterthwaite, M. A. (1975). 'Strategy-proofness and Arrow's conditions: existence and correspondence theorems for voting procedures and social welfare functions.' *Journal of Economic Theory*, vol. 10 (April), pp. 187–217.

Savage, L. J. (1954). *The Foundations of Statistics*. New York: Wiley.

Schmeidler, D. (1989). 'Subjective probability and expected utility without additivity.' *Econometrica*, vol. 57 (May), pp. 571–87.

Slovic, P. and Lichtenstein, S. (1983). 'Preference reversals: a broader perspective.' *American Economic Review*, vol. 73 (September), pp. 596–605.

Sonnenschein, H. F. (1971). 'Demand theory without transitive preferences, with applications to the theory of competitive equilibrium.' In *Preferences, Utility, and Demand* (ed. J. S. Chipman, L. Hurwicz, M. K. Richter and H. F. Sonnenschein), pp. 215–23. New York: Harcourt Brace Jovanovich.

Stigler, G. J. (1950). 'The development of utility theory: I; II.' *Journal of Political Economy*, vol. 58 (August), pp. 307–27; (October), pp. 373–96.

Suppes, P., Krantz, D. H., Luce, R. D. and Tversky, A. (1989). *Foundations of Measurement*, vol. II. New York: Academic Press.

Tversky, A. (1969). 'Intransitivity of preferences.' *Psychological Review*, vol. 76 (January), pp. 31–48.

—— (1972). 'Choice by elimination.' *Journal of Mathematical Psychology*, vol. 9 (November), pp. 341–67.

—— and Kahneman, D. (1986). 'Rational choice and the framing of decisions.' In *Rational Choice* (ed. R. M. Hogarth and M. W. Reder), pp. 67–94. Chicago: University of Chicago Press.

—— Slovic, P. and Kahneman, D. (1990). 'The causes of preference reversal.' *American Economic Review*, vol. 80 (March), pp. 204–17.

Vind, K. (1990). 'Independent preferences.' *Journal of Mathematical Economics* (in press).

von Neumann, J. and Morgenstern, O. (1944). *Theory of Games and Economic Behavior*. Princeton: Princeton University Press.

Wakker, P. P. (1989). *Additive Representations of Preferences*. Dordrecht: Kluwer Academic.

Whitmore, G. A. and Findlay, M. C. eds., (1978). *Stochastic Dominance*. Lexington, MA: Heath.

OLD WINE IN NEW BOTTLES

Milton Friedman

Economists generally desire increased intensity of State activities for social amelioration, that are not fully within the range of private effort: but they are opposed to the vast extension of State activities which is desired by Collectivists.

(Who said it and when? Answer at the end.)

One major conclusion emerges from browsing through past ECONOMIC JOURNALS as a prelude to peering into the next century: the substance of professional economic discussion has remained remarkably unchanged over the past century while at the same time the language in which economic analysis is presented has changed so drastically that few economists who contributed to the early volumes would have been able to read most articles in recent volumes. In addition, the scope of economic literature has narrowed in some dimensions, widened in others.

On substance, one indication is the difficulty that I suspect most readers will have in dating the quotation at the head of this article. As another, the first volume contained an article on profit-sharing, described as a 'peculiar method of industrial remuneration' (Schloss, 1891, p. 292). Volume 32 contains an article on profit-sharing which notes that, 'In recent years, many prominent public men of all parties have advocated profit-sharing' (Bowie, 1922, p. 467). Volume 98 contains an article on 'Profit-related pay' which begins, 'The case for profit sharing has attracted much recent attention' (Blanchflower and Oswald, 1988, p. 720). Additional articles on profit-sharing appear in volumes 99 and 100. The 1922 article does not refer to the 1891 article; the 1988, 1989, and 1990 articles do not refer to the 1922 article. The 1988 article refers to two other articles as providing 'surveys' of economic research on the issue, which the authors state has been 'predominantly theoretical' – true of neither the 1891 nor 1922 articles. The earliest reference in the two surveys (Blanchflower and Oswald, 1987, pp. 17–9; Estrin *et al.*, 1987, pp. 61–2) is to a 1972 JOURNAL article.

As another example, the first volume contains an article by Sidney Webb on 'The alleged differences in the wages paid to men and to women for similar work'. 'It is difficult', he writes, 'to extract any general conclusion from the foregoing facts. Women workers appear almost invariably to earn less than men except in a few instances of exceptional ability, and in a few occupations where sexual attraction enters in. Where the inferiority of earnings exists, it is almost always coexistent with an inferiority of work.... Summarizing roughly these suggestions, it may be said that women's inferiority of remuneration for equivalent work is, where it exists, the direct or indirect result, to a very large extent, of their past subjection; and that, dependent as it now mainly is upon

[33]

the influence of custom and public opinion, it might be largely removed by education and combination among women themselves' (1891, pp. 657, 661).

An article in volume 98 on 'Female relative pay and employment' concludes: '[C]hanges in the structure of the UK economy have been an important factor in explaining the rise in relative employment. They have however been less important in influencing relative earnings' (Borooah and Lee, 1988, p. 831). This conclusion could as well have been in an 1891 article, just as Webb's 1891 conclusion could have been in a 1988 article.

As a final indication of the slowly changing substance of economic analysis, the 32 items listed under the heading 'Original Articles' in volume 1 included eight that can be classified as dealing with labour, four each with money and doctrinal history, three with socialism, and one with tariffs. The 54 items listed in volume 99 under the heading 'Articles, Shorter Papers and Comments' included precisely the same number that can be classified as dealing with labour (8), doctrinal history (4), and tariffs (1); in addition, three can be classified as dealing with money, and one with socialism.[1]

The subjects covered, and even many of the conclusions reached, may have remained much the same but there are also striking differences. For one thing, the range of topics considered and the audience addressed have changed. The early volumes were something of a cross between a strictly professional journal and a journal of broad though specialised coverage, appealing to an audience like that served by, say, today's *Economist*. For example, the 'Original Articles' in the first volume included 'The difficulties of socialism' by the Right Hon. Leonard Courtney, M.P., and 'The McKinley tariff act' by Prof. F. W. Taussig (Professor of Economics at Harvard and editor of the *Quarterly Journal of Economics*, established four years before the ECONOMIC JOURNAL). 'Notes and Memoranda' in the very first issue (March, 1891) already include one on 'Trade and finance in 1891', another on 'The crisis of 1890', and still another on 'The Scottish railway strikes'. Later issues included 'Austrian' and 'Paris' correspondence and reports on 'The Argentine crisis' and 'The Portuguese crisis'. Such timely journalistic accounts have no counterpart in recent decades. In the early decades, 'Current Topics' covered legislative actions and noteworthy economic events at home and abroad. As the decades went on, 'Current Topics' came to refer exclusively to items of narrow professional interest: new subscribers to the JOURNAL, professional meetings, and the like.

'Reviews' show a similar drift toward a narrower orientation. In the early decades, a quarter to a third of the some 50 or 60 books reviewed are in foreign languages: mostly German, French, and Italian; in recent decades, fewer than a tenth; and in the 1989 volume, none. On the other hand, the sections on reviews and the listing of new books are least changed over the hundred-year period. Throughout, they have given the subscriber a readily accessible introduction to the content and character of the books being published in economics – and for the first 70 years to the coverage of the periodical literature as well, a function that has since been left to the *Journal of Economic Literature*.

[1] This count omits the twelve conference papers in the issue labelled a 'supplement'. None of them could easily be classified in the indicated categories.

The narrowly professional orientation of recent volumes has been reinforced by the change in language and techniques. Whatever the subject, the early articles are written in English. They could be read then and now by, and were accessible to, essentially all professional economists with command of the English language. Empirical data are plentiful, almost all descriptive, and presented in graphs and tables. Graphs also serve to facilitate exposition in theoretical articles. But mathematics and econometrics are rare. Not a single mathematical symbol intrudes into the first volume, even though the editor, Francis Ysidro Edgeworth, was a pioneer in both mathematical economics and mathematical statistics. Mathematical symbols appear on two pages in the second volume and one in the third, all three in contributions by Edgeworth. The restraints were eased in subsequent volumes, the number of pages with mathematical symbols being occasionally in double digits.[2] Even volume 40 (1930), under the editorship of John Maynard Keynes, himself no mean mathematician, has mathematical symbols on only one page.

The situation is very different after World War II. The change is least for the articles on doctrinal history. Those in volume 99 could have appeared in the first volume, except of course that one of their subjects, Lionel Robbins, had not yet been born, and the other, John Maynard Keynes, was eight years old. For the rest, the dominant language is mathematics and econometrics. Nearly half of the text pages devoted to articles and comments contain mathematics; others contain tables of a descriptive character, like those in the first volume, but also tables reporting the results of sophisticated econometric calculations. The English language has a minor supporting role.

The change is testimony to the increasing professionalisation of economics as a discipline, the growing number of academic economists, and their increasing specialisation. The representative subscriber to this JOURNAL in the early years may well have read many if not most of the articles and notes, as I found myself doing when I was browsing through the early volumes – a most enjoyable interlude, I may say. The representative subscriber to today's JOURNAL may skim many articles but is unlikely to read seriously more than a very few that happen to be in his special field of interest. To do more would be close to a full-time job and require a command of mathematical and econometric techniques that few of us possess.

As someone who has made extensive use in his own work of both mathematics and econometrics, and who shares Adam Smith's emphasis on specialisation of function as a source of efficiency, I regard the change in the character of economic literature as on the whole a good thing, reflecting the increasing maturity, sophistication, and power of our discipline. But it reflects more than that. The character of economic literature changed little for the first 60 years of the JOURNAL's existence. Since then, the change has paralleled the rise of the modern computer, and, I believe, owes much to that development.

Computers are a major productive resource for economics. But there can be

---

[2] As an amusing aside, of the 70 pages with mathematical symbols in the first 10 volumes of the JOURNAL (out of over 7,000), 30 were in contributions by Edgeworth, 10 by Irving Fisher, and 13 in an article by C. P. Sanger on 'Recent contributions to mathematical economics', leaving only 17 for all remaining authors.

too much even of a good thing. The computer revolution has, I believe, induced economists to carry reliance on mathematics and econometrics beyond the point of vanishing returns – something that is perhaps inevitable in the first flush of any revolution. It is enormously time-consuming to gather original data, even from archival sources let alone by direct observation, to piece together different sources, explore in detail their reliability and accuracy, and derive a full understanding of the historical and institutional circumstances under which they were generated. These considerations long rendered abstract theory, including mathematical economics, and doctrinal history the preferred areas for generating a record of publication to promote professional advancement. More recently, the easiest way to avoid perishing by not publishing is to access an existing data base, download a batch of data to your computer, and put the data through the econometric wringer with one or another of the statistical programs described in the recently added 'Software' section of the JOURNAL. A multiple regression that 45 years ago required three months for a skilled operator of a desk calculator, and 40 hours on the then most advanced large-scale computer, today takes me less than 30 seconds on my home computer (Friedman and Schwartz, 1991, Addendum). Needless to say, I personally regard that as a great boon and generate multiple regressions these days at a rate that I never would have contemplated three or four decades ago – and many more than I would if I followed my own prescription for proper research procedures.

The effect, I fear, has been to reduce the quality of much econometric research, a concern that has surfaced repeatedly in recent years, especially in articles critical of 'data mining' (as a small sample of an extensive literature, see Leamer, 1978, 1983; Cooley and LeRoy, 1981, 1986; McAleer *et al.*, 1985; Friedman and Schwartz, 1991). By now there is wide agreement that GIGO (garbage in, garbage out) is a real problem. But I suspect the reaction will be like that which Keynes anticipated in a highly critical note on Tinbergen's use of a system of simultaneous multiple regressions to test business cycle theories (one of the first comprehensive econometric models of the economy). Said Keynes (1939, p. 568), 'I have a feeling that Prof. Tinbergen may agree with much of my comment, but that his reaction will be to engage another ten computors and drown his sorrows in arithmetic' (needless to say, Keynes meant human computers not electronic marvels).

A similar criticism applies to the extensive use of mathematics, which again has greatly extended the power of economic analysis, but is often used to impress rather than inform. Results that might have been attainable only by sophisticated mathematics can nonetheless be explained in understandable English. Again and again, I have read articles written primarily in mathematics, in which the central conclusions and reasoning could readily have been restated in English, and the mathematics relegated to an appendix, making the article far more accessible to the reader. I have long agreed with the rules that Alfred Marshall, the leading figure in the founding of the Royal Economic Society, spelled out for the use of mathematics: '(1) Use mathematics as a shorthand language, rather than as an engine of inquiry. (2) Keep to them till you have done. (3) Translate into English. (4) Then illustrate by examples that are important in real life. (5) Burn in mathematics. (6) If you can't succeed in 4, burn 3. This last I did often' (Pigou, 1925, p. 427).

Closely related to the growing dominance of mathematics and econometrics is a notable increase in collaborative articles. All but two of the 112 articles in the first five volumes of the JOURNAL are by a single author, the two exceptions are by two authors and, revealingly, deal with descriptive statistical data. Only half of the 54 articles in volume 99 are by a single author, 23 by two authors, three by three authors, and one by five authors.

To summarise, there has been little change in the major issues occupying the attention of economists: they are very much the same as those that Adam Smith dealt with more than two centuries ago. Moreover, there has not been a major sea change in our understanding of those issues. We can still read the *Wealth of Nations* and David Hume's essays *Of Money* and *Of Interest* with pleasure and intellectual profit. Major improvements have been made in the 'engine of analysis', in Marshall's phrase, that we deploy to analyse those issues and to consider more specific and detailed questions. As a result, I believe that we have a fuller understanding of the basic economic forces than our predecessors did, and are able to apply the 'engine of analysis' to a broader range of issues – consider the branches of theory that have emerged dealing with industrial organisation, information, financial instruments, the family, crime, property rights, and, more generally, the largely new fields of public choice and law and economics.

A century after Adam Smith came the marginal revolution and explicit general equilibrium analysis, bringing the first major expansion in the use of mathematics in economic analysis. Marshall became the authority, at least for English-speaking economists, and Walras and Pareto for mathematical-speaking economists. Another half century, and the Keynesian revolution changed the language and tools with which economists analysed the aggregate economy, though it changed their substantive conclusions about the aggregate economy to a much lesser extent. More recently, the theory of games and the computer revolution, both linked with the name of John von Neumann, changed the language of discourse and the tools of analysis even more drastically. The pages of this JOURNAL mark these changes. Volume 2 contains an attack on Alfred Marshall by Rev. Prof. W. Cunningham and a reply by Marshall; volume 5 contains a note on 'Recent contributions to mathematical economics' by C. P. Sanger; volume 46 and subsequent volumes contain many attacks on Keynes' *General Theory* and replies by Keynes and others; volume 49 contains Keynes' criticism, already quoted, of Tinbergen's econometric model; and, finally, volume 99 contains 'A survey of some recent econometric methods' by A. P. Pagan and M. R. Wickens.

So much for the past century. What of the next? The current fashion prompts me to rush to the computer and see what econometric extrapolation can tell me. An obvious candidate is the number of pages in the four annual issues of the JOURNAL (that is, excluding supplements). The time pattern of 19 selected volumes from the first to the ninety-ninth is well fitted by a second-degree polynomial in time, both for the absolute number of pages and the logarithm of the number of pages (R^2s of 0·87 and 0·81 respectively). Not surprisingly, extrapolations to 2090 give very different predictions. You can take your pick between 3,946 pages and 23,866. And we can be reasonably confident that neither will be anywhere near the truth: qualitative prediction suggests that the number of paper pages will probably be zero long before 2090. The ECONOMIC JOURNAL will doubtless arrive in the form of the successor to the floppy disk and CD or perhaps solely in the form of electrical impulses coming through the air to the subscribers' home successor to today's computers. My regressions are a clear case of GIGO.

Similarly, any formal econometric extrapolation would suggest that single authorship will be completely replaced by collaboration and the language of words by mathematics. To quote an earlier tongue-in-cheek extrapolation by George Stigler (1965, p. 48), 'The science will have become completely mathematical by 2002–3 when (as Aaron Director has remarked) editors will be unable to read a non-mathematical article'.

Turning again to qualitative prediction, I draw upon a very different branch of economics, the study of cycles. Most phenomena have a tendency to overshoot, even when subject to a strong trend. I suspect that has happened already in the reliance on mathematics, econometrics, and joint authorship in the economic literature. These trends partly reflected an individually rational response to the market for economists, particularly the emphasis on publication relative to teaching and the tendency to count rather than evaluate publications. However, the market is now reacting, and adapting its criteria of judgment to the new circumstances – or so I believe, while recognising the danger of wishful thinking. I offer as tangible evidence the introduction of a new 'Policy Forum' section in the Centenary Volume of the JOURNAL. In the two issues available to me, the new section contains 64 pages, only one with any mathematical symbols. It contains tables and statistical analysis, but no sophisticated econometrics. The articles in the 'Policy Forum' would have been accessible to the subscribers to volume 1. Moreover, of six items, four are by single authors. However, this limited sample shows no lessening of professionalisation: the first 'Policy Forum' is devoted wholly to 'The market for economists in the UK' – perhaps at any time too important and sensitive a subject to be left to the tender mercies of the mathematicians and econometricians!

The JOURNAL may reach its subscribers 100 years from now in a very different form than it has for the past century, in ways that may be literally unimaginable to us, but I am confident that, if civilisation in anything like its present form survives, the issues dealt with will remain much the same. The economic problem will remain, in Lionel Robbins' (1935, p. 16) words, 'the relationship between ends and scarce means which have alternative uses'. It may be hoped that the available means will become more plentiful. However, the infinite capacity of human beings to expand their ends will assure that they are still scarce.[3] The ends may be very different, but they will still be numerous

---

[3] A fascinating example is provided by some comments of Schumpeter. In a book originally published in the United States in 1942, he wrote: 'If capitalism repeated its past performance [in the United States] for another half century starting with 1928, this would do away with anything that according to present

and differ from person to person, and group to group. So *the economic problem* will not vanish.

Similarly, mankind has not succeeded in evolving a satisfactory monetary system in several millennia. Here again, despite our greater scientific understanding of monetary matters, I doubt that a final solution will emerge by the end of the next century. Forms of industrial organisation will doubtless change but the problem of how people cooperate with one another will not disappear. Despite the widespread threat to the family as the basic economic and social unit, I doubt that a practicable alternative will emerge. Crime and relative poverty are almost sure to remain. And our successors will not lose their interest in what their predecessors wrote.

Conclusion: the subjects that were dealt with in the first and the ninety-ninth volume of the JOURNAL – labour, money, doctrinal history, and socialism – will in one form or another be represented in the 199th, though their precise content and the techniques employed in analysing them will be very different. In addition, the new fields that have been subjected to economic analysis in recent decades – financial instruments, law and legislation, the family, crime, public choice, property rights, costs of transactions – will be represented. Other fields will doubtless be added as economics continues to expand its empire. 'Green' economics is already clearly visible on the horizon, and no doubt other new areas will emerge in the course of time. The old and new issues will be analysed with a continually modernised engine of analysis, but with recognisably similar components of pure theory, descriptive statistics, and econometrics.

'When one looks back on a century of economic teaching and writing, the chief lesson should, I feel, be one of caution and modesty, and especially when we approach the burning issues of our own day. We economists... have been so often in the wrong!' (Ashley, 1907, pp. 487–8). Professor W. J. Ashley's conclusion in 1907 can serve as mine in 1990.

[Initial quotation: from Marshall (1907, p. 17).]

Hoover Institution, Stanford University

REFERENCES

Ashley, W. J. (1907). 'The present position of political economy.' ECONOMIC JOURNAL, vol. 17 (December), pp. 467–89.
Blanchflower, D. G. and Oswald, A. J. (1987). 'Profit sharing – Can it work?' *Oxford Economic Papers*, vol. 39 (March), pp. 1–19.
—— and —— (1988). 'Profit-related pay: prose discovered?' ECONOMIC JOURNAL, vol. 98 (September), pp. 720–30.
Borooah, V. K. and Lee, K. C. (1988). 'The effect of changes in Britain's industrial structure on female relative pay and employment.' ECONOMIC JOURNAL, vol. 98 (September), pp. 818–32.
Bowie, J. A. (1922). 'Profit-sharing and copartnership.' ECONOMIC JOURNAL, vol. 32 (December), pp. 466–76.

standards could be called poverty, even in the lowest strata of the population, pathological cases excepted' (1952, p. 66). This was based on his estimate that such a development would mean an average income per head in 1978 of 'about $1,300 *of 1928 purchasing power*' (p. 65, italics in original). In 1989 prices, the corresponding figure would be $9,500. Average income per head was $12,400 in 1978 in 1989 prices, or 30% above Schumpeter's extrapolation; and $14,502 in 1989, or 53% above Schumpeter's extrapolation. Yet, by our present standards, poverty is still very much with us.

Cooley, T. F. and LeRoy, S. F. (1981). 'Identification and estimation of money demand.' *American Economic Review*, vol. 71 (December), pp. 825–44.
—— and —— (1986). 'What will take the con out of econometrics? A reply to McAleer, Pagan, and Volker.' *American Economic Review*, vol. 76 (June), pp. 504–7.
Estrin, S., Grout, P. and Wadhwani, S. (1987). 'Profit sharing and employee share ownership.' *Economic Policy*, vol. 2 (April), pp. 13–52, 60–62.
Friedman, M. and Schwartz, A. J. (1991). 'Alternative approaches to analyzing economic data.' *American Economic Review*, forthcoming.
Keynes, J. M. (1939). 'Professor Tinbergen's method' (a review of J. Tinbergen, *A Method and Its Application to Investment Activity*). ECONOMIC JOURNAL, vol. 49 (September), pp. 558–68.
Leamer, E. E. (1978). *Specification Searches: Ad Hoc Inference with Non-experimental Data*. New York: Wiley.
—— (1983). 'Let's take the con out of econometrics.' *American Economic Review*, vol. 73 (March), pp. 31–43.
McAleer, M., Pagan, A. R., and Volker, P. A. (1985). 'What will take the con out of econometrics?' *American Economic Review*, vol. 75 (June), pp. 293–307.
Marshall, A. (1907). 'The social possibilities of economic chivalry.' ECONOMIC JOURNAL, vol. 17 (March), pp. 7–29.
Pigou, A. C. (ed.) (1925). *Memorials of Alfred Marshall*. London: Macmillan.
Robbins, L. (1935). *The Nature and Significance of Economic Science*, 2nd edition. London: Macmillan.
Schloss, D. F. (1891). 'The increase in industrial remuneration under profit-sharing.' ECONOMIC JOURNAL, vol. 1 (June), pp. 292–303.
Schumpeter, J. (1942). *Capitalism, Socialism, and Democracy*, 4th edition, 1952. London: George Allen & Unwin.
Stigler, G. J. (1965). *Essays in the History of Economics*. Chicago: University of Chicago Press.
Webb, S. (1891). 'The alleged differences in the wages paid to men and to women for similar work.' ECONOMIC JOURNAL, vol. 1 (December), pp. 635–62.

ECONOMICS IN THE CENTURY AHEAD

John Kenneth Galbraith

To speak of the prospect for economics in the century ahead – in the next hundred years of this JOURNAL – requires, along, no doubt, with a possibly excessive self-confidence, a fundamental decision. Are we concerned with a science or subject matter that is essentially static? Does economics explore and serve human motivations, aspirations and institutions that are ultimately constant? Does the subject change only as its unchanging context is more deeply explored and understood? Is there change only, or anyhow primarily, as the result of increasingly precise and technically more elegant examination and exposition?

Or, on the contrary, are we dealing with a subject matter that is in a constant state of transformation? Is the ultimate economic motivation subject to change? And, more particularly, are the economic institutions through which it is expressed and served also in process of change? If this last is the case, there is an inescapable need for continuing modification in content and conclusions and, needless to say, in the guidance that economists presume to offer both to individuals and to governing authority.

It will come as no great surprise that I see economics as in a continuing process of transformation. The other view, admittedly, has a powerful temptation; it assimilates economics to the hard sciences – physics, chemistry, biological sciences. Economists thus live in the universities in no less rigorous intellectual commitment than their fellow scholars. As a practical matter, it also ensures, or seems to ensure, that what is learned as a student or otherwise in early youth will remain relevant for a lifetime. And in scholarly writing and other interchange, since this allows of an infinity of technical refinement within an unchanging context and thus of a relatively objective gradation of professional achievement. For the successful, there is a rewarding sense of superiority as compared with those who have not similarly penetrated the complexities.

But, alas, if the basic subject matter is unstable, the result for those who think otherwise is a commitment to intellectual obsolescence. As regards either understanding or guiding the real economic world, it means increasing irrelevance. Economics that assumes transformation, change, can never be as tidy, secure and elegant as that which assumes and cultivates unchanging verity. It is, nonetheless, the economics to which I find myself committed. It is in this spirit that I contemplate the changes in our subject that are in prospect. The task is made somewhat easier because the circumstances forcing change are already evident. Lagging is the textbook and journal response.

The first of the controlling circumstances concerns the basic producing unit in the economic system. In the microeconomic orthodoxy this continues to be the profit-oriented, profit-maximising entrepreneurial firm which commands directly the capital that it employs. It may be a large limited company or corporation, but that makes no essential difference. It is the 'firm'. Competition is no longer, or anyhow not always, assumed; oligopoly or monopoly is fully admitted but with consequence only as regards price, social efficiency and income distribution.

In fact, as few will deny, the reality is the modern great corporate and management-controlled enterprise. In all mature capitalist countries these account for around two-thirds of nonagricultural production. In this enterprise the controlling management is presumed to maximise returns not on behalf of itself but, in a self-denying way, on behalf of stockholders, i.e. suppliers of capital. These, in the normal case, are both unknown to the managers and without any effective authority as regards the management of the firm.

That the great management-controlled enterprise with its distinctive motivation has not yet been assimilated to accepted microeconomics is, to say the least, bizarre. It is the accommodation by economists for which in the years to come one must most hope. Until then some of the most evident characteristics of the modern economy will continue to go unmentioned and unremarked in contemporary theory.

Thus power, its pursuit and its enjoyment, is a basic and admitted motivation in all corporate organisation. In his recently published memoir (*Father, Son & Co.*, New York: Bantam, 1990) Thomas J. Watson Jr., former head of IBM, says of his life in that notable enterprise, 'I learned a great deal about power, being subject to it, striving for it, inheriting it, wielding it and letting it go.' So much for a single-minded concentration on profit maximisation.

The power so sought and enjoyed is pursued and enjoyed for its own sake. It does not always, perhaps does not normally, serve simple profit maximisation. It may as well serve the scale and prestige of operations. Or the diverse revenues and enjoyments of management. Only as a minor concession to an inconvenient and eccentric voice does this enter into approved economic theory and instruction. Left out of that theory and teaching, in consequence, are some of the most pressing (and damaging) tendencies of modern economic behaviour – the empowered, entrenched and sometimes somnambulant management, corporate raiding, the leveraged buyout as protection, the massive and frequently deleterious substitution of debt for equity, profit maximisation effectively for company executives and their legal and financial allies and acolytes – all unrelated to economic performance and often notably in conflict therewith. None of this, to repeat, which is so evident in everyday observation, is present in accepted microeconomic theory. Can one avoid hoping that in the developing economics of the firm it will play a part and that its insusceptibility to refined theoretical and mathematical method will not bar its consideration? That reality is complex is not a sufficient excuse for failing to deal with the economic world as it is.

Nor is this all. The great enterprises that embrace so large a part of modern economic life are subject to the basic tendencies and constraints of all great organisations – in less engaging language, to the basic tendencies of bureaucracy. These, in turn, can be stolidly in conflict with profit maximisation. Such firms regularly substitute established policy for profit-maximising change; they proliferate personnel, for it is by the number of subordinates that power and prestige are assessed; they measure intelligence according to what most conforms to the intelligence of those making the assessment. From this, then, comes the corporate sclerosis of older business enterprises, the antithesis of effective profit maximisation. In the older capitalist countries, these are matters for everyday observation and comment. On them turns much of the discussion of the effectiveness of national economies. One must hope that in years to come, at whatever inconvenience to formal theory, the view of the firm will be broadened to incorporate what is so evident and important in the experience of our time.

There could be some of my general mood who will disagree with my urging and my hope. They will say that were many, perhaps a majority, of economists not attracted to technically fascinating irrelevancies and thus rendered silent, too many voices would be heard on public policy. And the voices of those of us who do so speak would be lost in the din. My answer, proffered in what, I trust, is a characteristically generous way, is that this is a risk we should run.

I have referred to microeconomics. I would hope that in the century ahead the present sharp dichotomy as between microeconomics and macroeconomics would blur and disappear. Microeconomic interaction between prices and wages has been an urgent cause of inflation. This has been suppressed in practice either by restraint in negotiation or formal public action, i.e. a passive or deliberate incomes policy, or by a socially aggressive macroeconomic policy operating through unemployment and weakened trade union (and employer) power. It is implicit in much established theory that only macroeconomic action – monetary and fiscal restraint – accords with the basic principles of the market system. Only this is relevant macroeconomic policy. This limitation on thought I hope to see abandoned. The stark separation of microeconomics from macroeconomics in its bearing on public policy stands as one of the more damaging errors of modern economics.

The foregoing brings me to my next hope for the coming years, one of no excessive novelty: it is that the political context of economics will increasingly be recognised.

Anciently classical economics was seen as a stern limitation on state intrusion upon the market economy. If selectively, it still so serves. Less recognised is the way conventional theory acts as a political and social cover for the exercise of corporate influence and authority. If the business firm is safely subordinate to the market, the clear implication is that it is broadly powerless in the world at large. While I believe that we suffer far more from corporate lethargy and incompetence in the older capitalist countries than from the exercise of corporate power, it should not be the service of economics that it conceals the latter. The modern great corporation has a commanding role as regards prices paid and prices received, and its influence extends on to shaping the demand that it serves and on to the state. It should not be the service of economics that it casts a cloak over the exercise of political influence for economic ends. This has been strongly its service in the United States in past years and, if perhaps more subtly, also in Britain.

The economists associated with the administration of Mr Reagan were eloquent, even passionate, in their emphasis on free market principles, as, with perhaps marginally more sophistication, are those now of Mr Bush. This economic rhetoric has, in turn, been a cover for the greatest resort to international trade restrictions – tariffs and numerical quotas – since the 1930s. And for unparalleled subsidies to financial institutions, notably the now infamous savings and loan associations. Also for large subsidies to sometimes larcenous housing and real estate interests. Also for massive support to the defence establishment, with its powerful economic presence in Washington. And very specifically for tax action on behalf of the influentially affluent. I would hope that in the years ahead we would be more alert to, and more relentlessly critical of, the use of economic concepts as a cover, however transparent, for political purpose.

The more flagrant of economic service to politics in these last years has not, indeed, entirely escaped professional criticism. Justifying the American administration's desire to reduce taxes on its affluent supporters, one notable economic construct has held that the resulting release of incentive and investment would ensure against any reduction in aggregate revenue. The more general case for improved economic incentives has contended that the rich were not saving and investing because of undue taxation and too little revenue, and the poor, in contrast, needed less government support and the spur of their own poverty. These unduly convenient constructs have, to the credit of economists, been regarded with well-justified professional contempt. I would hope for a similar and even sharper reaction in the future.

Specifically, I would hope for less professional tolerance of the politically convenient proposition that a certain minimum level of unemployment, not necessarily low, is economically essential. Also in the United States, as perhaps in Britain, economics has been unduly, if not universally, accommodating to the political pressure for low taxation and high real interest rates as the basic policy against inflation. High interest rates operate against inflation by limiting that part of aggregate demand that comes from productive investment. And they accord income to the economically passive rentier class. To this policy, broadly denoted as monetarism, which is so favourable to the affluent and rentier interest, economics, as I have said, has been unduly accommodating. Appropriate taxation has a far more productive effect.

In modern life no clear line separates economics from political interest. The two live in inevitable juxtaposition. I do not wish to see economics indifferent to larger political and social concerns. Economics, as I have urged, should not be a soulless abstraction; it is in the service of the larger social good as the individual in question sees and defines it. But in the years ahead I hope that economic conclusions will be less subservient to political need and convenience. We must not in the future spare those who, whether innocently or deliberately, engineer or accept such accommodation.

However, as the economist must not accommodate to political convenience, so he or she must not be indifferent to the political context and its social and humane constraints.

As this is written, economic designs are being advanced in Eastern Europe and the Soviet Union for a return to a market economy. That a movement in this direction is necessary, even inevitable, is not in doubt. Both the incentive basis and management structure of comprehensive socialism have been shown to be gravely at fault. Also its planning and command structure does not serve the infinitely diverse and unstable wants of the modern consumer goods economy. Inflation, which is manifested in socialist countries in long lines at the shops, has been endemic as income has regularly been supplied in excess of the supply of goods. But economic proposals being advanced and in some cases, as in Poland, adopted have been gravely indifferent to social and political consequences. What has been called shock therapy is politically acceptable only to those not experiencing it; in consequence, much welcome liberalisation in politics and personal expression is being associated with painful economic deprivation and hardship. Economics, to repeat, must not be the servant of political ends. It must, however, accept pragmatic adjustment to larger political and social needs and constraints.

There is here an error that I trust will be avoided. That is the tendency to identify ideological rigour with wise economic policy. Lecturing in Eastern Europe in the autumn of 1989, I was asked in a reproachful way why I did not urge the economics of Professor Friedrich Hayek as the alternative to the economic system there so obviously failing. I replied that this was not a design which, in its rejection of regulatory, welfare and other ameliorating action by the state, we in the United States or elsewhere in the nonsocialist world would find tolerable.

There is an undoubted satisfaction in seeing economic life and policy as existing within stern parameters. So it was with those who once avowed firm socialist principles; so it is with those who now avow stringent capitalist or free enterprise principles. I would hope that in the future this would be recognised as simply an alluring escape from thought. The only humane course in economic policy is to assess individual economic action not in accordance with broad rules but in accordance with specific effects. This is mentally far more tedious. It is, however, because of such assessment and the resulting action that what is still frequently called capitalism has survived. And it should not be wholly a matter for professional regret that this places a far greater responsibility on those who call themselves economists. Not much intelligence is required for the application of the seemingly immutable rules; rhetoric and indignant condemnation of deviation can then replace thought. Far more is required of those who bring information and analysis to bear on the particular case.

Economics in the time immediately ahead will have a primary focus on the erstwhile socialist world. This is not to suggest that the economic problem is solved in the capitalist lands. Nowhere in the world are economists by way of becoming the predictable and commonplace figures that Keynes identified with dentistry. There is, however the possibility, indeed perhaps the probability, that the nonsocialist economic systems have developed a certain resilience that acts against their most feared, most decisive danger, namely the deep and politically and socially devastating depression. It is a matter of elementary personal caution that one avoid prediction. I accept the possibility of recession. Yet over the last forty-five years these economies have shown a remarkable overall stability, which includes an impressive ability to withstand bad economic guidance or, on occasion, no visible guidance at all.

In contrast, the Central European countries, the USSR and China must make their way from a system that all too evidently does not work to the pragmatic structure that serves Western Europe, the United States and the Pacific lands. This is a perilous passage, one no country has yet had the experience of navigating. We do not know of the problems and the pain. So it is here that the attention of economists and economic discussion in the next years will be focussed. That this great transition will be the centre of economic attention well into the next century is, perhaps, the one forecast that can now be made with safety.

I conclude with the hope that economics in the future will not be confined in its concern to the relatively affluent countries. Beyond the developed world, that of erstwhile socialism and modern welfare capitalism, lies the large world of still relentless poverty. From living in past years in that world, I am far from happy about the long arm of economics as it is extended thereto. Far too often it sought to transfer both the doctrine and the physical investment relevant only to more developed countries. There was debate over free enterprise or socialism where neither was relevant. Airports, dams and industrial plants were seen as both the symbols and the substance of development. Stable, predictable government operating within the limits of sharply circumscribed administrative capacity and a strong emphasis on public education were the far greater, far more relevant needs. This would once have been assumed. In our time, I remind as often before, no literate population is poor, no illiterate population is other than poor. Perhaps poverty and illiteracy have larger causes; nonetheless, this unshakable association should remain always in mind.

I come to a word in summary. In the nonsocialist world economics must, above all, come abreast of the modern institutional structure, not be in the service of politics but be responsive to larger social needs and be subject to overriding public and social constraints. The erstwhile socialist world, which will be a major focus of attention, must find the uncharted and possibly perilous path not to classical capitalism but to the pragmatic compromise that, in fact, is the model it sees. And in the Third World, as it is called, there must be a new attention to the requirements for development – education and stable government – that were once considered essential and that remain so in a time when other, later action, notably the transfer of industrial plant and technology, are too alluring. Let it be called, if we insist, investment in human capital. Let us stay with the simple fact that development and stable government both require well-cultivated human intelligence.

Harvard University

THE NEXT HUNDRED YEARS

Frank Hahn

I am pretty certain that the following prediction will prove to be correct: theorising of the 'pure' sort will become both less enjoyable and less and less possible. In the remainder of this note I shall give my reasons for making this prediction.

I do not share the view that pure theory is scholastic and so by implication bound to be irrelevant to the world. It is not my contention that it will wither under the scorn of practical men or women. The reasons for its demise are all 'internal' to pure theory itself. By this I mean that there will be an increasing realisation by theorists that rather radical changes in questions and methods are required if they are to deliver, not practical, but theoretically useful, results. This change in method will, I maintain, be a change which will deprive theorists of much pleasure.

Roughly speaking I mean by pure theory the activity of deducing implications from a small number of fundamental axioms. A theorist investigating special cases derived from special assumptions will ensure that the latter do not contradict these axioms. With surprising frequency this leads to beauty (Arrow's Theorem, The Core, etc.) and to surprise. The symmetry of the substitution term, the excess burden of indirect taxation and the two Welfare Theorems are examples. I have elsewhere (Hahn, 1984) argued at some length that it has also been crucial to our understanding of decentralised economies. Altogether then, an activity congenial to those who prefer proof to speculation and who derive satisfaction by subjecting their thinking to the discipline of the demands of consistency and coherence.

But a thriving subject will know at each stage of its development what the next crucial questions are. Pure theory is no exception. But it so happens that it is becoming ever more clear that almost none of them can be answered by the old procedures. Instead of theorems we shall need simulations, instead of simple transparent axioms there looms the likelihood of psychological, sociological and historical postulates. These new roads will find willing and happy travellers, but it is unlikely that those with the temperament and facilities of mid-twentieth-century theorists will find this a congenial road. There will be a change of personnel, and economics will become a 'softer' subject than it now is. That may, indeed surely will, be desirable for all sorts of reasons, but I am supposed to be predicting, not evaluating.

Consider the axiom of rationality. As increasingly complex questions began to be investigated it has become clearer than it was when Simon first raised his objections that it may be *theoretically* as well as empirically unsatisfactory. Certainly it was realised that the problem the rational agent was supposed to solve had to be computable. Not all are. If computable, there are strong grounds for demanding 'computable in finite time' (or finite number of operations). But even so, computing is like working and so a subject for choice. On the other hand, until a computation has been performed its outcome is unknown and so therefore its potential benefit. The first reaction of theorists to such difficulties is to stick as closely as possible to the familiar. So the agent is modelled like a finite machine. But the subject of 'bounded rationality' is on the agenda, and I predict that it will soon escape the 'machine' into the realm of 'rules of thumb' and their simulation.

Even more serious is the realisation that the axiom has not yielded the hoped-for fruits. For instance, in game theory it has not sufficed to generate an agreed solution concept. Already there is talk of 'salient' solutions, which is not exactly a precise concept. Not only are solution concepts in dispute; for any one of them there are typically a number (sometimes very many) candidates. This led to a large literature on 'refinements', which illustrated that theorists were reluctant to follow more promising but uncongenial routes. These rather obviously demanded consideration of actual, say evolutionary, processes whose outcome might be one of the equilibria. Work here has started, but I conjecture that it will yield much activity on computers and few theorems.

What is true in game theory also applies to General Equilibrium analysis. We hailed Debreu's (1970) demonstration that almost always the number of equilibria is finite, but it still left us potentially with a very large number of them. Recently in models of incomplete markets (see below), even that result has had to be modified, and a large continuum of equilibria is possible. In a sense all of this shows that we have been on the right track: there are many possible worlds. But to explain any one of them we need to know how it came to be. History dependence stares us in the face (David, 1985; Arthur, 1989), but it is not the stuff of pure theory. Apart from anything else the analysis will quickly make analytical methods impossible. Some general insight will be gained from special simple examples, but economists will soon want to move on from these.

In this respect the signs are that the subject will return to its Marshallian affinities to biology. Evolutionary theories are beginning to flourish, and they are not the sort of theories we have had hitherto. In particular, biologists have always known that, say, the giraffe was not inevitable. There are many routes evolution could have taken even in stationary environments. But wildly complex systems need simulating. Interestingly enough, ideas from evolution are being applied to the learning (and behaviour) of the individual agent. There has been much interest in evolutionary algorithms which are designed for the computer. There are convergence theorems and there no doubt will be more and better ones. But while there will be work for the computer scientist, I very much doubt that economists will be able to establish general propositions in any but very special examples. Again I do not judge – simulation, especially when based on good data, is a perfectly respectable and probably fruitful activity.

I have just referred to learning by individual agents. For a while rational expectation theorists believed that they could skip this stage and concentrate their attention on situations where everything that could be learned had already been learned. But the large multiplicity of such situations as well as the possibility that some of these allowed agents to live in an essentially fictitious world (sunspot equilibria) has convinced pure theorists (if not all macroeconomists), that the learning stage cannot be skipped. At present some interesting models of this are being investigated (e.g. Woodford, 1988), but they are special cases and contain much which pure theorists are wont to call 'ad hockery'. That is inevitable in a situation where there is no agreement on what should be meant by 'rational learning'. (Bayesian learning is an obvious candidate but not free from objections.)

These are some of the 'grand' questions which most theorists know to be next on the agenda, and which I have argued will inevitably lead to deep changes in the manner of theorising. Paradoxically I am confirmed in this view by some of the more recent attempts to stem the tide. After all in other spheres, say religion, one often encounters increased orthodoxy amongst some just when religion is on the decline. Thus we have seen economists abandoning attempts to understand the central question of our subject, namely: how do decentralised choices interact and perhaps get coordinated in favour of a theory according to which an economy is to be understood as the outcome of the maximisation of a representative agent's utility over an infinite future? Apart from purely theoretical objections it is clear that this sort of thing heralds the decadence of endeavour just as clearly as Trajan's column heralded the decadence of Rome. It is the last twitch and gasp of a dying method. It rescues rational choice by ignoring every one of the questions pressing for attention. Moreover, those who pursue this line defend it on the grounds that it 'fits the data'. Nothing could illustrate better than this that the habits of proof and argument are gone.

There is another class of questions which have been brought to the forefront by recent theoretical work. One of these concerns the objectives of firms, the reason for their existence and the manner of their decision taking. Each of these questions will require modes of analysis quite different from those which have dominated this century.

The objective 'maximise profit' has been much debated with reference to its realism; to the theorist however its lack of meaning when 'markets are not complete' is more threatening. To reinterpret as 'maximise expected profit' requires the special *ad hoc* assumption of risk neutrality which is not deducible from the basic axioms. Equally serious difficulties arise here when markets are not perfect. If firms are, as in theory, owned by households, their motives require representation in a firm's moves, and since only in complete perfect market situations will shareholders be unanimous, no obvious traditional route of answering the question presents itself. There is here a clear invitation to add social and historical elements to an answer.

When we ask why firms exist we think of transaction costs and of increasing returns. Neither is well understood and both, except for trivial cases, resist incorporation into traditional modes of analysis. Moreover, there is unlikely to be any necessity for firms to exist. There could for instance be cooperatives or indeed no firms at all. Once again historical modes of analysis will eventually seem to be unavoidable.

As to a firm's organisation, we know that 'the entrepreneur' will not do and that understanding will require not only organisation, information and team theory but almost surely social psychology and an account of historical development.

Evidently one could go on in this vein for a long time. My point has not been that twentieth-century theory sheds no light, nor indeed that its methods will not continue to provide some illumination. But it is my prediction that the latter will increasingly be found to be too faint in the search for answers to questions which have quite naturally arisen from twentieth-century theoretical developments. Not only will our successors have to be far less concerned with the general (leave alone the 'generic') than we have been, they will have to bring to the particular problems they will study particular histories and methods capable of dealing with the complexity of the particular, such as computer simulation. Not for them the grand unifying theory of particle physics which seems to beckon physicists. Not for them, or at least less frequently for them, the pleasures of theorems and proof. Instead the uncertain embrace of history and sociology and biology. Unfortunately, as recent work by biologists shows, these subjects are still in a state in which they can learn from our own past work rather than teach us new tricks. Our successors will be tempted by grand and woolly theories to escape the tedium of the computer. We must hope that they will on the whole resist it and patiently wait for a new dawn such as shone on those of us who came to economic theory after the last war.

Cambridge University

REFERENCES

Arthur, W. B. (1989). 'Competing technologies, increasing returns, and lock-in by historical events.' ECONOMIC JOURNAL, vol. 90, pp. 116–31.
David, P. (1985). 'Clio and the economics of QWERTY.' *American Economic Review Proceedings*, vol. 75, pp. 332–7.
Debreu, G. (1970). 'Economies with a finite set of equilibria.' *Econometrica*, vol. 38, pp. 387–92.
Hahn, F. H. (1984). 'In praise of economic theory.' (Jevons Lecture). London: University College London.
Woodford, M. (1988). 'Learning to live with sunspots.' Mimeo, Chicago.

ECONOMETRICS: RETROSPECT AND PROSPECT

Jack Johnston

Econometrics is certainly a child of the past 100 years. Looking back one sees an infant of mixed pedigree, an intellectual mongrel in fact, taking its first steps with one hand clutching some numbers painfully transcribed on to pieces of paper and the other grasping for early mechanical calculators, the beloved Monroes, Marchants and Facits, with their cogs and wheels clanking merrily away: cogs and wheels which took hours to produce what a modern PC delivers in seconds. The infant had a lofty ambition: to find a quantitative resolution of the mysteries of the economic universe, or at least of some parts thereof. Were there empirical counterparts to the graceful demand and cost curves, which adorned the economics treatises? Could the Greek letters in the mathematical constructs of the more sophisticated economic theorists be replaced by numbers? Were there laws of motion of the economic system waiting to be discovered? Could the path of the economic system be changed by purposive action, based on sound empirical research, so that the economist might advise the Chancellor of the Exchequer not just in what direction he should move but approximately what distance down the recommended road he should travel? Finally, and most daunting of all, could one discriminate between the theories of Professor Tweedledum and those of Professor Tweedledee?

Perhaps this ambitious list of objectives comes more from the perfect vision of hindsight than from an accurate reading of the infant's plans, but it is not an inaccurate reflection of the objectives of mainstream econometricians in the 'glory days' of the subject in the quarter century from, say, 1950 to 1975. The econometrician tackled his formidable task by gradually cobbling together a set of disparate elements. From the economist he took, when possible, a mathematical specification of a presumably relevant 'model' or 'theory'. That specification was hardly ever a finished product, ready for the econometrician's adoption, since the overwhelming preoccupation of economic theorists has been with the determinants of equilibria, whether short or long run. Sadly, an equilibrium, like the conjoining of the lovers on Keats' Grecian Urn, is never attained but only sought after. As Joan Robinson once said:

> Economic life is continually lurching from one out-of-equilibrium position to another (Robinson, 1960).

and there is no reason to doubt the current validity of this statement. Thus economic data reflect such lurching and not the elusive equilibria. The econometrician's equations must consequently reflect adjustment paths towards possibly changing equilibrium positions. So far the formulation of such paths has not received the same theoretical attention as the determinants of equilibrium.

Next the econometrician has had to draw on published statistical data as the raw material for his estimation and testing procedures. Seldom has such data been produced in response to a design dictated by the research requirements of economists. Mostly the available data base is a by-product of the administrative needs of government and business. As a consequence there is no necessary congruence between the data and theoretical constructs, which happen to share the same label. Perhaps, more importantly, much crucial data is not available in published form and may not exist at all. This is particularly true of 'expectational' data. To quote Joan Robinson again, writing in a style reminiscent of student debates in the Oxford Union:

> ... the causal elements in the situation are expectations; the evidence can never catch them. We are looking in a dark room for a black cat which left before we got there. (Robinson, 1960).

To the more extreme rational expectation theorists the lack of data on expectations is no problem. In their world all economic agents are endowed with the complete blueprint for the black cat, so they can literally 'see' it in the dark.

Thirdly, the econometrician took over the inference procedures of classical statistics. These procedures had direct relevance and validity for experimental situations and thus required considerable modification and development for application to non-experimental economic data. However, there is still considerable controversy over appropriate statistical methodologies in econometrics, as will be detailed below.

The infant has now reached early middle age. Some would suggest that he is already experiencing a 'mid-life' crisis. What is his present condition? What are his future prospects?

The present condition is characterised by three important features. First there is an explosion of computer power at the finger tips of any econometrician – be he ever so humble. Secondly, a cornucopia of computerised data bases is also available at finger's end, containing deep seams for happy data miners. Thirdly, the number of suggested estimation, testing and diagnostic procedures has proliferated, perhaps to the point where even econometric theorists are not fully cogniscant of the nature, advantages and disadvantages of the various procedures, and certainly beyond the point where the average applied econometrician can hope to make sensible judgments about what research procedure to implement. It is thus all too possible for someone to activate an econometric software package, of which he has only a dim understanding, to apply it to data of whose nature and provenance he is ignorant, and then to draw conclusions about an economic situation, whose historical and institutional realities he has, perhaps, not studied in any depth. The literature must surely contain more than a few nonsense regressions which have survived the editorial process, and have not yet been consigned to the econometric graveyard.

Despite the above comments there has been a substantial amount of 'state of the art' applied econometric work, which has quantified many aspects of, at least, the industrialised economies. A valuable single reference for some major applied areas is Part 8 of Griliches and Intriligator (1986). The applied work ranges from multifarious single equation studies to economy-wide models, containing literally thousands of equations. In his contribution to the Griliches-Intriligator volume Klein notes:

> The Wharton Quarterly Model, regularly used for short run business cycle analysis had 1,000 equations in 1980, and the medium term Wharton Annual Model had 1,595 equations, exclusive of input-output relationships. The world system of Project Link has more than 15,000 equations at the present time and is still growing. (*op. cit.* p. 2067).

One impression which surfaces repeatedly in any perusal of applied work is the *fragility* of estimated relationships. By and large these relationships appear to be time specific, data specific and country or region specific. Why should one expect otherwise? Should one expect, for example, a stable demand function for apples? If so, would one expect that function to encompass the behaviour of Eve in the Garden of Eden and that of her present-day sisters, such as the Newport Beach matrons strolling the aisles of the up-scale super markets in Southern California? The question need only be posed to provide the answer. Yet a few years ago enthusiastic, if not indeed fanatical, monetarist colleagues used to assure me that the demand function for money was the one basic and stable relationship, the rock underpinning the macro-economy. Along came financial deregulation in the United States and that was the end of that proposition. A similar fate befell the Phillips Curve, which disintegrated soon after being exposed to the light of day.

Evidence of so-called instability might be intepreted alternatively as evidence of inadequate specification of the relationship. The original Phillips Curve requires to be augmented by an expected inflation component. Linear relations need perhaps to be replaced by nonlinear ones and so forth. These qualifications are certainly valid, but there is no reason to expect the *conditional* nature of economic relations to go away. The point was put eloquently by Lord Robbins, when speculating on the differences between economics and the natural sciences:

> The influence of the Reformation made no change in the forces of gravity. But it certainly must have changed the demand for fish on Fridays. (Robbins, 1981).

It is surely too much to expect the econometrician to develop a 'super' demand equation for fish, which contains within itself an explanation of the Reformation. The numerical equivalents of the Greek alphabet are thus subject to change, whether from structural shifts, slow evolution or random perturbations. One must test continually for the structural shifts and try harder to incorporate the others into the modelling process.

The same fragility affects the performance of the large macro models, as is evidenced by the 'add on' factors and other subjective adjustments that the model builders employ in making their forecasts. It is impossible to regularly test hundreds of equations for specification errors. However the models tend to be re-estimated frequently, giving chase to en evolving world, in an attempt to keep the dynamic picture of the economy up to date.

THE FUTURE

One might envisage an economy in which a robotic, automated productive and distributive system is controlled by a relatively small number of people sitting at their video display terminals in decentralised work stations. Sampling and aggregative processes applied to the data in this economy-wide computer network provide government workers at their VDT's with instantaneous and accurate statistics on the behaviour of the economy. The economists (the term now being synonymous with econometricians) are likewise hooked into their computers and are busy analysing this feast of data to infer the decision processes at work and forecast the evolution of the economy. This, of course, is pure fantasy and I do not have any idea what the economy will look like one hundred years from now, still less what our professional successors will be doing. However, if we set a modest objective of improving the quality of econometric work in the near term, there are a few things that might be done soon. The following tentative suggestions are offered in that spirit.

(i) *Lines of Communication Between Econometric Theorists and Applied Econometricians*

This is something of a Chiefs v. Indians problem. The Chiefs are supposed to tell the Indians what to do. However, the Indians have difficulty comprehending the messages. A visitor from Mars, asked to explain the activities of this tribe, might well advance a maximum likelihood proposition that the objective of the Chiefs is to communicate with and make a big impression on a sub-set of other Chiefs, and the Devil take the Indians. The Indians, for their part, being confused about the instructions from on high and nervous about the reaction of the Chiefs, do not render a complete and faithful account of all their activities but offer up only a sub-set of their results. Thus there are faults on both sides, but ones which could easily be corrected. Editors of journals which concentrate on theoretical articles might well require the authors of theoretical papers to append one page addressed primarily to the Indians. That page would outline the operational steps required to implement their procedure and the likely comparative advantages and disadvantages of so doing. This would increase the likelihood of new theoretical procedures being adopted and evaluated in the real world. The Indians, for their part, feeling more confident about the beneficent intentions of the Chiefs, should provide more complete reports of their investigative activities. This two-way interchange would enhance the prospects of the profession learning by doing and incidentally learning more about the workings of the economy.

(ii) *The Balance Between Theoretical and Applied Work in Econometrics*

This is a standard topic for geriatric Jeremiads, deploring the alleged distressingly low proportion of applied to theoretical work. No one knows the optimal proportion for these activities in the economy as whole, still less in the academic sector, where the abuse is usually thought to be most prevalent. Presumably academic econometricians have learnt sufficient economics to be maximising some utility function subject to perceived constraints. Thus a division of intellectual labour evolves naturally. If, however, it is true that good empirical work requires greater inputs of time, computation and effort than does purely theoretical work, and if academic advancement depends mainly on output then the academic sector might generate an excess supply of theoretical work, some of which may be of trivial significance for real life applications. One solution to such a problem would be to evaluate research activity by 'inputs', as is done for the measurement of government services in the national income accounts. Academic politicians and administrators could joyfully spend many committee hours evaluating the quantity and quality of research inputs just as they now do with research outputs. However, the provision of sound empirical work is not the responsibility of Academe alone. Government, business, unions and other groups all have their own needs for such information and responsibility for obtaining it.

(iii) *Resolution of Doctrinal Disputes*

Econometrics is now enshrined along with Micro and Macro in the modern trinity at the core of graduate instruction at all the major schools. The mix and flavour, both within and between the three subjects, vary across institutions. In econometric methodology there are three major 'sects', namely the Bayesians, the (confused) Classicals, and finally the (Minnesota) Agnostics. The major bibles for the Bayesian believers are Zellner (1971) and Leamer (1978). The Classicals were formerly the dominant tribe, specifying maintained hypotheses on the basis of economic theory, estimating parameters and carrying out various tests with 't', F and χ^2 statistics etc. If the maintained hypothesis is not correct, the test procedures may be invalid and the associated critical values incorrect. Charges of data mining and other abuses have confused this tribe and they are presently in some disarray. They may be rejuvenated by the work of Hendry (1989) and his associates. One may approach Hendry's work through his software manual and the references therein or await the publication of Hendry, *Lectures on Econometric Methodology* (forthcoming). The essence of the approach is to 'test, test, and test'. This generates 't', F and other statistics galore, and it is easily possible to generate more test statistics than there are data points in the sample. It is still somewhat unclear, at least to this Indian, by what processes, subjective or otherwise, this battery of test statistics is to be digested and interpreted. At any rate the surviving Classicals are offered a feast of their favourite delicacies, instead of being restricted to a single serving as in days gone by. The (Minnesota) Agnostics, (Sims, 1980) have little confidence in the ability of economic theory to specify the form of relationships and advocate *vector autoregressions* (VAR's). With a minimum of theoretical restrictions VAR's are plagued by collinearity, too many coefficients and too few degrees of freedom. The Ghost of Koopmans in the Elysian fields is probably writing a new review article entitled, 'Estimation without Theory'.

To cope with these problems the Agnostics themselves recommend the injection of some Bayesian priors into the analysis.

The only solution to doctrinal disputes is intellectual Darwinism. It is to be hoped that the next few decades will show which approach best helps our successors solve their problems. In the meantime all sensible graduate students should have a catholic approach to econometric methodology.

Envoi and *Bon Voyage*

University of California, Irvine

REFERENCES

Griliches, Z. and Intriligator, M. D. (1986). *Handbook of Econometrics*, vol. 3, Amsterdam: North Holland.
Hendry, D. F. (1989). *PC-GIVE. An Interactive Econometric Modelling System*, Institute of Economics and Statistics, University of Oxford.
Keats, J. (1982). *John Keats: Complete Poems*, Harvard University Press. 'Ode on a Grecian urn.' Pp. 282–3.
Leamer, E. E. (1978). *Specification Searches*, New York: Wiley.
Robbins, Lord. (1981). 'Economics and political economy.' *American Economic Review*, vol. 71, pp. 1–10.
Robinson, J. (1960). 'The present position of econometrics: a discussion.' *Journal of the Royal Statistical Society*, Series A, vol. 123, pp. 274–8.
Sims, C. A. (1980). 'Macroeconomics and reality.' *Econometrica*, vol. 48, pp. 1–49.
Zellner, A. (1971). *An Introduction to Bayesian Inference in Econometrics*, New York: Wiley.

ECONOMICS AND BUSINESS

John A. Kay

THE ECONOMICS OF INDUSTRY

If you ask most businessmen what they think economics is about, their answer will be economic forecasting. They do not think very much of economic forecasting – although they go on thinking they need it – and so they do not think very much of economists. Every day they are concerned to analyse their costs – which is done by their accountants. They determine their prices – this is the responsibility of their marketing department. They need to interpret the business environment they face – the task of their corporate planners and strategic advisers. The economic input into any of these functions is minimal. Yet costs, prices, industries and markets are the very lifeblood of microeconomics, just as inflation, output and growth are the lifeblood of macroeconomics. Economics dominates public policy and every country's chief executive regards his (or her) macroeconomic adviser as a vital aide. But economics has almost no influence on business policy, and in only a small minority of companies does the chief executive have an economic adviser at all.

The evolution of microeconomics over the past century provides a partial answer. 1990 is not only the centenary of the ECONOMIC JOURNAL; it is also the centenary of the first edition of Alfred Marshall's *Principles of Economics*. It was Marshall who set the agenda for much of the economics that was to occupy this JOURNAL for the subsequent 100 years. Marshall's analysis, and his understanding of the commerce of his day, was sophisticated and wide ranging. Indeed Marshall probably knew more about the day to day functioning of business than any leading economist this century. Yet his approach barely scratched the surface of the firm. Marshall's key tool of analysis is 'the representative firm'. His famous metaphor of the trees in the forest is designed precisely to play down the role of individual agents and the importance of their distinctive characteristics. It is no accident that his second landmark work is entitled *The Economics of Industry*, not the economics of the firm. The imperfect competition revolution of Chamberlain and Joan Robinson changed this direction little. In the models they develop, firms do differ from each other, but the ways in which they do so are essentially trivial.

THE STRUCTURE–CONDUCT–PERFORMANCE PARADIGM

Since the Second World War, the dominant tradition in industrial organisation has been based on the strongly empirical structure–conduct–performance paradigm. The focus of this work is clearly set out by Bain (1959):

> I am concerned with the environmental setting within which enterprises operate and in how they behave in these settings as producers, sellers and buyers. By contrast, I do not take an internal approach, more appropriate

to the field of management science, such as could inquire how enterprises do and should behave in ordering their internal operations and would attempt to instruct them accordingly… my primary unit for analysis is the industry or competing group of firms, rather than the individual firm or the economy wide aggregate of enterprises (pp. vii–viii).

Fig. 1, drawn from Scherer's (1970) definitive survey of that tradition, illustrates its essential features. All of the factors in it are external to the firm:

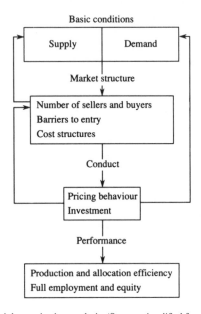

Fig. 1. A model of industrial organisation analysis. (Source: simplified from Scherer, 1980: fig. 1.1.)

nothing explains why one firm in an industry differs from another. True, Scherer's work is also a rich encyclopedia of information about American business, but it is precisely that which distinguishes it so clearly from other contributions in its genre. His unit of analysis is emphatically the industry, not the firm. For industrial economists in this tradition (and, indeed for those of the Chicago school which represented its principal alternative) the policy issues of interest were those of public policy, not business policy.

There have, of course, been different schools and dissonant voices. There are the critics of Marshallian analytic microeconomics. Hall and Hitch asked businessmen what they knew, or thought, of many standard economic concepts; and discovered that the answer to both questions was very little. Hall and Hitch took this to be a criticism of economists: most economists have taken it to be a criticism of businessmen. Both sides are, to a degree, justified. The fact that a sales manager cannot describe a marginal cost curve does not mean that it does not help to describe his behaviour, any more than the fact that an athlete does not know why he runs so fast invalidates the study of physiology.

But the magnitude of gap between the study of economics and the approach to the same topics within business illustrates at least a failure of communication and probably a faiiure of relevance by the economics profession.

There is also a more institutional tradition. Coase's articles on *The Nature of the Firm* remains seminal, but the fact that we turn so often to an article which is now 50 years old is a measure of the lack of progress on that particular subject as well as a measure of the classic status of the work. The approach that sees the firm as essentially a mechanism of maximisation – a black box or production function – has had its critics, most profoundly Simon, most eloquently Galbraith. At the same time, Oliver Williamson has almost single-handedly developed a wide-ranging body of analysis which bears directly on the choices facing the individual firm, rooted in the analysis of transactions costs and structures of property rights. But all of these have been, until recently, outside the mainstream of developments in industrial economics.

This inability, or unwillingness, to probe within the boundaries of the firm itself has serious weaknesses even in its own terms. If opportunities are equally available to all they are available to no one in particular. This problem, most clearly articulated by Richardson (1960), lies a little beneath the surface. But the failure to resolve it creates a theory of industrial organisation of limited value to practical businessmen. Reviewing the state of oligopoly theory in 1975 Joskow comments that 'the ultimate test of the utility to the various models is whether they prove useful to people involved in analyzing problems involving actual markets or groups of markets. I suggest that not only aren't they particularly useful but also that they aren't really used.'

THE DEVELOPMENT OF BUSINESS STRATEGY

The vacuum that this leaves has been filled. Igor Ansoff is generally credited with founding the subject of corporate strategy. Although such a development is clearly foreshadowed by Chandler's contributions to business history, Ansoff (1965) is explicit that his work is motivated by the deficiencies of contemporary microeconomics:

> Study of the firm has been the long time concern of the economics profession. Unfortunately for our present purpose, the so-called *microeconomic* theory of the firm which occupies much of the economists' thought and attention, sheds relatively little light on decision-making processes in a real world firm (p. 16).

It cannot be said that the development of a distinct discipline of strategy has enjoyed much success. The tools of the strategist – the experience curve and the portfolio matrix – are jejeune at best, and much of what passes for strategy is platitude or pious exhortation. The most substantial body of empirical research to be found under the heading of strategy is based on the PIMS database (Buzzell and Gale, 1987) and would fit comfortably into the structure–conduct–performance tradition. The most widely read and influential management book of the 1980s is probably *In Search of Excellence*, a journalistic account of the characteristics of leading American corporations (Peters and

Waterman, 1982). The two most important contributors to the development of strategic thinking in the last decade are probably Porter and Moss Kanter, whose work has recognisable antecedents in economics and organisational sociology respectively. Strategy has even developed its own counter-culture, based largely around the engagingly eccentric Henry Mintzberg, who denies the possibility, or at least the relevance, of a rational strategy process.[1]

Michael Porter stands out from this field in having taken economics to business leaders and in having based strategy firmly in economics. Yet the economics he uses is economics with which Bain and Mason would have been comfortable and familiar. Porter's 'five forces' – suppliers, substitution, entry, customers, rivalry – have an obvious affinity with Scherer's S–C–P presentation in Fig. 1. And this should come as no surprise, since what Porter has done is to cross the Charles River, metaphorically and literally, and bring together the traditions of Harvard economics with those of its Business School. It is notable, but consequential, that the approach is decidedly less successful when applied to the firm (in *Competitive Advantage*, 1985) than when applied to the industry (in *Competitive Strategy*, 1980).

The absence of a well-ordered body of knowledge is most clearly reflected in the way in which the subject is taught. This is based largely on the case method – a kind of classroom learning by doing. No one teaches physics by cases and, interestingly, the technique is not much used in law either. But if economics might lay claim to providing that well ordered body of knowledge which strategy lacks, it is not a claim that has been widely recognised. While business education as a whole has been expanding, the role of formal economics within it has generally been contracting.

THE NEW INDUSTRIAL ECONOMICS

But while all this has been going on, and following directly on the pessimistic comments of Joskow cited above, the subject of industrial economics itself has undergone massive changes. Those that are relevant to the themes of this article fall into two broad areas. Each reflects the resurgence of formal methods in industrial economics: in reaction to, or perhaps in development of, the strongly empirical traditions of the structure–conduct–performance paradigm.

One of these areas is the development of models rooted in game theory. An economist who knew nothing of business strategy might well suppose that it would be centred around the theory of games. He would be quite mistaken. A recent volume (Oster, 1990) is the only major text book on strategy I know even to mention the subject and even that apologises for its novel content by beginning with the slightly shamefaced confession that 'this is a book about competitive strategy by an economist'. Now it is perhaps true that game theory has never quite lived up to the potential which its initial development appeared to offer. One recent text on the subject (Rasmussen, 1989) describes it as the Argentina of economics, in terms of the gap between potential and achievement. If same theory seemed to offer the key to analysing oligopolistic

---

[1] See, for example, Porter (1980, 1985, 1990), Moss Kanter (1983, 1989) and Mintzberg (1976, 1985).

interactions, the lock proved obdurately hard to turn. But from the mid 1970s it did begin to move, and modern textbook in industrial organisation such as Tirole (1988) are very largely based on game theory, at least in a broad sense.

The second important area of change is in that group of issues concerned with asymmetry of information, with principals and agents and with the nature of contracts and ownership. This area of study is currently developing in many different directions, and at present enjoys little coherence taken as a whole. This hardly matters. It is evidently a fertile area of study and has attracted many of the most fertile minds in the profession. It holds out the prospect of a theory of the internal organisation of firms, and of the relationships which is both between firms more comprehensive and more powerful than anything that has existed until now.

THE USES OF MODELS

If strategy has boomed in the last two decades, so has the activity of modelling. All sophisticated firms now have sophisticated models of their operations. Most of these models are of a very different kind to the models typically built by economists. They are deterministic, they are numerical, they are complex, and they are used for computer simulation of future scenarios.

In the early 1970s, this activity was the province of specialists, because the computing power required was so substantial that only skills in new types of program languages made the development of such models feasible. But computing power is no longer a problem, and the development of spreadsheets means that anyone can become a modeller.

This activity has developed to meet a perceived need for forecasts. And forecasts are what the models provide. Output in 1995, costs in 1997, profits in 1999, all come in pages of computer printout at the touch of a button. It is as easy to see why, in a turbulent world, everyone would like the aid of a crystal ball. Yet it is genuinely unclear – even to those who commission it – what this activity is for. Ask a businessman what he would do, if he were given a completely accurate prediction of what his profits would be in 1999. It relieves the task of management hardly at all. If we knew everything about the future, that would relieve the task of management, but only because the task of management would already have been done. As 'Back to the Future' films demonstrate, there is a problem about the role of an individual in a future which is already determined.

The question to which the businessman wants an answer is not 'what does the future hold?' but 'how will my actions affect the future?' It has not been well understood that answering the first is not an essential preliminary to answering the second, and, moreover, that a model developed to answer the first is not necessarily well adapted to answering the second. I could establish how braking affects the motion of my car by inviting a motor engineer to predict the position of the car with and without the application of force to the brake pedal. But it is not a very good way of arriving at the answer. It does not give it very precisely and it does not clarify the distinction between applying the brakes and making a hole in the petrol tank, each of which may have very similar short term effects on the position of the car. The better approach is not to model the car, but to try to understand the braking system – to focus on the element of interest, not to describe the structure as a whole.

The analogy makes the point seem obvious, but it seems to be not at all obvious. The usual purpose of modelling is not to make predictions, but to enhance our understanding of complex systems. The most useful model – and the test of such a model is utility, not truth or falsehood – is the minimal model necessary to capture the essence of the problem. Such approach is quite alien to the professional modeller who objects that the minimal model leaves many things out. How can you model the brake system, he asks, without also modelling the accelerator? If you want to predict what will happen to the car, the objection is well founded. If you want to understand the brake system, it is a red herring. The purpose of modelling complex structures such as firms is not to predict the future – in which neither group of models are much use – but to illuminate the structure of the problem, and here the model that has an analytic solution wins every time against the model which needs three hours of mainframe time for every simulation. It does appear that economists have acquired the most sophisticated understanding of how models can, and cannot, be deployed in the social sciences: it also appears that they have kept that understanding firmly to themselves.

THE FUTURE OF ECONOMICS IN BUSINESS

The firm is a collection of contracts. Its internal organisation is a set of arrangements between principals and agents. Its relationships with its competitors are non-cooperative games and those with its suppliers and customers are cooperative games. All these are subjects which have been at the centre of research in economic theory in the past fifteen years. The key issue for the development of microeconomics in the next century is whether they can be expressed and developed in ways which gives them relevance to business policy. This requires change in the attitudes of both businessmen and economists.

It is, of course, easier to say what businessmen must do. Distinguish insight from cliché. Discover that learning comes not from hearing the felicitous reiteration of what one has oneself just said – the mainstay of most consultancy and business seminars – but from experiencing challenges to one's pre-conceptions. Most of this will happen as the educational level of management rises.

Microeconomics has potentially the same role to play in relation to management issues that macroeconomics currently has for political issues. Because of the ways in which the subject has evolved over the past 100 years, it has conspicuously failed to play that role. Today businessmen's expectations of what economics can offer are not related to microeconomics at all – they look to economists mainly for their forecasts (and are inclined to look at them less).

Yet the present state of knowledge in microeconomic theory is one which makes the time particularly apposite to assert that economics has a much wider range of practical uses. Economics is the natural integrative discipline for much of management science. But its past relative neglect of the firm as the unit of organisation has severely limited the role which it has to play. That is now changing, and that can mean that economics in the next hundred years will have a quite different, and much wider, range of policy applications than those it has exercised in the century that has passed.

The two key groups of question of interest to businessmen – the internal organisation of the firm and its relationship between its suppliers and customers, and the nature of strategic interactions between small groups of firms – are clearly on the agenda of modern economics in a manner which has not been true for most of the last century. First year students are still puzzled when they are faced with models of atomistic perfect competition and wonder which real world industries this actually describes. It is a safe bet that they will not be presented with the same material in the next century.

London Business School

REFERENCES

Ansoff, H. I. (1965). *Corporate Strategy*. McGraw Hill.
Bain, J. S. (1959). *Industrial Organisation*. New York: Wiley.
Buzzell, R. D. and Gale, B. T. (1987). *The PIMS Principles*. New York: Free Press.
Chamberlain, E. H. (1933). *The Theory of Monopolistic Competition*. Cambridge, Mass: Harvard University Press.
Chandler, A. D. (1962). *Strategy and Structure*. Cambridge, Mass: MIT Press.
Coase, R. H. (1937). 'The nature of the firm.' *Economica* vol. 4, pp. 386–405.
Forrester, J. W. (1961). *Industrial Dynamics*. Cambridge, Mass: MIT Press.
Galbraith, J. K. (1964). *The New Industrial State*. Boston: Houghton Mifflin.
Hall, R. J. and Hitch, C. J. (1939). 'Price theory and business behaviour.' *Oxford Economic Papers*, No. 2, May.
Hart, O. and Holstrom, B. (1987). 'The theory of contracts.' In *Advances in Economic Theory* (ed. T. Bewley). Cambridge: Cambridge University Press.
Joskow, P. (1975). 'Firm decision making process and oligopoly theory.' *American Economic Review Papers and Proceedings*, pp. 270–9.
Marshall, A. (1890). *Principles of Economics*. London: Macmillan.
Mintzberg, H. (1976). 'Planning on the left side and managing on the right.' *Harvard Business Review* (July/August).
—— (1985). 'Of strategies, deliberate and emergent.' *Strategic Management Journal*, pp. 257–72.
Moss Kanter, R. (1983). *The Charge Masters*. London: Allen and Unwin.
—— (1989). *When Giants Learn to Dance*. New York: Simon and Schuster.
Oster, S. (1990). *Modern Competitive Analysis*. New York: Oxford University Press.
Peters, T. J. and Waterman, R. H. (1982). *In Search of Excellence*. New York: Harper and Row.
Porter, M. E. (1980). *Competitive Strategy*. New York: Free Press.
—— (1985). *Competitive Advantage*. New York: Free Press.
—— (1990). *The Competitive Advantage of Nations*. New York: Free Press.
Rasmussen, E. (1989). *Games and Information*. Oxford: Blackwell.
Richardson, G. B. (1960). *Information and Investment*. Oxford: Oxford University Press.
Scherer, F. M. (1970). *Industrial Market Structure and Economic Performance*. Rand McNally.
Simon, H. A. (1957). *Models of Man*. New York: Wiley.
—— (1961). *Administrative Behaviour*. New York: Macmillan.
Tirole, J. (1988). *The Theory of Industrial Organisation*. Cambridge, Mass: MIT Press.
Williamson, O. (1975). *Markets and Hierarchies*. New York: Free Press.
—— (1985). *The Economic Institutions of Capitalism*. New York: Free Press.

THE NEXT FIFTY YEARS*

E. Malinvaud

1940–1990, this was a longer period than the one during which I dared to identify myself as an economist. Pretending that I can now forecast what a second life would be, if God would permit, shows that I am still as bold as a young man can be. Although pleasing, the hypothesis on my forecasting ability is no more true than many other hypotheses one can read in professional economic journals. But the rules of our games require that we study the implications of false hypotheses. So, let me go on.

When first thinking about the next fifty years, I saw them as quite gloomy: the challenges will be so serious and we are so badly prepared! But history and personal experience taught me that people do not like Cassandras. Thus pushed by a strong incentive, I gazed more intensely through the fog until I could see behind it a bright future. A good methodology for prospective work requires, however, that before speaking about the future I give at least a brief look at the past.

I. THE PAST

Perhaps the main concern in this JOURNAL is to consider economic science from within so as to see how research evolves, what it achieves, how the main paradigms change, and so on. On this occasion I believe it is more proper at the beginning to question whether economics meets with the expectations one entertains about its ability to contribute to solving some of the problems raised by the organisation of our society. From this point of view the past fifty years were obviously marked first by a wave of optimism, then by the painful realisation that most of the initial beliefs were the product of delusion. This applies whether one considers the broad development issues or the more modest current problems of industrial countries, within which most economists are living.

The following sentences express, admittedly with a bit of caricature, beliefs that were entertained by large and influential groups of economists in the fifties about what the progress of economics would permit: it will lead to international economic order; it will gear development in the Third World; it will show the way to good socio-economic performance in alternative systems to capitalism. Economists are certainly not the only ones to be taken as responsible for subsequent events, which seemed to invalidate such beliefs; however, seen in retrospect, the beliefs appear to have been mainly unwarranted, following from wishful thinking and from bold or loose extrapolations of what economics really knew.

---

* Professor Malinvaud half-accepted my invitation to contribute to this volume: unwilling to speculate over the whole of the next century, we compromised on one half of it; to me, half of Malinvaud is preferable to none. JDH.

The same sequence of confidence and disappointment occurred with respect to the role of economic management in market economies, whether it concerned allocation of resources, distribution of welfare or macroeconomic stabilisation. What happened on this score is still more significant for our present purpose than experience with broader issues. Indeed, initial beliefs derived from properly formulated theories and from sensible ideas on their relevance, as well as on the orders of magnitude of the main effects involved. But one had later to realise that public management never is a purely economic matter and cannot be immune from political interference, if only because the notion of an objective to be achieved can seldom be precisely defined beforehand. More importantly, side effects that had been taken as negligible turned out to be determinant and to require consideration on a par with what had been taken as the main effects. The turnover in the dominant paradigms inspiring theoretical research cannot be fully neglected here, but on the whole ability or inability to solve the real problems played a larger role than fashions in academic research.

II. CHALLENGES OF THE FUTURE

During the next fifty years the world will change. So far as one can tell today, human societies will face huge problems, some of which reacting on priorities that ought to be respectively assigned to different economic questions. Here are three trends that I consider as particularly critical.

First the limitation of resources will increasingly raise concern. From the industrial revolution up to recently, resource pessimism was expressed several times and later found to have been unwarranted because discoveries and technical progress had been grossly underestimated. This experience makes us conscious of the great uncertainties surrounding any assessment on such matters. But it does not rule out that pessimism may increase and appear better justified during the coming decades. Signs at present all point in this direction. World population keeps increasing fast and is not likely to slow down its pace quickly. Parts of the Earth's surface are becoming barren. The environment is deteriorating in many places. Worries about the global climate are spreading. No important breakthrough was achieved for decades over new methods thanks to which human beings could exploit now unused resources. I do not want to contribute to the dramatisation of these signs; resources are still plentiful; but they are perceived as progressively becoming less so; no-one knows whether the pleasant but unproven assumption of the Brundtland Report (1987)[1] ('development is sustainable') will have wide and long support.

Secondly, acute problems may result from inequality of conditions. Indeed, the trend toward a greater degree of inequality is apparent. Within Western countries it may be transitory after a long period in the opposite direction; part of it is due to the abnormal unemployment of the 1980s, which will of course keep receding. But persistence of poverty, the development of an underclass

---

[1] World Commission on Environment and Development, *Our Common Future*, also called *The Brundtland Report*, United Nations, 1987.

and the chronic reappearance of various kinds of segregation, which are also due to non-economic factors, remain disturbing since they are so much at variance with the Western social philosophy. Clarifying the economic factors in such trends and proposing corrective actions will be challenging.

The most disturbing problems are, however, likely to follow from international inequalities. Coexistence of affluent and poor countries was often a major reason for armed conflicts. The South, often overpopulated and exposed to tragedies, will look with less and less sympathy toward the rich North. How economic action can alleviate the tensions and help development will remain a pressing question.

Thirdly, the integration of markets throughout the main regions of the world is likely to pose new challenges. I do not want to deny the many benefits to be reaped from this integration, particularly so in Europe. The microeconomic advantages are obvious and will contribute to create a favourable environment for a new phase of world growth. But it would be irresponsible to ignore the risk of systemic malfunction, as market institutions are becoming more and more complex. The occurrence of financial crises that nobody would be ready to control may have a low probability; economists ought nevertheless not to rule it out of their thoughts.

III. ECONOMICS IS BADLY PREPARED

I am afraid that the prevailing state of mind in the profession tends to turn attention away from the challenges I perceive. What happened during the recent past explains why the old concept of a spontaneous Natural Order has revived. It inspires the research and teaching of some of the most creative and powerful people among us. But it is clearly inappropriate for dealing with the problems I listed in the preceding section, none of which can be properly solved by the free operation of unregulated markets.

The same historical experience has discredited the alternative philosophy of confidence in beneficial public action that was adopted fifty years ago by quite a few in my generation. Such being the situation, it does require a strong character for a young economist to adopt a problematic that could be said to depend on this philosophy.

The risk therefore seriously exists that the discipline progressively loses touch with real problems, develops on its own into a scholastic and becomes less and less significant for the layman's concerns. Many of us think they detect signs of such an evolution when they see that great efforts are being spent for solving problems whose ultimate relevance can only be very indirect.

This vision may, however, be unduly pessimistic. It may follow from an incorrect understanding of the true stakes of some research projects, from a misplaced emphasis on writings that do not deserve much attention and from the oversight of promising works that pave the way to future important progress. Admitting that indeed my worries originated from a misperception of the most urgent needs and/or of the potentialities of economics for facing them, I shall now try to explain how our science ought, according to me, to develop.

IV. ECONOMICS WILL BE REFOCUSED

Progress of the discipline may be identified with a strengthening of its theoretical base, which should exhibit more unity, should better fit the facts and should be made more appropriate to its many uses. But this will not be achieved during the coming decades along the same lines as it was during the previous ones. Signs of change are already apparent whether one considers model building, data analysing or policy advising.

We shall progressively have a richer system of theoretical models. Work on general theories will not be negligible, but advance will mainly come from the setting up and study of constellations of specific models, each one being appropriate for dealing with some particular aspects of the phenomena, the articulation between models being well charted. Each one of these models will make strong simplifications, even for analytical convenience; one may say it will present only a prototype of the real economy. Indeed, the world we have to understand is quite complex and fundamental notions, which were still obscure not very long ago, have been clarified. Very general models no longer suffice for the more specific questions we now have to consider; they have to be supplemented by more operational models, whose usefulness and limitations will become familiar.

The quantification of economics and the diffusion of econometrics were definite and irreversible acquisitions. But the profession must still secure a stricter deontology for its dealing with data. All the more so as economists will never work with 'exact laws'; clearly an approximate fit has a dubious value as long as it is not duplicated or somehow enlightened by other evidence: in econometrics as in the court 'testis unus, testis nullus'. The collective inductive work of estimation and testing will go on, even if at times it appears tedious. It will use a more diversified set of data sources and recognise for instance that a direct knowledge of motivation is often accessible. Even when they contradict previously held ideas, results will be cumulative and make our empirical knowledge progressively less spotty and more precise. We shall obtain a better characterisation of constraints and behaviour, measure the order of magnitude of many elasticities, locate the reliable and risky aggregations, and so on. The outcome of this work will in particular be to tell us the worth of each one of the operational models that will enrich our tool kit.

After a period of doubts the usefulness of economics as a normative science will again be recognised. A new doctrine for macroeconomic policy making will emerge; it will be less simple-minded and more cautious than the one following in the older days from vulgar Keynesianism; but it will not recommend abstention under any set of circumstances, while it will also pay great attention to market incentives. Similarly economists will again have a role to play in the choice of public projects and taxation rules. Stress will everywhere be laid on the international aspects of policies, since these aspects will be dominant features of the challenges people will have to face.

V. ECONOMICS WILL BE A LESS ISOLATED SCIENCE

During the past decades economic logic was put to work on phenomena that belong to the realms of other social sciences: demography, politics, sociology,…Specialists of these disciplines have to say how much they may benefit from these intrusions; so far as I understand, the gains are significant. Time is now coming when reverse flows are going to be found interesting for economics. More and more people among us will recognise the limits of the dominant concepts of economic rationality and economic equilibrium; without abjuring their faith in the value of these concepts, they will realise that exclusive reliance on them is not always warranted. Psychologists, sociologists, political scientists will offer us a rich body of evidence on when and how economic behaviour and economic interactions systematically deviate from the patterns implied by our paradigms. Eventually the profession will find these contributions useful and even palatable.

Simultaneously economists will more and more often collaborate with others on policy issues. Problems tend to be increasingly multisided in our complex world; costs and benefits of alternative solutions may be quite subtle; they may fall on distant and far apart periods, as well as on different nations or different social groups. In all these cases economic analysis is required in order to appraise proposals made by scientists. Conversely in order to decide on many issues posed to the economist supplementary information on physical, technological, institutional or social constraints is required. Interdisciplinary collaboration will thus have to become much more frequent; we see it already at work for instance in the management of the environment or in the study of public issues by national academies. This is just a beginning.

College de France

GENERAL EQUILIBRIUM THEORY IN THE TWENTY-FIRST CENTURY

Michio Morishima

In trying to predict what the shape of economic theory will be in the twenty-first century, I am going to take as my time period the latter half of the century, and to limit my consideration to the field of General Equilibrium Theory (GET), the area within which I have up to now been conducting research. The purpose of GET is to try to clarify how the social economy works. Models are constructed, and these are then strictly and rigorously subjected to theoretical analysis. In order to do this, it is necessary to start off with a broad vision of the movement of the economy, such as is portrayed, for example, in macroeconomics. GET then elaborates on this at the microeconomic level, with the aim of supplying a microeconomic foundation to the macroeconomic vision. GET owes a great deal to developments in macroeconomic theory; in the latter part of the last century theorists such as Marx and Walras refined Ricardo's economics (I regard the theories of Marx and Walras as old GET), while in the second half of this century Hicks, Patinkin and Malivaud have been inspired by the theories of Keynes, and Arrow–Debreu and Arrow–Hahn have axiomatised Hicks' theory to form new GET.

Given the complexity of society, GET has tended hitherto to deal with a model constructed on the basis of an exaggerated and deformed view of economic society, shedding light on only a few facets of that society. Ricardo and Walras looked at the question of how population and capital must adapt within a given area of land; Marx looked at the exploitation of one class by another, while the focal point of the models conceived by Walras, Hicks and Leontief was the repercussion of prices and outputs from one sector of the economy to another. Böhm-Bawerk's, Wicksell's and Hicks' analyses concerned the time structure of the modern production system – for example what length of roundabout production is the most appropriate, and when machines and capital equipment should be discarded and replaced. All of these views are entirely pertinent, but each by itself is essentially a distortion, seeking out no more than a single facet of reality. We need a comprehensive multiple-facet model; the various theories must not just be advocated by separate schools, but must be brought into synthesis.

In reaching such a synthesis, however, conflicting views will have to be harmonised. We are only too aware how scholars are divided between approval and disapproval of exploitation theory, and there are doubtless a host of other views which are mutually contradictory if we examine them in more detail, and which will need to be rationalised. Unlike physics, economics has unfortunately developed in a direction far removed from its empirical source, and GET in particular, as the core of economic theory, has become a mathematical social philosophy. In spite of its scientific presentation, the Arrow–Hahn book[1] may remind us of Baruch Spinoza's *Ethica Ordine Geometrico Demonstrata*.

I have discussed myself in a separate essay[2] how Japanese mathematics (or *wasan*) in the Tokugawa period, though it had attained a high level of sophistication, came to a wretched end due to its total absence of interaction with natural science. It turned into a technique for the setting of puzzles, and the *wasan* scholars were reduced to being the playmates of culture-loving samurai and members of the newly risen merchant class, just like the masters of the tea ceremony, of flower arrangement and of the *haiku*. At the same time, the mathematics itself regressed. The following words by John von Neumann can be read as a warning against decadence of this kind: 'At a great distance from its empirical source, or after much "abstract" inbreeding, a mathematical subject is in danger of degeneration.'[3] In fact, GET economists, along with the specialists in von Neumann economics who are just one element of them, have sunk into excessive mental aestheticism. If this bad habit is not corrected, and if what von Neumann said is right, then the twenty-first century will see the degeneration of their subject.

In the models of theorists such as Hicks, Arrow, Debreu and Hahn which are the focal influences in GET, not just households but firms as well are assumed to act as pricetaker. These models are exactly applicable only to agriculture, forestry, fishing and part of the mining sector, industries whose outputs account at the very most for 20 % of GDP in most modern industrial economies. In most remaining industries, individual enterprises make decisions on the price of their respective outputs, according to the mark-up theory, either of the version called the full-cost principle or of the version known as the marginal-cost principle. Competition is carried on through devising methods of production or methods of selling which will permit a lower mark-up rate.

Within these industries there used to be a fair number of industries where prices were determined by haggling of the GET type. In the case of taxi fares, for example, negotiation over the price on the street actually disappeared as meters were installed in all the taxicabs. This means that methods of determining prices differ according to the stage of technological development. With technological development, communication of a kind hitherto impossible is available at a low price, and hence becomes accessible to a large number of people. This in turn means that the price of many commodities – such as equities and foreign currency – is determined by methods very different from those postulated under GET. For example, under GET price determination is carried on in a situation of universal knowledge in a perfectly open market which can be entered by anyone, while the banks' foreign exchange dealers conduct price negotiations over the telephone without the intervention of a

[1] K. J. Arrow and F. H. Hahn, *General Competitive Analysis*, Amsterdam: North-Holland (1971).

[2] M. Morishima, 'The good and bad use of mathematics', in *Economics in Disarray*, P. Wiles and G. Routh ed., Oxford: Basil Blackwell (1984).

[3] M. Dore, S. Chakravarty and R. Goodwin, *John von Neumann and Modern Economics*, Oxford: Clarendon Press (1989), p. xiv. Notwithstanding a citation of this kind at the start of this volume, the empirical content of the various pieces contained in it is surprisingly thin and meagre.

third party.[4] However, this kind of chain of activity, where prices are determined in isolation, ultimately causes the price to converge on an equilibrium price. To obtain this effect each dealer may not negotiate in a selfish fashion over the price, but must keep to the established rules, and it is essential for GET to clarify the nature of the rules which will bring about price stability. Thus the institutional elements of the economy are important. It is not surprising to see that the theory of stability, that mountain of empty theorising accumulated between the mid 1940s and the late 1960s, was a total failure.

And that is not all. As methods of preserving goods are developed, the ways of determining their prices also change. The cut-price sale of strawberries on the street in the evenings, for example, is likely to disappear once we reach the stage where strawberries can be perfectly preserved, and the price of strawberries will be determined, like those of manufactured products, according to the full-cost principle. In so far as these sorts of method of determining prices are dependent on technology, price theory too must inevitably change in accordance with the stage of technological development. Those who might be referred to as neoclassical economists have not up to now made any positive attempt to come to terms with the full-cost principle, and it will become abundantly clear in the twenty-first century that such a conservative attitude is out of tune with the times.[5] The eyes with which we look at an economy differ depending on the theory that we use, and in the case of economics a theory is never totally self-sufficient and autonomous, but dependent on material conditions (especially on technology).

It is also the case that the world of GET is in fact a dream world, a world which is not totally workable in the context of actual society. The number of actors on the stage in this GET world are far too few. The old general equilibrium theorists were strongly aware of this. Walras, for example, in his *Elements of Pure Economics*, emphasised the existence not only of capitalists, landlords and workers, but of a fourth group as well, namely entrepreneurs, who acted as independent agents. Moreover, in Schumpeter's *Theorie der Wirtschaftlichen Entwicklung* (1911), not only did the author stress the importance of entrepreneurs, but bankers were brought on to the scene for the first time. Entrepreneurs without bankers are like soldiers without weapons; without bankers it is extremely hard for entrepreneurs to discharge their own functions.

This kind of trend showed that GET was progressing in the right direction. With the new GET, however, both entrepreneurs and bankers have virtually ceased to exist. There are no innovations nor founding of new enterprises, and the head of each enterprise earns his profits by operating production possibility sets given to him, i.e. bequeathed to him by his ancestors in the past. This is a reversion to a truly medieval, hereditary economy if ever there was one. I will

---

[4] For how the foreign exchange markets actually work, and what sort of rules the dealers have to adhere to, see, for example, M. Morishima, *The Economics of Industrial Society*, Cambridge University Press (1984), pp. 99–132. For the structure of other markets, there is a splendid account in Hicks' *A Market Theory of Money*, Oxford: Clarendon Press (1989).

[5] My criticism is directed at neoclassical economists, but the Sraffians are far worse in their disregard of empirical content.

grant that such a retrogressive approach is an easy path if one wants to construct a model axiomatically, and it may also be of some use as a temporary means of facilitating the dichotomising method, whereby entrepreneurs and bankers are put to sleep for a while. (I also give due credit to the fact that GET now has monetary theory as one of its elements, even if it is a monetary theory whose entrepreneurs and bankers are either absent or asleep.) Nevertheless, once the existence of equilibrium in this fictional world has been proved, GET theorists go crazy. They pursue their model too far, under the illusion that by clarifying its optimum properties they have also clarified the optimality of the modern capitalist economy, in which entrepreneurs and bankers play such an important role, whereas all they have in fact done is to clarify the optimality of a hereditary economy.

GET, moreover, following the fundamental premise of seventeenth- and eighteenth-century English rationalism, makes the assumption that each agent acts in accordance with the principles of utility maximisation and profit maximisation. As long as the economies with which we are dealing are those of Western countries (especially those of North Europe and North America), there was no particular objection to this in the twentieth century, but during the course of the twenty-first century the countries of Asia, starting with Japan, and of South America, are likely to become the objects of GET analysis. When that happens, if we continue to act upon the same assumptions as we do now, GET will in these countries no longer be able to play the role of an instrument of economic analysis and a theoretical system capable of cultivating a vision of the economy. It will be too far removed from their own reality. It will come, therefore, to be regarded merely as an instrument for training students' power of logic. Peoples possessing a philosophy (or a set of guiding principles) very different from Western European rationalism, have already acquired the skills needed to operate capitalism or highly productive economies which can compete effectively with capitalist ones. In the context of this development it is essential for GET to throw off its adherence to eighteenth-century Western rationalism, to attempt to become more universal, and to consider of its own volition the kind of ethos appropriate to an economic system with a high degree of productivity.

It goes without saying that as long as people's work ethics are different, the industrial organisation constructed upon them will be different as well. GET needs to maintain a relationship of close cooperation with both sociology and social psychology, and we need to look very deeply into the sociological aspects of the GET system. The bureaucratic operation of enterprises and industries should be paid more attention in GET analysis, and at the same time even research into family relationships is likely to become a research topic within GET, as the twenty-first century will see the flourishing of small, family-based enterprises in the wake of robotisation. It would be difficult to find anything differing more between North and South Europe, and between Oriental and Occidental countries, than family relationships. Here, too, is something that cannot be easily determined by principles of utility maximisation and profit maximisation.

The question of convergence between the economies of Western Europe and those of Eastern Europe has been much discussed, and in the twenty-first century the issue of convergence between the eastern and western hemispheres is likely to become a research topic as well. That means, in essence, a convergence of cultures. Should the various disciplines which concern themselves with trends in society come in this way to be more aware of the differences between cultures and to look at the issue of convergence of different cultures, then GET, too, must go along with this trend, overcome the limitations of Western European rationalism, and look closely at the differing kinds of ethos which may be compatible with capitalism or with the operation of a modern social economy.

The issue of the appropriateness of various kinds of ethos to modern technology was one which deeply concerned Max Weber. It was at the beginning of this century that he first posed this question, at a time, perhaps, when the issue was somewhat premature. It was a time when the Christian cultural area, in particular the countries with a strong protestant tradition, had almost total command over modern technology, and of the countries outside this area only Japan had entered into this privileged company. Even in the case of Japan, it was not clear whether or not the country was well established as a group member.

For that reason the issue was discussed in the context of inadequate empirical materials. It was extremely difficult, therefore, to reach any sort of scientific verdict on the argument, and the result was inevitably that the debate advanced in a very ideological fashion. Now in the twenty-first century we will have at our disposal the results of substantial empirical observations, and be able to discuss objectively how economic systems change according to the different ethos. Not just that, we shall be able to discuss on the basis of empirical evidence the reverse relationship, namely how technology influences an ethos, whether it brings about convergence of ethos, and stimulates a degree of uniformity. If it is to be able to examine this sort of range of questions, then GET must become truly multi-disciplinary by being more closely tied to sociology and other disciplines.

Of the two pillars of economics – mathematical analysis and social scientific analysis – it is the latter which will become relatively more important in the twenty-first century, and it must become so, at least as far as GET is concerned. What must be emphasised, however, is that there is no question of my making this prediction on the basis of any 'anti-mathematics' sentiment. In June 1900 Walras wrote: 'The twentieth century, which is not far off, will feel the need...of entrusting the social sciences to men of general culture who are accustomed to thinking *both* inductively and deductively and who are familiar with reason *as well as* experience'[6] (my italics). What I am saying here is very much the same thing. However, whereas in his time mathematics lagged behind in becoming widely used, and he was urging mathematicalisation, in the contemporary world it has gone too far, leading theorists to have an

---

[6] Leon Walras, *Elements of Pure Economics*, London: George Allen and Unwin (1954), p. 48.

inadequate concern for actuality. I, therefore, am arguing for rather the opposite. No pillars can serve together to support a building, but should one become too big and too strong the other will become correspondingly weak, and the building will collapse. Clearly, a strong and healthy construction cannot be founded upon such a basis.

Whether or not my prediction comes true will depend upon the good sense of all GET theorists in the future, but various encouraging things have occurred which make me feel optimistic. One such factor is the appearance during the 1980s of works such as A. M. Okun's *Prices and Quantities*[7] and Hicks' *Market Theory*, mentioned above, works which could well serve as a starting point for the kind of GET which I have in mind. I know of course that one section of GET scholars may regard with hostility those who make statements such as I have made above, on the grounds of their loyalty to mathematics. Scholars of this group expend their energies on competing with each other in demonstrations of intellectual and theoretical ability, and regard as their inferiors those who contend the need to observe the real world. This phenomenon is a palpable symptom of scientific degeneration.

However, should there by any chance appear a group of brave souls who are prepared to forgo the easy pleasure of demonstrating their mathematical abilities and to hone the skill of building a model on the basis of empirical observation, the history of theory will move off in a completely different direction. The new empirical model itself must come first; its axiomatisation and mathematical refinement must be the second stage.

London School of Economics and Political Science

---

[7] A. M. Okun, *Prices and Quantities*, Oxford: Basil Blackwell (1981). My own *Industrial Society*, referred to previously, also describes this kind of schema. A recent addition to this stream is R. M. Solow, *The Labour Market as a Social Institution*, Oxford, Basil Blackwell (1990).

PROGRESS AND MICROECONOMIC DATA*

Andrew J. Oswald

In my day the Economics journals were relevant. They were full of information about real firms, workers and consumers. Now there's nothing but obscure algebra. Imagine what it is going to be like in a hundred years...

Archetypal critic

Is Economics going in the right direction? Some people think not. Wassily Leontief (1982) has argued that our discipline has deteriorated into a second-rate branch of applied mathematics in which, unscientifically, researchers eschew empirical investigation. James Heckman (1986, p. 384) says that the subject is 'widely perceived to be discredited because it has so little empirical content and cares so little about developing it'. John Pencavel (1989, p. 1) concludes that economists do not want applied work to be done, because it is likely to reveal the irrelevance of their hypotheses and undermine their ability to derive sweeping implications from theoretical models. Theodore Morgan's (1988) study shows that in Economics half of all published papers use no data, whereas in Physics it is only 12% and in Chemistry approximately zero. In private conversation it is common to hear applied economists ridicule the 'chalk scribbles' of theorists and impugn their motives. Partly because of such concerns, the American Economic Association recently instituted an inquiry into the state of economics as taught in US graduate schools.

One theoretical objection to all this is that research in economics is generated in a form of free market and is therefore likely to be efficient. Those doing the important work should earn the highest salaries and get promoted most quickly; economists engaged in boring research should be penalised. Adam Smith's hand ought to be leaning on mine.

Although Dr Pangloss might agree with this view, it does not cut much ice with sceptics. Free markets, they say, can go wrong. Academic economics has entered into a downward spiral in which, because a post-war generation of mathematicians hold power, formal analytical ability is the criterion for advancement. Believing themselves to be an elite, the ruling class aim to create future generations in their own image. They do this by accepting for publication only certain kinds of articles, by recommending for promotion young mathematical economists, and by changing graduate courses to stress technical skills at which they excel. This moulding of the subject is possible because academic economists' behaviour is not constrained, like that of commercial companies, by outside customer pressure. Academic economics is

* For helpful suggestions I am grateful to Graham Beaver, Joan Beaver, Danny Blanchflower, Alan Carruth, John Hey and Coral Oswald. Opinions are mine alone.

bankrupt but will not die. University professors laugh, cynically or in self-delusion, all the way to the bank.

I do not know how best to address this complex question, nor precisely where I stand on it (though my sympathies are with the critics). However, it seems clear that the matter will not be clarified by a list of prejudices or platitudes. It is natural to ask if there are any data that bear on the issue.

I. THE STUDY

In this short paper I report the results of an examination of all full-length articles published in regular issues of the ECONOMIC JOURNAL between 1959 and 1990. The focus of my study is articles which use empirical microeconomic information (micro data, in the current jargon). Theorists and applied researchers should presumably be able to agree that it is desirable to have research using data at the least aggregated level. Empirical inquiries at the micro level ought to fit in naturally with the microeconomic models which appear to dominate theoretical research, and help to build an empirical microeconomic foundation for aggregate economics. Stafford (1986) identifies a post-war growth of research using micro data in labour economics and suggests that it is this kind of change that will prevent the demise of scientific economics. In this spirit, I try to consider the following question. Compared with today, did a previous generation have journals full of practical articles based on data for real firms and people?

I went through each issue of the JOURNAL from March 1959 to the June issue of 1990, which was the most recent issue at the time of the project. Because of the nature of the exercise, I was unwilling to assign the job to a research assistant. Apart from counting the numbers of articles, I noted those papers which used micro data, namely, non-aggregated data on the actions of microeconomic agents like firms, plants, workers, consumers, unions, subjects in experimental situations, and even laboratory pigeons. The main kinds of relevant data were:

  (i) case studies done by the authors,
  (ii) small sample surveys or experiments carried out by the authors,
  (iii) computerised survey data sets not collected directly by the authors themselves.

I did not include aggregated data of the kind used in most macroeconomics and international trade, nor industry-level aggregates as employed especially in industrial and labour economics.

In a small number of cases it was hard to decide how to classify a piece of research. Should one include a study that uses consumer survey data at almost, but not quite, its fully disaggregated individual level? What of an aggregate time series study that incorporates in an incidental way a minute questionnaire survey, or a case study of a firm in which almost no data are used or reported? Generally I gave such studies the benefit of the doubt and included them, because I was concerned that to exclude these papers would bias the results against the earlier literature in which computer data sets were not so easily acquired. However, the Appendix, which is constructed to allow others to check my calculations, marks these borderline cases with an asterisk. Those who wish to do so may verify that the key conclusions of the paper are insensitive to the exclusion of the marginal cases.

The years 1959–90 were chosen to allow a full three decades of data after correcting for a three year moving average. The raw data are given in the Appendix.

Summing within decades, the proportions of articles based on micro data were as follows.

Proportion of ECONOMIC JOURNAL *articles using microeconomic data*

1960–1969	1970–1979	1980–1989
5%	15%	17%

This leads to the paper's first conclusion. I find nothing to support the view, captured in a provocative way in the archetypal quote at the front of the paper, that ECONOMIC JOURNAL authors have systematically turned away from the study of microeconomic data on real economic agents. Rather, the news is, from most economists' perspective, fairly encouraging The JOURNAL now publishes proportionally three times as many empirical papers based on micro data as it did three decades ago.

It is revealing, however, to study the time series statistics. These are plotted in Fig. 1. To smooth out some of the fluctuations in a comparatively volatile series, Fig. 1 reports a three year moving average.

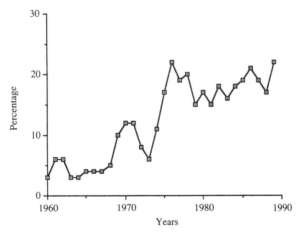

Fig. 1. Proportion of articles using microeconomic data (3 year moving average).

Fig. 1 shows that from 1960 to the end of the 1980s there was strong growth in the proportion of papers using microeconomic data. During the 1960s the numbers rarely exceeded one paper in twenty; then, in the early part of the next decade, the percentage doubled; by the 1980s it was fluctuating around what appears to be a steady percentage of approximately one in five of all published articles. Although a linear regression produces a statistically significant time trend, inspection of Fig. 1 suggests that these data are more consistent with a mid-1970s jump in the amount of research based upon micro data. Whilst more degrees of freedom would be welcome, there is little sign of a continuing upward trend in empirical microeconomic research. The 1976 figure, for example, is identical to that in 1989. One speculative interpretation of this – in line with neoclassical economics' stress on technology – is that a revolution in computing power changed the equilibrium once and for all. My own guess had been that the data would reveal a powerful and continuing upward trend.

Before concluding, it may be necessary, at the risk of stating the obvious, to record the following points. First, most of us believe that economics needs theory as well as empirical evidence, and also recognise that applied work can degenerate into an unhelpful cataloguing of correlations. The key and difficult question is that of the optimal division between theoretical and empirical research. Second, the ECONOMIC JOURNAL is only one journal and it is possible that the results found here do not generalise to others. Third, various kinds of valuable empirical research are not covered in this study. Fourth, the data I have collected cover only one third of the JOURNAL's history. Fifth, the quote with which this paper begins is phrased, as a form of debating device, in a deliberately simple and provocative way. I am aware that many critics have more subtle objections than are encapsulated by it.

II. CONCLUSIONS

This paper has examined the contents of full-length articles published in regular issues of this JOURNAL from 1959 to 1990. Contrary to the archetypal critical view quoted at the beginning, I do not find evidence of a decline in empirical research on firms, workers and consumers. The reverse is true. Thirty years ago, 3% of articles used microeconomic data. Today the figure is approximately 20%.

If this is a ray of sunshine, my judgement is that it does not come out of a cloudless sky. As Morgan (1988) demonstrates, half the articles published in the *American Economic Review* and the ECONOMIC JOURNAL do not use data of any kind. Moreover, the results in my paper seem to suggest, in contrast to what I had expected, that we are not seeing exponential growth in research drawing upon micro data: around the mid-1970s the proportion of such work levelled out at about one article in five. This suggests that economics is in an equilibrium in which large numbers of researchers treat the subject as if it were a kind of mathematical philosophy. I find it hard to believe that this is a desirable state of affairs.

Dartmouth College, NBER and London School of Economics

REFERENCES

Heckman, J. (1986). *Who's Who in Economics* (ed. M. Blaug). Cambridge: MIT Press.

Leontief, W. (1982). 'Academic economics.' *Science*, vol. 127, pp. 104–7.
Morgan, T. (1988). 'Theory versus empiricism in academic economics: update and comparisons.' *Journal of Economic Perspectives*, vol. 2, pp. 159–64.
Pencavel, J. H. (1989). Chapter 3 ('Trade union objectives') of unpublished book manuscript.
Stafford, F. (1986). 'Forestalling the demise of empirical economics: the role of micro data in labor economics research. In *Handbook of Labour Economics*, vol. 1 (ed. O. Ashenfelter and R. Layard). Amsterdam: North Holland Publishing.

DATA APPENDIX

To allow others to check my calculations and assumptions, I list here, in order, (i) the years covered, (ii) the proportion of articles analysing micro data in each year, and (iii) the names of the authors of those papers that use micro data. As explained in the text, I assign a * after the author's name if I judge that that article uses micro data but I consider it possible that others might judge differently. For example, an entry reading '*1999*: 0·035, Smith and Jones, Alexander(*)' means that in year 1999 three and a half percent of articles used microeconomic data and this was a total of two articles, one by Smith and Jones and the other by Alexander, where the classification of Alexander's article as using micro data might be considered by some to be mildly controversial.

All Notes, Presidential addresses, Surveys and Supplements were excluded from the analysis. The raw data are as follows.

1959: zero, zero.

1960: zero, zero. *1961*: 0·083, Butler, Fisher, Kilby. *1962*: 0·094, Grossfield(*), McLelland(*), Farrell(*). *1963*: zero, zero. *1964*: 0·042, Helleiner(*). *1965*: 0·034, Kreinin(*). *1966*: 0·037, Grossfield and Heath(*). *1967*: 0·038, Maddala and Knight(*). *1968*: 0·037, Meek and Watts *1969*: 0·069, Rowley(*), Hartley.

1970: 0·190, Alemson, Selby Smith, Kothari(*), Briston and Tomkins. *1971*: 0·107, Sutherland(*), Radice, Adelman and Dalton. *1972*: 0·059, MacKay and Reid, Cowling and Cubbin. *1973*: 0·061, Wilkinson, Benishay. *1974*: 0·071, Muellbauer(*), Brown and Levin. *1975*: 0·185, Layard and Verry, Cosh, Singh, Stoneman(*), Meeks and Whittington. *1976*: 0·241, Pack, Huang, Firth(*), Hart, Shorrocks, Levitt, Chiplin and Sloane. *1977*: 0·250, Utton, Teece(*), Solomon and Forsyth, Muellbauer(*), Jones and Backus, Morawetz *et al*. *1978*: 0·094, MacLennan, Booth and Coats, McGregor. *1979*: 0·250, Nguyen and Martinez-Salvidar, Beckerman(*), Creedy and Hart, Forsund and Hjalmarsson, Firth, Fry, Doherty(*).

1980: 0·111, Hocking(*), Greenhalgh, Nickell, Harrigan *et al*.(*) *1981*: 0·154, Binswanger, Hughes and McCormick, Mansfield *et al*., Schaefer(*), Green, Fenn. *1982*: 0·189, King and Dicks-Mireaux, Shorrocks, Hemming and Kay, Blundell and Walker, Gort and Klepper(*), Mookherjee and Shorrocks(*), Allen. *1983*: 0·206, Plott, Hemming and Harvey, Levy, Zabalza, Cubbin and Leech, Stewart, Pittman. *1984*: 0·100, Stewart and Greenhalgh, Brubaker, Blundell and Ray, Carter. *1985*: 0·238, Ravallion, Jones-Lee *et al*., West *et al*. Cable, Micklewright, Christofides, Narendranathan *et al*., Lucas, Truong and Hensher, Butler and Worrall. *1986*: 0·18, Bailey, Kay and Thompson, Dimson and Fraletti, Masson, McCormick, Kooreman and Kapteyn, Stark *et al*., Gort and Wall(*), Borooah and Sharpe(*), Blake *et al.*, Schankerman and Pakes(*). *1987*: 0·163, Stewart, Knight and Sabot, Harrison *et al.*, Lowenstein, Battalio, Miller, Dolton and Makepeace. *1988*: 0·162, Anderson and Gilbert(*), Blanchflower and Oswald, Fenn and Veljanowski, Bean and Turnbull(*), Rosenzweig, Ravallion. *1989*: 0·182, Dyer *et al.*, Cable and Wilson, Taylor(*), Cohen and Levinthal, Baker *et al.*, Pissarides and Wadsworth, Baden-Fuller, Bover.

1990 (2 issues only): 0·33, Wadhwani and Wall, Levis, Phipps, Harrison and Morgan, Nickell and Wadhwani, Blackaby and Manning, Cable and Wilson, Johnes.

PROSPECTS FOR ECONOMICS*

John Pencavel

In any discussion about the state of economics, there are two, closely related, classes of issues: the state of the profession and the state of ideas. In what follows, I shall meander between conjectures about the future of the profession and conjectures about the future of economic ideas. Though, in principle, these are distinct classes of issues, my meanders will hopelessly blur them. This is not surprising: however much we may try to restrict out sights exclusively to the analysis of ideas and arguments, we never quite dissociate them from their social context. Indeed, scientific endeavour is embodied in the work of scientists and the intellectual enterprise does not exist outside of the people and their organisations.

A recurring theme in what follows is the increasing size and diversity of economics in the future. Along almost any dimension – topics studied, analytical approaches, institutional affiliations, specialist associations – the enterprise of economics will become bigger and more varied. A larger, more heterogeneous, discipline does not necessarily imply greater competition in the process of scientific discovery and the dissemination of ideas, but in fact economic science will become an even more competitive activity than it is now. A rough pyramidal hierarchy will persist, but there will be a much wider base with many minarets representing local confluences of authority. In fact, I am emulating most soothsayers here by projecting into the future some trends evident from the past one hundred years of economics. What are these trends?

EXTRAPOLATING TRENDS?

The most obvious change in the profession has been in its size. There were surely less than one thousand economists in Britain a century ago and perhaps the same number in the United States. The study of economics was restricted to a few countries mostly in West and Central Europe and in English-speaking societies of North America and Australasia. The focal points of the profession remain West Europe and North America even though in every country today there are people designating themselves as economists. In the future, insofar as the international concentration of wealth becomes less marked over time so (with perhaps a generational lag) will the concentration of economists. North America and West Europe will remain centres of scholarship and instruction, but their relative influence will decline.

The past hundred years have witnessed a terrific growth in the demand for and supply of economists. Should we expect this to continue? I think so.[1] We

---

* In writing this essay, I have benefited from conversations with Paul A. David and Victor R. Fuchs.
[1] At least a growth in absolute numbers, not in proportionate rates of change.

have been remarkably successful in leading both public and private organisations to believe we can provide useful services for them. The pressures on various organisations and individuals to be seen courting and acting upon expert advice are considerable and certain attributes of economists have resulted in their filling this role in many cases.

These attributes consist, first, of a coherent and robust set of principles on which to base a study of human behaviour. Notwithstanding extensive criticism of conventional models of economic behaviour, economists' first basic principles have appealed to the demand for information by a wide variety of agencies and organisations. Perhaps the activities of economists should be seen as simply providing justification for and blessing of the natural instincts of these organisations[2] or perhaps there is real value added to the work economists do. In either event, the perceived relevance of these principles is one important component explaining economists' success.

Another feature that has served economics well is the remarkable spread of mathematical methods of reasoning among economists. Of course, there are cases where the use of mathematics has no more than repeated in unnecessarily formal and forbidding terms an argument that could be made more simply and honestly without mathematics. There are also cases in which vacuous or trivial ideas have been camouflaged by forbidding and empty formalism. But in many cases, mathematics has effected a great economy of reasoning and has allowed deductions that would have been virtually impossible without it.

I do not believe that past trends in the use of mathematics in economics will continue into the future. There is no question that there will always be a very important role for mathematical reasoning in economics and a heavy reliance will be continue to be placed on mathematics in expressing and reporting on frontier research. Indeed, more than is the case now, conversations among economists will be expressed mathematically. However, I do not expect the profession to allocate its honours increasingly to those offering more and more abstract characterisations of economic behaviour. As mathematical reasoning becomes ever more commonplace, so the scarcity value of original and relevant ideas will become manifest.

By comparison with other social sciences, economics has been in the vanguard of applied mathematics and, in an increasingly quantitative age, this has allowed it to score many points over rival disciplines. I shall be surprised if economists' edge over other social scientists in the use of mathematical reasoning is going to persist. Other social scientists are aware of the rewards economists have earned from being mathematically literate and in the future these other social scientists can be expected to acquire the skills enabling them to compete more successfully for them. There is nothing intrinsic about the sort of problems economists work on that endows them with a natural advantage

---

[2] 'It is precisely the pursuit of profit which destroys the prestige of the business man. While wealth can buy all forms of respect, it never finds them freely given. It was the task of the economists to overcome these sentiments and justify the ways of Mammon to man. No one likes to have a bad conscience. Pure cynicism is rather rare... It is the business of economists, not to tell us what we do, but to show why what we are doing anyway is in accord with proper principles' (Robinson, 1962, p. 21).

in the mathematical expression of their arguments. So this attribute of economists' considerable professional success during the past decades will surely be of less importance in the future. Economics will then fall back exclusively on its particular set of beliefs.

THE EVOLUTION OF BELIEFS

It is difficult to forecast how economists' beliefs will change. Our current stock of beliefs is the product of our experiences and of our interpretation of these experiences as provided by economics research. Economics is, of course, an empirical science – it seeks to understand the world we live in or have lived in – and, if we were to trace through the genealogical lines far enough, we would find that all economics research has distinct roots in quite basic questions about the actual operation of economies and about economic behaviour. However, in some research, the genealogical tree has to be followed through very many generations before these empirical roots are exposed. In these cases, 'internally propelled' research, the motivation for an article or monograph is provided by unresolved issues and particular puzzles unearthed in previous economics research and the links to the underlying empirical questions are obscure and difficult to fathom. By contrast, the motivation for 'externally propelled' economics research derives immediately from some observed behaviour.

This distinction between internally and externally propelled economics research is, of course, one of degree, not of kind. It turns on the length of the genealogical lines between current work and its empirical underpinnings and the tracing of these lines is sometimes difficult and arbitrary. The distinction is certainly not one between theoretical and empirical research: many theoretical papers are prompted not by X's last paper, but by some observed anomaly or perceived pattern for which elements of an explanation is offered. Correspondingly, much work in empirical economics has lost touch with the questions originally instigating the line of work and it takes the form of organising data differently (with perhaps different statistical techniques) or of exploiting new bodies of data without addressing the fundamental issues.

Necessarily, it is difficult to foretell the direction both of internally and of externally propelled research. In the case of the former, there is a large stochastic and unpredictable component in the processes describing its evolution. Externally propelled research is going to be affected substantially by our particular experiences which, of course, are also unknown at the moment. But this serves to point out that the most obvious contribution to scholarship available to economics a century hence is simply provided by the passage of time and the experiences over that time. In one hundred years we shall have one hundred more years of accumulated data on behaviour provided we bother to accumulate it in a usable form! A cynic will wonder whether this will effect much change in economic ideas and beliefs, but I have little doubt that the experiences provided by the workings of economies will help immeasurably in understanding behaviour.

The particular form of that learning will depend on those experiences: little will be learned about hyperinflation if no economy experiences the ravages of hyperinflation. But in studying the evolution of economies over this period and in collecting and examining data about the operation of these economies, the economist one hundred years from now should have a bounty of information from which to draw. This should result in a substantial change in economic thinking and I expect a number of fashionable ideas today will be seen, in retrospect, as fanciful and ridiculous.

This will be the case unless the 'middle ground' of economics research is largely deserted. By the middle ground, I mean research that systematically and honestly confronts hypotheses about behaviour with experimental and nonexperimental observations. And confrontation means not merely using data to calibrate a model's parameters (although there is a very important role for this), but also genuine attempts to corroborate and falsify conjectures about behaviour. This style of research seems to be becoming less fashionable and increasingly economists are moving to the research wings where a given intellectual effort produces quicker or more certain returns in the form of publications.

Occupying the wings are pure theory and pure data analysis. In one wing are theorists developing 'toy models' where drastic assumptions are made to yield implications, sometimes sweeping and sometimes bland, whose empirical relevance is rarely examined in a systematic manner. Given the ingenuity of economists, it is not difficult to organise the elements of the theory so that some correspondence with the facts can be claimed. The result is a profusion of explanations with little organised attempt to shift through and determine which demand our serious attention. On the other research wing are economists devoted to the computation of more and more correlations among various variables in the vague (usually unspoken) belief that these correlations speak for themselves when adjudicating among rival explanations. In fact, all observations speak to us only through our analytic and preanalytic vision and judgements about the relevance of certain theories usually require more explicit attention to their formulation.

Of course, variations in individual preferences and the benefits from division of labour explain why economists specialise in pure theory or pure empirical research. It is surely undesirable, even if it were feasible, to expect all economists to match theories with observations in all their research. I am simply expressing the view that much of advance in economic science will come from those trying to fuse theory with data yet there are centrifugal pressures attracting economists away from the centre and toward the rims. The resolution of these pressures will have important effects on how rapidly our core beliefs will evolve.

Will our core beliefs today be a part of our core beliefs in one hundred years? This would be easier to answer if economists were agreed today on what constitutes the core beliefs of the discipline. To many, these beliefs centre on the notion of constrained optimisation by self-interested individuals and a great deal of effort has been devoted to defending this notion. Expressed this way, with the objectives and constraints unspecified, the idea is obviously empty of content; any observed behaviour is consistent with such a vague principle. It is made useful by placing some structure on it, but insofar as any observed behaviour can be ultimately rationalised in terms of constrained optimisation it is not clear why we should want to identify it as a core belief.

If, as I expect, economists become less wedded to a narrow interpretation of self-interested behaviour, then they will draw increasingly on ideas and perspectives from other social sciences. We are well aware of the inroads that economics has made in recent decades in studying issues that were once the exclusive purview of social psychologists, political scientists, sociologists, and other social scientists. I expect that in the future we shall see more examples of the reverse – of economists exploiting concepts, modes of reasoning, and research results from other social sciences. I expect and hope we shall contribute in a substantive fashion to that research and not merely rehearse for an audience of economists arguments already expressed elsewhere.

THE PROFESSION

If this is the case, then we should expect to see the distinctions among the social sciences becoming increasingly fuzzy. Economists will continue to take their core beliefs to the study of non-traditional topics, but also economists' somewhat condescending attitudes toward other social science research will moderate. We will become more willing to entertain other types of argument and to draw upon these to forward our own research. As a result, economists will be an increasingly heterogeneous assortment of scholars. Indeed, it will become difficult to identify exactly what common elements bind us all. The set of problems we will study will be very large (not restricted, for instance, to the study of human beings) and our approach to these problems will be diverse.

In such circumstances, for those economists housed in universities, I anticipate a good deal of segregation: either on the basis of topics studied (for instance, human resources or technological change or international finance) or on the basis of approach (especially the degree to which the narrow interpretation of self-seeking behaviour is adopted), distinct departments of economics will exist, all housed in an overarching School of Economics.

Another dimension of this segregation is that teaching and research activities will be dissociated even more than they are now. Economists will be increasingly drawn to work in teams and institutes will need to underwrite the fixed costs of joint research. In such circumstances, current university appointment and tenure procedures will come under strain as the single investigator-teacher model of learning copes with the team product feature of research.

As our most basic notions – the operation of supply and demand in competitive markets, the principle of comparative advantage in explaining exchange, the concept of the division of labour, and so on – receive further endorsement and verification through accumulated experiences, so they will achieve more in the way of parity with ideas from the physical sciences. Thus, in one hundred years, our most fundamental ideas will constitute part of what will be regarded as essential material in the education of, say, eleven-year-old children. Partly as a consequence, the general level of understanding of economics in society will be substantially greater than its woeful level today.

If our wealth accumulates at the rate of the last century, a larger fraction of economists will find opportunities to undertake research outside universities. Research institutes – some attached to universities and some not – will proliferate. There will be extensive opportunities for individuals as individuals to fund their own research, independent of universities or any formal organisations. A whole spectrum of different contracts will emerge: some economists will be closely tied to their employer university, bank, research institute, or government agency; other economists will form a looser association with these and perhaps other organisations.

If the profession will grow in size and diversity in the way described in the preceding paragraphs, then the problem will present itself to each individual of being informed of ongoing research. The problems exist already, but with the huge growth in the discipline they will become immense and completely intractable. There will be a great demand for information presented succinctly that helps to keep scholars abreast of developments beyond their specialty. But the concept of specialty will itself change: today we think of the broad categories of economics – international trade, industrial organisation, econometrics, and so on – as constituting the typical areas of specialisation for economists; within a few decades, the areas of specialisation will consist of what are now very detailed subcategories within these broad areas. Specialisation will attain new heights.

Journals (some appearing in electronic form) will proliferate and with greater frequency, a reflection of the subdivision of the discipline into its various specialties and of the keener competition for priority. Publications containing information about ongoing research such as that provided today by the *Journal of Economic Literature* will appear weekly if indeed they appear in printed form at all. The technological developments facilitating the dissemination of information one hundred years from now are difficult to envisage, but we can be pretty sure there will be a terrific demand for information of the sort that will keep economists cognisant of research in their own and related fields.

These developments also indicate greater decentralisation within the discipline. It will be simply impossible for economists to be at all well-informed of developments in more than a few narrow fields of the subject. An attempt to make substantive contributions to many fields of economics is likely to result in an embarrassing display of ignorance. Where no one can be well versed in ongoing research in more than a few fields, the profession will assume a more pluralistic character. Very many different institutions, journals, meetings, and people will jostle for the profession's prizes and authority and yet, in this fragmented world of specialisation, it will be increasingly difficult for any one of us to arbitrate scientific disputes and award intellectual honours.[3]

---

[3] Will the major professional associations establish standing committees acting as tribunals to adjudicate scientific malpractice?

THE PROSPECT

The historical evolution of a science – the topic of this brief essay – may be understood through the development of its principles and through the changing features of its profession. It is necessarily impossible to detail the way in which our central ideas will change other than to conjecture that our current basic concepts will remain critical and fundamental. Our scientific achievements will depend on the extent to which we candidly pit our theories against observations and on the ability of our models to withstand these encounters.

With respect to the changing social character of economics, the interesting intellectual puzzle posed by scientific professions resembles the classical problem of laissez-faire: how is it that coherent intellectual enterprise and progress to emerge from the autonomous activities of individual scientists driven by diverse goals?[4] The answer lies in the practices, organisations, and conventions that regulate the exchange of ideas and information among economists. These include commonly shared methodological precepts as well as their institutional form such as the nature of professional organisations, their journals, awards, and so on. Most of us devote little energy to understanding these institutions yet these can have a tremendous impact on the character of scientific change. There have been many instances in the history of science of the arbitrary exercise of professional authority and, no doubt, there will be more examples in the future. The distinction between the promotion of a particular way of thinking about a problem and the promulgation of dogma is not always clear though it is faced daily by journal editors in evaluating referee reports and in making decisions about what to publish.

Professional tyranny is less likely where the institutional form of the discipline is pluralistic – where there are many associations of scientists, many journals for the dissemination of ideas, many alternative sources of employment, many ways to acquire the status of a member of the discipline, and, in short, where the discipline's institutions take on a competitive form. Whether the discipline will continue to take on this form, as I have assumed throughout the discussion above, depends not only on the actions of the members of the discipline itself, but also on the attitudes and activities of society as a whole. In other words, ultimately the evolution of the discipline depends in its most fundamental sense on the evolution of the larger society of which it is a part.

Stanford University

REFERENCE

Robinson, Joan (1962). *Economic Philosophy*. New York: Anchor Books.

[4] The analogy may be pursued farther: the collective outcome of these individual efforts may be quite different from those anticipated and intended by the individuals.

ECONOMICS IN 2090: THE VIEWS OF AN EXPERIMENTALIST

Charles R. Plott

The tone of this essay is optimistic. The rapid rate of growth of rigorous theory that has occurred in the past several decades has caused considerable concern in some quarters. The pessimist's view, which I do not share, is that this growth is symptomatic of an increasing irrelevance of economics. Pessimists see the technical discussions in the literature as representing scholarly self-indulgence that is tolerated, if not promoted, by questionable journalistic editorial policies and by an academic tenure process that demands only volumes of publications. According to the pessimistic view, the next century will demand wholesale reform. My optimism results from a completely different interpretation of the circumstances as they apply.

BASIC ASSUMPTIONS

My optimism is based upon three types of assumptions. First, the existing trend toward specialisation and formalisation will continue. This tendency reflects improvement in the ability of economists to think through and communicate about the immensely complex phenomena that economics attempts to elucidate. The theoretical activity is helping to isolate the logical principles that provide building blocks for ideas about how things work.

The second assumption upon which my optimistic view is based is that the laboratory experimental foundations for economics that are now being formed will stand the test of time and many replications over the decades. Thus far, experimental results in economics have proved to be amazingly robust but a degree of scepticism seems to reside in the minds of all scientists and I am no different in that respect. Consequently, the validity and reliability of existing results are listed as assumptions. It is the potential implications of this laboratory experimental approach to economics that I wish to explore.

The third assumption is not divorced from the other two. The assumption is that over the next several decades public funding for basic research in economics and the other social sciences will substantially increase to levels comparable to other sciences. The resources that have been available to support basic research in economics are almost nonexistent when compared to other fields of science. Such striking asymmetries in the policies of governmental funding agencies have had a substantial impact on both the research and the researchers in economics and the social sciences in general. Research of the future will be expensive both in terms of equipment and data collection, and economics will need to attract the very best scientific talent. The assumption is that within the next few decades the biases that exist now in the scientific research establishment will be removed and that the science of economics will be allowed to develop naturally along with the others.

HOW ARE THE KEY ASSUMPTIONS RELATED?

Theory and experiments are related in several ways. The directions taken by current theorising will set the stage for experimental work for the next several decades. Almost all of modern microeconomic theory remains as a challenge to experimentalists. In almost every field of economics the most central and major propositions have not yet been examined by experimental testing. As microeconomics finds its way deeper into political science, organisational behaviour and into the nature of the law, a sufficient number of questions will be generated to challenge experimentalists well into the twenty-first century. The questions posed by the theory of repeated games and games with asymmetric information will require another several man-decades of experimental efforts. The ideas of psychologists are being felt as they push both theorists and experimentalists to add concepts of perception and cognition to the models. The developments in mathematics, especially in the field of computation, are extremely important because these tools will enable researchers to grind out the predictions of specific features of models, the implications of which would otherwise be impossible to determine.

Theory and experiments are related in a second way. Theory, on the one hand, usually involves sweeping statements about broad classes of phenomena. For example, the law of supply and demand and the resulting notion of an equilibrium price are supposed to be characteristic of markets regardless of the item that is being bought and sold. Experiments, on the other hand, are very special cases of phenomena. They are usually very simple relative to phenomena that are found naturally occurring. This simplicity is both the strength and the weakness of experimental methods. Strength follows from the fact that simplicity permits a clear view of unfolding behaviours. Weakness follows from the fact that any finite number of experiments leaves unexamined the infinite number of other cases that remain. It is at this point that the theory provides strengths that the experimental method lacks. The theory that successfully finds experimental support in the simple cases suggests what will happen in the others. Thus, theory and experiments are important partners in economics and the development of one will help the advance of the other as the next century approaches.

WHERE ARE WE NOW?

The past century seems to have crystallised thoughts around two separate sets of basic principles. One set is applied to markets or other types of groups of individuals and the other set is applied only at the individual level of analysis. Experimental support exists for both sets of principles. This is not to say that the models work perfectly or that paradoxes are not abundant. Indeed, nothing works perfectly. Nevertheless a body of experimental evidence is evolving which strongly suggests that economic theory is on the right track.

Perhaps the most powerful notion at the group level is the concept of an equilibrium. Equilibration of decision processes is an observable, wide-ranging and documented phenomenon. Several models capture the idea. Examples are competitive equilibria, cores of cooperative game models and Nash equilibria of noncooperative game models. Such models generally involve no principles of dynamics at all and instead suggest only a final 'resting place' of social activities. By contrast, actual decision processes are bristling with dynamics. Nothing rests. Nevertheless movement is drawn to the areas that the models identify as equilibria. Single markets, multiple markets, voting processes, bidding processes, etc., etc. when placed in a stationary environment exhibit an equilibration tendency. This idea of an equilibrium, which is central to modern economic thought is closely connected to behaviourial facts. Obviously, the question posed for the researchers of the future is 'why?'

Equilibration at a market or at a 'group' level of analysis suggests something about the changes and the dynamics taking place at the individual level of analysis. For purposes of a discussion about dynamics, it is useful to partition the theory of individual behaviour into three parts: a theory of preference or interest; a theory of beliefs and expectations; and, a theory of choice and decision.

The theory of choice and decision consists of principles which define a process that facilitates the selection of the 'acceptable' or the 'best' options. Of course, the concepts of 'acceptable' or 'best' are themselves derived from attitudes captured by the other two parts of the theory of individual behaviour. For example, the choice could be the maximal elements of a binary (preference) relation or the maximising arguments of a scalar (utility) function. Of course principles of maximisation are just one approach to this part of the theory. Other logics exist that equally capture a concept of 'rationality' but no aspect of choice theory, part of the general theory of behaviour, seems to contain dynamic elements that could be utilised in a theory of equilibration and change. Similarly another part of the broad theory of individual behaviour, the theory of preference (or utility) does not seem capable of capturing the nature of dynamics. The dynamics of individual change are currently captured only in the theory of beliefs. The theory of beliefs is essentially a theory of subjective probability that has the capacity to evolve in accord with Bayes law and related formal constructions. At this time the other two parts of the theory, the theory of choice and the theory of preference, seem to have nothing special to contribute to the problem of dynamics.

The gaps that exist in the general theory of individual behaviour seem sufficiently obvious. However, when the theory is modified by caveats pertaining to perception and the nature of cognition, a surprising level of consensus exists among researchers. Solid experimental evidence exists for all the basic elements of parts of the theory even though there exist active controversies about many important details. The seeds of neither a wholesale rejection of the theory nor a revolution in the nature of the theory can be found in what is known now. It is the gaps, and not an alternative way of thinking, that will demand the attention of the future theorists.

WHAT ABOUT 2090?

From the above thoughts it is possible to venture a guess about the nature of three different aspects of economics: basic research, policy-related research, and economics in the classroom.

A major effort of basic researchers will be at the individual level of analysis. The current emphasis on the development and evolution of beliefs (subjective probabilities) will have expanded to a consideration of the development and evolution of attitudes in general. Preference formation and change will be the issue and researchers will be pushed to inquire about chemical, biochemical and physiological influences on preference formation. Already economists have experimented with the structure of preferences in lower forms of animals. Concepts of preference and optimisation are beginning to appear in biology. Existing research suggests that the concept of preference could serve as a background theory of behaviour across animal species and research on animals will be an important source of information.

Theories of cognition will play an important role in the economics of individual decision and choice. Already concepts of decision rules, heuristics, and resulting 'biases' are seeping into the literature. It should not be long until the focus turns to behavioural theories about how people decide to decide. The choice of methods, decision aids, organisation and the decision rules that individuals acquire to compensate and/or complement their intuitive decisions will be a major research issue.

The problem of deciding how to decide will be of interest to scholars who study social decisions as well as those who study individual decisions. Individual behaviour within the context of a fixed process, or rules of the game, will have advanced considerably. On the other hand, the nature of individual choice of process, a set of rules and institutions that will operate when one's preferences are different from those that exist at the time of choice, will still be a perplexing challenge. Theories of moral behaviour and values that are popular now will be popular in 2090. Some scholars think that such notions like morality and fairness are fundamental to the choice of process. However, I hold very little hope that current ideas about the possible influence of moral attitudes on behaviour will become sufficiently refined to produce useful results for economics. We will know much more about models of games in which the outcomes are games. We will know much more about the choice of institutions and organisation as a form of manipulation and/or control of other people. That is, organisation as a means to an end will be understood but the preference for organisation as an end in itself will not be understood.

At this point, two implications can be drawn about the nature of economics of the future. First, the involvement of the life sciences will foster a degree of specialisation beyond the imagination of most economists. Special areas will exist depending upon the relationship of the senses (sight, hearing, etc.) to choice and upon the relationship of physiological functions (perception, memory, etc.) to choice. Secondly, the nature of theories at the market or group level could be profoundly influenced by a deeper understanding of the individual. In particular, greater detail about the nature of choice at the individual level of behaviour will provide the theoretical handles for more refined models of the equilibration process and about the nature of equilibrium itself. How such developments will effect models that have a substantial strategic component is not clear. As game theory is conceived now the existence of common knowledge about principles of individual behaviour (i.e., rationality) is fundamental to the logical structure of the theory. How a process account of rationality, one that involves biases and approximations, might influence the theory of games is by no means clear.

The nature of applied work in economics will be substantially influenced by the basic research. The influence of special institutional properties of decision-making processes on the dynamics of equilibration has been clearly established. It follows that researchers will be actively exploring typologies of institutions and documenting their influences in the context of experiments as well as in the context of naturally occurring history. No doubt much academic specialisation will be based on types of institutions and this specialisation will facilitate much more interactions among accounting, law, and economics than now exists. However, a major change in applied work will be in the area of policy analysis.

Policy analysis will reflect the influence of several substantial fields of theory that are beginning to converge. Mechanism theory, public choice, social choice theory and incentive compatibility all have similar background philosophies about the nature of policy analysis. The choice of policies is viewed as choices of process and institutions through which decisions evolve. This philosophy changes the research emphasis from the development of information needed by a person who makes day-to-day judgements to a study of the incentives of the people who make such judgements in a bureaucratic context. The public sector is viewed more like an agent which acts for a principle which consists of other individuals in the public at large. The relationships between the two, as defined by the institutional environment is the variable to be researched. How will the public sector behave in response to differing modes of organisation, voting processes, constitutions, or mechanisms as some would prefer to call them? The policy process (mechanism, institution) is supposed to choose differently among options according to the background situation (environment, individual preferences, opportunities). The policy problem is to find an institution (process, mechanism) that responds appropriately according to some pre-specified ideas about how the system should respond. It is recognised that decisions made within the process would involve conflicts and gaming and that the mechanism should reflect that possibility. Hence the concepts of incentive compatibility and incentive compatible mechanisms are appropriate. The outcomes expected of the process should not require that people involved in the process act against their own self interest. That is, incentive compatibility places a constraint on the types of processes that might be considered as solutions to any given policy problem. By 2090 many other types of behavioural constraints will be used in addition to, or even replacing, the concept of incentive compatibility that is used now.

Theory will enable researchers to use mathematical tools to scan all logically conceivable types of processes that satisfy the behavioural constraints and the normative performance characteristics desired of the process. The resulting process, discovered by theoretical means, will generally have no historical predecessors. Such theoretical processes might appear to be different than anything that has ever existed before even though theoretically they have the properties that are desired. Such newly imagined processes could involve individuals voting directly using some unusual type of voting process, or they could involve individuals instructing computer robots how to act on their behalf in a process that proceeds at the speed of light. They might involve rules, institutions or actions operating in ways that differ substantially from what might be suggested by intuition or experience. For example one might be able to imagine decentralised processes that are able to solve problems that are currently solved only by managerial and military types of organisations.

Such new and unusual processes are not likely to be adopted simply because some theory says they will work. It is at this point that experimental methods will be a valuable aid to the policy process. Experimental techniques will be able to provide the testing and experience with the operation of such processes before implementation. Experimental 'testbedding' will be widely used. The idea will be to use experimental techniques to create a challenging economic environment. The test 'policy' will be implemented and tested in that environment. If the policy passes the first test it will graduate to more complicated tests presumably undergoing modification as it proceeds. Field tests will be one of the stages. With sufficient testing to remove the 'bugs' the process will be implemented. Thus, policy analysis will be substantially complemented by the application of laboratory experimental techniques.

Economics in the classroom will be completely different. Laboratory methods will involve teaching on an experimental basis similar to what occurs now in the natural sciences. Students will learn about principles of economics from their own experiences and not only from the experiences of other people as reported in books or pages of statistics. Experimental research will proceed in a nationwide, if not worldwide, laboratory system. Different sites will be connected by computerised and other electronic hookups that allow the simultaneous interaction of some students while other students watch in real time.

Students will still experience the operation of the law of supply and demand in single and in multiple markets. They will experience the equilibration process. They will use their own introspection to try to understand what makes markets work much the same way we do now. The convergence process they experience will be the same one that we see now. One of the processes that they use to bring demand and supply into balance, the open outcry system, will still be around. The classroom instructor will be able to pose a question about that particular process much the same way as we pose it now. In spite of what will be known about individual choice behaviour, the process of market convergence will still contain many mysteries in 2090.

California Institute of Technology

THE ECONOMICS OF THE NEXT CENTURY*

Sir Austin Robinson

I

We have been celebrating this year the centenary of the Royal Economic Society. As we start its second century it is interesting to speculate where that second century may take us. It would, in my view, be absurd to assume that the United Kingdom will continue to change between 1990 and 2090 at a rate exactly similar to that by which it has grown between 1890 and 1990. But if we are to establish possible orders of magnitude it is relevant to have in mind what has happened between 1890 and 1990.

If one starts from statistical measures, the gross domestic product at constant prices of 1990 is about 6·7 times that of 1890. The per capita gross domestic product of 1990 is about 3·8 times that of 1890. But to say that is almost meaningless. We live in a quite different world. My own memories go back to about 1901. Perhaps I can best illustrate from a few years earlier. When I showed signs of arriving in the world at the inconvenient hour of 2 a.m. on a November morning in 1897 at my mother's family home in a Surrey vicarage a couple of miles outside Farnham, my grandfather was sent off to run to fetch the doctor and the gardener to harness the pony and take the trap to bring the doctor and his equipment. There were no telephones, certainly none in a country vicarage. There were no cars. There were few hospitals. Few of the life-saving drugs existed. The infant mortality rate was fifteen times that of today.

On the other hand Britain then still had strong claims to be regarded as 'top nation'. Only one North American country could compete. This was in part the outcome of the military history of the eighteenth and nineteenth centuries. It was in far greater degree the result of the technological history of the eighteenth and nineteenth centuries. Down to 1700 it would be no great exaggeration to say that the technical development of the world was not very far from equal. The Venetians, the Spanish and Portuguese, it is true, had had temporary leaderships in ship design and navigation. The Chinese and Indians had their own national technologies but were about abreast of the Europeans in textiles. There were no very wide differences in methods of metal manufacture. Nor in techniques of agriculture. The age before 1700 may be described as the Age of Technical Equality.

Then came the first generation since the time of the Romans of major technical advances – the construction of canals, the mining and shipment of coal, greatly improved methods of making iron and steel, the railway, the first agricultural revolution, and textile inventions, the steamship, the steam-engine and many other inventions. The significant point in regard to all of these

---

* The author does not wish to implicate anyone else in his thinking. The editor has invited him to 'think long-term and be expansive'. The author has taken him at his word.

innovations is that they were all first developed in one or two of a small group of four or five European or North American countries and the majority of them in Britain. Most of them required highly specialised machinery which could only be produced with the know-how only available in the particular country that was responsible for the invention. The natural consequence was the concentration in those four or five countries of exports both of the products of the new inventions, textiles in particular, and also of exports of the new machinery to some of the countries which were being undercut and were anxious to continue to compete at least in their own markets. This was the Age of Inequality. The innovating countries, and particularly the United Kingdom, had considerable export surpluses, had increased imports of feed and raw materials, enjoyed a reduction of death rates and infant mortality resulting in a considerable growth of population; income per head began to rise progressively.

Most of the major innovations mentioned above had, as I have said, been made in the United Kingdom and before 1850. After 1850 inventions and discoveries continued. Those which most significantly changed the pattern of life included the harnessing of electricity in the 1850s, the invention of the internal combustion engine in the 1880s and the pneumatic tyre in the 1890s.

But it was their applications rather than the inventions that were important. One may dispute about who it was who made the initial discovery. But one thing is clear. The leadership in the development of applications of electricity, in its generation, in lighting, in sound equipment, in calculating equipment, was initially in the United States and only later extended to the United Kingdom, Germany, France and other countries. The same is true of the other great advances of this period, the automobile and aviation, though in the latter case the initial development was largely in France. I would regard the period 1850 to 1920 as the Age of Continued Inequality with a changed division of the advantages of leadership between the leading four. It still remained true that the greater part of the advanced technical equipment of the world was made by one or other of the four leaders. It still remained true that they could afford to import food, if they needed it, and raw materials and minor manufactures. But for the United Kingdom this had become less easy. While textile exports had been equivalent to 75 % of the total in 1800 and 50 % in 1900, they were little more than 30 % by 1937.

But already by 1913 the Age of Diminishing Inequality was beginning. During the war years of 1914–18 all four of the industrial leaders were preoccupied with producing war equipment. Countries that had depended on them for imported manufactures lost their source of supply and, because of difficulties of transport, also their markets for the primary products with which they had mainly paid for their imports. They began to supply themselves, and when the war was over they did not return to their pre-war sources. And as a by-product of this they developed adequate, though less sophisticated, capacity to make machinery for themselves. Thus the post-1913 exports of the big four of the goods they had exported in 1900 contracted severely. Their problem was now whether or not they could continue the process of a hundred years earlier and find new products, wanted the world over, which they alone had the skills and know-how to produce, and which the less-developed countries needed but did not yet have the skills and know-how to produce.

The inventors of the period 1913–90 have in fact succeeded to some extent in doing this. Predominant among the new advanced country exports have been automobiles and lorries, electricity generating plant, radios, televisions, refrigerators, cookers, computers, man-made fibres and products made from them. But a more significant change has been taking place: the number of advanced countries, seeking to live in this way, has begun to increase significantly. The earliest in the field were Sweden, the Netherlands, Belgium and Switzerland. Later but by far the largest is Japan. More recently one must add Hong Kong, Singapore, Taiwan and South Korea. This greatly widened and much more fierce competition has effectively brought to an end the Age of Inequality. We are now back again in a second Age of Equality.

It is relevant to ask how this change, seriously adverse to the interests of the advanced countries of the nineteenth century, has come about. Backward countries during the Age of Inequality were backward because they lacked one or other, or indeed all, of certain things: managerial skills and know-how in their entrepreneurs and managers; adequate operational intelligence and skills in a potential labour force; an adequate supply of monetary capital funds; sufficiently up-to-date fixed capital equipment. Through the nineteenth century a country such as India was permanently handicapped by poor management, not very skilled operational labour, shortage of capital, out-of-date machinery, inadequate infrastructure. That situation is now completely changed. Higher education in most of the formerly backward countries is immensely improved and many of those likely to hold higher posts in industrial management will have received education abroad in one of the technically advanced countries. The level of education of the potential skilled labour force is now not significantly inferior to that of some of their European counterparts. What is much more important is that the emergence of the multi-national firm has provided manufacturing units in many of the backward countries with financial resources and experienced financial management, fixed capital equipment, and access to advanced country market almost equivalent to those possessed by similar units in the advanced countries. When one visits a newly constructed unit in Taiwan one wishes that the similar units in the United Kingdom were as well equipped. At the same time, one knows that a significant part of the export market for industrial machinery served in the past by Britain was that to less developed countries which were short of capital but had low real wages and thus were wishing to begin manufacture with equipment simpler and cheaper than that suitable to the wage levels and interest rates of advanced countries – the machinery, that is to say, that was being discarded in the more advanced countries. Such machinery is now losing its markets and those that remain are increasingly served by exports of machinery made in less developed countries.

In some cases, in engineering in particular, technical progress, improvements of the strength and durability of materials, reductions in the necessary size of products have enabled advanced countries to retain the production and export of another generation of certain products. But in more instances (the cotton textile industry is a good example) the predominant manufacture of simpler products is passed down at intervals from country to country as technical success in other more advanced countries leads to higher real wages and inability to continue to compete in export markets. One has seen the major concentration of the cotton industry move from Lancashire to Japan and more recently from Japan, with that country's engineering progress, to Hong Kong, Indonesia and other newcomers with India finding it harder to maintain its place.

May I sum up the experience of the past century during the existence of the Royal Economic Society. It was a century following a period of great change. Britain had enjoyed during the century 1750–1850 a continuing but constantly changing growth of exports and an export-led industrial expansion, subject at intervals to political or military interruptions but with the longer term expansion predominating. With rising real incomes and falling infant mortality and death rates, population grew more rapidly and was increasingly located in the areas of the rapidly expanding coal-mining, iron and steel manufacture, shipbuilding and the textile industries, concentrated near the ports that handled their materials and exports. This phase of export-led expansion reached its peak about 1880. From then on the ratio of British exports to G.D.P. began to decline.

One needs to remember that both Adam Smith, evolving his thinking in the 1760s and 1770s, and Alfred Marshall doing his basic thinking in the 1860s and 1870s were doing their thinking in what was at that time the leading country in a world of inequality, in which the mobility of technology was very limited and in which wage bargaining was also limited to the extent that it was reasonable to assume that real wages, combined with exchange rates, readily and quickly reflected the true world scarcities of those skills. In the very different world of today, in which technology and capital are very mobile, in which education has made the transfer of skills very much more rapid and in which wage bargaining has become an annual and often acrimonious operation, it is less obvious than it was that the price system will now always produce the economically most desirable answer for a country that is well down the scale in the order of size of national income and international bargaining strength. It is time that economists gave more thought to the universal validity of principles evolved for a leading country.

One needs in particular to remember that the extent of the benefit of international trade depends on the extent of the difference of the relative productivities of two countries in producing the products concerned. If the ratios of productivities are the same in both countries and there are no abnormalities of wage-bargaining or exchange rates, there will be no benefit from trade. I have been arguing that the great inequalities of 1750 to 1850 are disappearing; thus the benefits of international trade are diminishing.

It remains among all orthodox economists nothing less than sacrilege to suggest that anything other than complete freedom of trade should ever be considered. As a small northern island we must always import both certain essential materials and some very desirable semi-tropical foodstuffs. It remains, however, that other countries of much the same size which have been less impeccable in their devotion to free trade have suffered less from problems of the balance of payments, have been less obliged to restrict investment in order to reduce imports by reducing incomes, and have thus outstripped us in growth of income-per-head. While I would still welcome international trade to the limit of our foreign earnings in conditions of full employment, I would not regard it as sacrilege in a world of declining inequality to take steps to substitute home production for imports to the extent necessary to give us a favourable balance of payments, a low interest rate and more rapid growth.

If, as I would expect, it is rather unlikely that Britain will enjoy an export-led expansion of the dimensions of those that we enjoyed in the world before 1913, and assuming a progressively falling ratio of exports to gross domestic product, one must concentrate on the home market and try to see the pattern and possible orders of magnitude of its growth. Gross domestic product grew by 32% between 1920 and 1937, an annual rate of about 1·6%. It grew by 70% between 1953 and 1973, the year of the world crisis following the foundation of OPEC, an annual rate of about 2·7%. (It is arguable that the last year or two of this were a period of over-heating.) It has grown by 31·5% between 1973 and 1988, an annual rate of about 1·8%. The rate of growth between 1978 and 1988, the first few years of which were years of recovery to the level of 1973, has been 2·3%. Over the years since 1953 we would like to think that we have learned a lot about running a modern economy but our growth has nonetheless been slower than that of any of the other major economies. My working guess – it can be no more – is that over the next fifty years the average growth of G.D.P. will be about 2·5%, that is about 28% a decade. This is slightly slower than we have achieved in the past. But through the nineteenth century Britain had the great advantage of being the country with the highest average income per head. This meant that during the periods of rapid growth it was in Britain that it first became profitable to develop the new products with a high income elasticity or to develop the large scale manufacture of goods which had hitherto been made by hand for the rich but could now be afforded by the middle classes. As other less wealthy countries increased their income per head their first resort was then in many cases to import already available British exports. But this advantage depended on British leadership in income per head. When Britain surrendered the lead to the United States and progressively fell to somewhere around twelfth in the order of real income per head, this earlier advantage changed into a handicap as the most modern and best manufactures of new products came to be found in the United States or Japan.

May I sum up? It is physically possible and should be administratively possible to continue growth of real production and consumption at the present 2·5% per annum, equivalent to about 28% per decade. This would mean that we may reach the present standard of the U.S.A. by about 2015 and by 2050, still within the life-span of those graduating this year, have a level of income twice that of the United States today. With a roughly constant population that does not present problems of normal food supply. It does not present problems of building materials. It probably does not present problems of the normal industrial raw materials. It is more difficult to say whether there will be adequate supplies of some of the inputs of the rapidly growing chemical industries. The two serious scarcities are likely to be energy and space. The consumption of electricity in the twelve countries that compose E.E.C. has risen on average by 5·3% per annum over the past thirty years. We know how a continuation of that rate of growth may be made technically possible. I believe that we shall in the course of time be less reluctant to use it.

II

With this thinking in mind what can one expect to happen during the second century of the Royal Economic Society? One thing is clear: it is virtually impossible that we can repeat over any long period an export-led growth at all similar to that which we enjoyed on a diminishing scale over almost the first half of the Society's present existence before 1939. The remarkable thing over that period (see Appendix 1) is the succession of different products which from 1750 to 1938 formed the main bulk of British visible exports; first woollens, then cottons, with metals and engineering products steadily growing in importance and with coal, chemicals and other exports finally outstripping textiles by 1913. And now the textile exports have almost vanished. One can see the dramatic effects of each of the two great wars. But it was economic progress in other countries, and particularly in what in 1938 we regarded as the undeveloped world, which has in fact dictated the changes in the pattern of our economy.

If one looks forward, the first and most important factor in determining our future economic problems is the change from population growth to a static or slowly declining total population, with an almost constant sector of working age, a declining number under 15 and a growing number over 65. What is hard to predict is what will be the combined effect on the total working population of the increasing desire of women to work, the pressures for earlier retirement and the success or failure in dealing with unemployment in a world of more rapid technical change. I have, moreover, a suspicion that if 60 becomes a normal age of retirement from one's ordinary career there will be a large number of people between 60 and 70 who are quickly bored with doing nothing, would welcome an addition to income, and will be looking for less onerous or part-time work, probably in some local service.

What will be the pattern of employment? One must assume that, as in all countries, progress will mean a further decline of the proportion of primary production, which is already very small, a further reduction of the proportion of secondary, manufacturing, employment though this has already gone very far. Within manufacturing an increasing proportion will be in the construction of capital equipment. As in all countries the proportion of the occupied population engaged in tertiary occupations, services of all kinds, will increase.

This includes distribution services, secretarial services, banks and finance, travel and transport generally, teaching, publishing, house agents, legal services and countless other similar activities.

One has to ask where geographically this will happen. For some inexplicable reason economists have in recent years increasingly neglected the problems and implications of the location of industry and have implicitly abstracted from their influence; it was only for a few years in the 1950s that the government took the problem seriously and recognised the conflict between private and public interest resulting from a choice of location. It must be borne in mind that almost all the tertiary activities are provided directly to the purchaser and the products must be located close to where the purchaser is located.

The location of purchases is in the short period dictated by the location of the stock of houses. If one looks at the present pattern of the nation's stock of houses and the related shops, roads, railways and social amenities, it can be seen at once that they primarily represent the location of the nation's mid-Victorian activities, the manufacture of textiles, the making of steel, the mining of coal, the building of ships, the export and import of goods by sea. The location of the present stock of housing bears little relation to the needs and desires of the present world and still less to the probable needs of 2050 or 2090 with a Channel tunnel. The present generation has improvised a solution by a widespread adoption of commuting from home to work and back over longer and longer distances; in this way housing built for a less efficient agriculture or for now obsolete industries has become available for distant tertiary occupants. But this process is exhaustible. During the coming century much rehousing will be necessary, including the further creation, as in the 1950s, of new cities. Indeed the better housing of the nation and the better location of growing activities is likely to become the predominant problem of the economy.

Where will the new tertiary employment be located? Obviously services in the main must follow the pattern of the population to be served; they are not significantly influenced, as were Victorian secondary activities, by the pattern of resources. But increasingly tertiary activities are being provided by large companies or organisations with a central organisation, involving meetings and consultations, and increasingly this means a growth of London despite its inefficiencies and shorter effective working day as the consequence of travel to work. London alone, served by its eight radiating railway lines, is the only possible place to site a truly central organisation. For many activities, particularly of a financial character, London is the great world centre, with its long traditions and experience. But it is legitimate to ask whether it will remain necessary in the changed conditions of 2000 or 2050 for London to add to its increasing duties as a financial centre and the centre of national government additionally that of being the national shopping centre, that of being the national arts centre, that of being an important educational centre, and that of being a first recipient of immigrant population to the extent that it is today.

With increasing income per head combined with more equal income distribution, local and regional shops are already today more able to cover the demand even of higher-income groups. The television set in one's home has largely taken the place of the theatre; Stratford-on-Avon and Glyndebourne have taught one that London is not an imperative location of high-quality theatre or opera. I believe that by 2050 the number of Londoners with a passionate conviction that one cannot live a civilised life anywhere else will have begun to decline, and the number of employers prepared to move their offices out of London will have increased, to the great benefit of those who really need to work in London. If this does not happen, as I would expect, voluntarily I would expect political pressure to press for some element of compulsion.

If a considerable increase in a better located housing stock would not only increase productive efficiency but also reflect what I believe to correspond with the highest income elasticity, what are the dimensions of the problem? In 1986 (and things have not since changed significantly) a U.K. population of $56\frac{3}{4}$ millions was accommodated in $21\frac{3}{4}$ million households, an average of 2·6 per household. Of these 2·6 some small proportion of sons and daughters would have preferred to have a home of their own; some Londoners have both a main country household and a London flat. With a population including more in the over 65 category and fewer under 15 we shall need more households for a given population.

How many houses do we need to meet the potential demand also in respect of quality and location. May I first discuss quality? A very considerable proportion of the present housing stock was built either in the inter-war years or in the period 1955–70 and despite improvements reflect the standards and tastes of a much lower real income per head than that of today. More relevant, the pattern of personal consumption has already shifted into activities (or in-activities) conducted in the home – watching the television, reading, cooking, washing, and other activities facilitated by modern equipment that are already almost universal. Longer life expectations combined with earlier retirement will make the space and comfort of the home increasingly desirable. A large proportion of the present stock of houses is incapable of adequate improvement as well as unsatisfactorily located.

My own guess (it can be no more) is that of the present stock of about 22 million houses at least 6 million should, to meet the demands of 2000, be replaced. How long will that take? In the 1970s we were increasing the stock of houses in Great Britain by about 200,000 to 250,000 a year by building 300,000 to 350,000 new houses and demolishing around 100,000 a year. More recently the annual new building has been nearly halved and the demolishings almost proportionately reduced. If we could revert to the levels of the 1860s or 1870s it would take 25 to 30 years to solve the housing problem. If one projects our present slower progress it would take 30 to 35 years. And in 30 to 35 years our present concepts of what represents an acceptable house will, with a much higher average standard of living, again be sadly obsolete. There is, in my view, a strong case for helping private builders of houses to build somewhat in advance of their immediate standards.

Where should these houses be built? What shall we be consuming in 50 or 100 years time? Where will manufacture be located? The only sensible answer is that we cannot know. But I think we can learn a little from the past. When one's income increases by 10% one does not increase all one's expenditures by 10%. Some forms of consumption have an income-elasticity below 1; some have an income elasticity above 1. The consumption expenditures with a high income elasticity at present include housing, mainly frustrated by various controls, automobiles and their use and maintenance, certain electrical equipment, clothing, and various services, including foreign travel. The consumption expenditures with a low present income-elasticity (below 1) include food and somewhat surprisingly alcohol as well as tobacco.

Can one project the present income-elasticities and regard them as immutable? I would say 'no'. Some forms of durable goods which serve as domestic equipment (refrigerators, gas or electric cookers, washing machines, telephones for example) are already almost universal, whatever the income of the household. These within the next half century will almost certainly reach a very low income-elasticity. Of all households, over 60% in the United Kingdom and nearly 90% in the United States now own one or more cars; it seems probable that within 25 years the income-elasticity for automobiles will have fallen considerably, with such elasticity as remains largely concentrated on quality. In the United States there remains a high income-elasticity for large freezers which can be replenished by visits in an automobile to the shop at infrequent intervals; but the freezer requires the space of an American cellar and is inconsistent with the present British tendency to escape the obligations of cooking by weekly purchases of semi-prepared food; there is here a possible but uncertain future field of high income-elasticity.

But this serves very well to illustrate the factors determining the income elasticity of demand. When a new product is first invented there is an immediate small demand at a high price while its efficacy is established; there is a large demand while its initial sale spread and immense price reductions makes it almost universal; it retreats thereafter to a limited market dictated by replacement demand and thus determined by the working life of the product. The working life itself depends primarily on the extent to which unreliable parts can or cannot be replaced.

If one tries to see how the increment of real consumers' expenditure over the years 1977 to 1987 was distributed, one finds that very few products had a high income elasticity. Consumers' expenditure in total, measured at constant prices, increased over the decade by about 35·5%. Expenditure on food increased by about 9%, that on alcohol by less than 8%, that on tobacco fell by 20%. Expenditure on furniture increased a little over 16%. The only fields of expenditure that increased by more than the average 35·5% were cars and clothing. The constant-price expenditure on cars more than doubled (208% of that of 1977). That on clothing increased by a little over 70%. Expenditures on certain unspecified goods and services also showed high income elasticities.

Can this pattern of recent growth give us trustworthy guidance regarding the pattern of future growth? One must, I think be very careful about projecting it. During the three decades 1956–86 we moved from 25 cars per 100 households to 63 cars per 100 households. In the United States the number of cars per 100 households seems to have stabilised at about 85 to 90 cars per 100 households. If one takes account of households of the elderly and households in very large cities where a car is not convenient, a somewhat similar limitation of growth and a transition to a replacement and quality-improvement demand seems probable within the next decade or so.

It thus seems likely that the principal components of a greatly increased real consumption per head by the middle of the next century, apart from clothing will be completely new products or services corresponding in their own generation to the television or the refrigerator in the post-war period.

There are two additional reasons for caution – the effects of income distribution and the effects of age distribution. The income distribution of 1988 was extraordinarily different from that of 1939. In 1988 many of the professional classes had real incomes scarcely equivalent to those of 1938. This has been in part the result of less bargaining power; it is to a greater extent the natural and proper result of much increased educational facilities and the much increased entry of women. These members of the professional classes no longer have the high position in the local hierarchy that they had when I was young or the capacity to build large houses, buy smart clothes and employ two or three servants. They will never recover that privilege. They are now in the forefront of the market for labour-saving inventions. Their large houses are beyond the means of their children and are being converted into flats for another generation.

The future consequences of age distribution are more complex. It seems likely that by the mid-2000s the pattern of life of the ordinary citizen will be divided into three segments: 0–20 (or a year or two later) the phase of growth and education; the period 20–60 the phase of normal work; the period of 60–about 85 (the expectation of life at 60 is already over 16 years) the phase of retirement. If, with constantly improving medical skills, most retired people live on average till their late 80s we have to ask what load we are imposing on the segment of 20–60. At present a work force representing about 52 % of the population provides not only for themselves but also for children and retired drawn from about 48 % of the population. My calculations for the 2000s suggest a work force drawn from 45 % of the population trying to support not only themselves but also children and retired representing 55 % of the population. Between 20 and 60 a man or woman must not only gain experience of work; they must also directly or through taxation acquire and furnish a home, marry, provide for the birth and education of children, provide for the capital equipment one uses, provide for the infrastructure and defence of one's country. Are we imposing too heavy a burden on too few?

III

What about the economists in this future world? I have stressed the dramatic and continuing changes in the structure of the British economy over the past two hundred years and the perpetual need to adjust to these changes. I expect similar changes to continue with similar need to adjust. It is the economist's responsibility to provide foresight. Hardly any problem is not easier to solve if it is foreseen and more time is given to find a solution. Governments seldom look forward beyond the next election. Their economic advisers must concern themselves primarily with the urgent problems of the moment. Too many of the research institutes have a similar short time horizon. I would argue the case for more concern with long term trends and long term problems.

Some of the problems of the next century can already be foreseen. Sometime within the next century we shall come near to exhausting the world's more easily available stocks of oil. Are we doing enough research on a new instrument of personal transport? We are exhausting rapidly the world's stock of timber. Are we doing enough to develop new forms of paper, new materials for house-building and furniture construction? One of the successes of the past fifty years has been the development, largely under wartime shortages, of new substitute materials. Why is that not continuing? Is research planning sufficiently guided by foresight?

If, as I believe, one of the primary demands of a richer population is likely to be better and rather more spacious housing, are we doing enough research on techniques of housebuilding? Granted that the post-war prefab was too metallic, was not acceptable as a long-term solution. But was the whole concept of mass-produced components wrong?

Of all longer-term problems that of the balance of payments is far the most serious. A relatively small potential deficit can lead to the imposition of brakes on the economy which have wholly disproportionate effects by contracting current consumption and incentives to invest and grow. I believe that, in a world of rapid technical change and rapid potential growth, foreign trade policy needs to be considered as objectively and dispassionately as any other branch of economics.

If I may sum up; the experience of the past two centuries has been one of continuing and dramatic change. The Britain of Adam Smith lived on modest exports of woollens. Total exports were only about 8% of G.D.P.; of those exports about 78% were woollens in 1750. By 1850, a few years before Alfred Marshall was beginning his thinking, Britain had exports equivalent to 12% of G.D.P.; now cottons provided 55% of the whole. By the foundation of the R.E.S. in 1890 exports were still about 15–16% of G.D.P., with cottons now providing 40% of the whole and metals and engineering providing 28%. By 1937, greatly changed by the war of 1914–18 and the subsequent adjustments, exports were down to about 13% of G.D.P. with cottons down to 9% of the whole and metals and engineering up to 48%. It is the difficulty, perhaps the impossibility, of finding another range of products that we might dominate in the same way that we dominated successive products in the nineteenth century that creates our present difficulties.

If potential growth of productivity during the next century can be considerable, who will be the beneficiaries? It is most unrealistic to assume that all classes and all occupations will benefit equally. It is relevant merely as a warning to consider what has happened in the fifty years 1938–88. If I may trust estimates published in the Economist Diary, the benefits of the increased productivity of those years went primarily (as was eminently desirable) to those who in 1938 one regarded as ill-paid. The real incomes of miners are more than three times those of 1938; those of factory workers, agricultural workers, railway employees are more than twice what their predecessors got in 1938; the real incomes of shop assistants, bank clerks, have increased only by some 20% to 30%; the real income of teachers and doctors have barely remained constant; the real incomes of senior civil servants and university professors are shown as having declined, but it is difficult to be sure that one is comparing like with like; their numbers and responsibilities have changed greatly over the fifty years; in 1938 they were few and carried heavy responsibilities, today they are many and share responsibilities.

The explanation of this anomaly is not far to seek. The increase of income per head has gone primarily to those engaged in manual-working occupations. During the past fifty years their real incomes have increased, very properly, by more than 100% and in some cases by nearly 200%. During the same period the real income of the professional classes has in almost all cases increased by less than 25% and have in a few cases actually declined. The reasons are obvious. Very widespread education coupled with the ambition to earn a professional-class income has made it possible to recruit new entrants into professional occupations at the old level of earnings. The academics are not alone in the stagnation of their real incomes.

That apart, academics are poor bargainers for their private incomes. What is clear is that many of us are more concerned with our standing in the community, the interest of our jobs, the sort of home we have the income to create, the sort of education and prospects of employment that we can get for our children. These aspects of welfare are almost impossible to quantify and are not the automatic result of a deluge of physical goods. One has to ask whether we can all simultaneously and equally enjoy public respect and a high standing in the community or whether these personal ambitions are inevitably competitive and reserved for the few, as I believe them to be. Thus though I feel confident that in 2050 or 3000 those who survive that long will be increasingly supplied with a greater plenitude of physical goods than they can use, I feel far from certain that they will be happier.

Sidney Sussex College, Cambridge

Appendix
Orders of magnitude of Major Components
1750–1990

Population* 1800 = 100		Gross Domestic Product (at constant prices) 1800 = 100	Exports as % of G.D.P.	Proportion of total exports (%)				
				Woollens	Cottons	Metals and Engin- eering	Coal	Others
1750	74	(50)	(9)	75	5	14	2	1
1800	100	100	8	43	32	17	3	1
1850	198	460	12	16	55	20	2	7
1880	283	810	15	12	48	25	5	10
1890	314	1,180	15	12	40	28	9	11
1913	390	1,930	15	9	41	22	16	12
1937	438	2,780	13	9	22	47	12	10
1965	501	4,860	16	3	6	47	1	43
1990	540	7,950	17	1	1	42	1	55

Warning note:
I have myself constructed this table solely in order to establish orders of magnitude. It is drawn from a large number of sources and I have linked separate estimates for separate limited periods. Figures in some cases have been rounded. While it is believed that it establishes orders of magnitude, any serious scholar concerned with details should check from original sources.

* England, Wales and Scotland.

GAME THEORY AS A PART OF EMPIRICAL ECONOMICS

Alvin E. Roth

There is something slightly madcap in agreeing to make a hundred year prophecy about a field of study less than fifty years old, particularly a field that has undergone considerable evolution in that time. Yet this is the situation of game theory. Although it has antecedents going back much further (e.g. in the work of Cournot, Edgeworth and Zeuthen), game theory did not become a coherent field until the publication in 1944 of von Neumann and Morgenstern's *Theory of Games and Economic Behavior*. And many of the extensions and reformulations that shaped modern game theory came only in the 1950s and 60s, in the work of Aumann, Harsanyi, Nash, Shapley, Selten, and others.

I will also speculate about the future of experimental economics, which is one of the tools – but by no means the only one – that I anticipate will play an important role in helping game theory bridge the gap between the study of ideally rational behaviour and the study of actual behaviour. Although it too has older antecedents, experimental economics is also a fairly new line of work, having originated more or less contemporaneously with game theory. Indeed, many of the earliest experimental economists are today known primarily as distinguished game theorists, and were drawn to experimentation by the chance to test game theoretic predictions, and observe unpredicted behaviour, in a controlled environment (see e.g. the experimental work in the 1950s and 60s of Maschler, Nash, Schelling, Shubik, and Selten).[1]

Since the safest part of a long term forecast is the far future, let me state at the outset that I am cautiously optimistic that, a hundred years from now, game theory will have become the backbone of a kind of micro-economic engineering that will have roughly the relation to the economic theory and laboratory experimentation of the time that chemical engineering has to chemical theory and bench chemistry. Game theory is, after all, the part of economic theory that focuses not merely on the strategic behaviour of individuals in economic environments, but also on other issues that will be critical in the design of economic institutions, such as how information is distributed (e.g. Harsanyi, 1967–68; Aumann, 1976), the influence of players' expectations and beliefs (e.g. Kreps and Wilson, 1982), and the tension between equilibrium and efficiency (e.g. Myerson and Satterthwaite, 1983). And game theory has already achieved important insights into issues such as the design of contracts and allocation mechanisms which take into account the sometimes counterintuitive ways in which individual incentives operate in environments having decision makers with different information and objectives.

---

[1] E.g. Kalisch *et al.* (1954), Schelling (1957), Sauermann and Selten (1959) Shubik (1962), Maschler (1965).

However if we do *not* take steps in the direction of adding a solid empirical base to game theory, but instead continue to rely on game theory primarily for conceptual insights (deep and satisfying as these may be), then it is likely that long before a hundred years game theory will have experienced sharply diminishing returns. In this respect, I think the next hundred years will likely bring about a change in the way theoretical and empirical work are related in economics generally, and that, if not, then the entire discipline of economics may also fail to realise its potential.

The problem as I see it is that empirical work in economics has focused disproportionately on economically important questions. In case this does not seem like a heavy indictment, let me explain. While answering questions about important parts of the economy is a good thing for economists to try to do, it need not be the activity that best fosters the growth of theory, or fosters the growth of the best theory. And the relative neglect of empirical work directed primarily at testing and developing economic theory may therefore slow the growth of practical economic knowledge, since sound theory is of incalculable practical value.

Suppose, by analogy, that physical scientists had focused almost exclusively on important practical concerns like communication and illumination, to the detriment of more 'basic' science such as research on electricity and magnetism. We would likely have known much less today about radios and electric lights, which are not simply improvements on carrier pigeons and kerosene lamps. And, without the aid of experiments designed to elucidate basic phenomena far removed from immediate practical concerns, knowledge of electricity and magnetism would have accumulated much more slowly. Yet, in economics, 'basic science' is done disproportionately by theorists, who must rely for their empirical bearings on data collected for more immediately practical purposes.

However my optimism that in the future we will see more empirical work pointedly directed at theoretical issues is based on the fact that work of this sort has already begun to thrive. To illustrate what I mean, I will briefly mention some of the areas in which such work has been done. And then I will try my hand at the riskier part of prophecy, namely forecasting what will be some of the most productive avenues of work in the near and intermediate term.[2]

CONFRONTING THEORY WITH EVIDENCE IN THE LAB AND IN THE FIELD

(A) Laboratory Studies

Expected utility theory, as formulated by von Neumann and Morgenstern, was one of the first subjects in economics to attract the sustained attention of experimenters. From the very beginning this effort has both provided indications of the extent to which the predictions of the theory are approximate guides to individual choice behaviour (e.g. Mosteller and Nogee, 1951), and

---

[2] Twenty-first century readers should note that the omission of many of the most productive avenues of research that emerged during the years following this article is due to the severe space limitations under which the prophet laboured.

identified particular situations in which a significant proportion of subjects consistently violate the predictions of the theory (e.g. Allais, 1953). And this experimental work has fed back into the theoretical literature, giving rise to new theories of individual choice and to experimental tests of those theories (e.g. Loomes and Sugden, 1987). At the same time, experimental techniques have been developed which allow theories stated in terms of individuals' expected utility to be examined under controlled conditions. For example, Becker *et al.* (1964) described an experimental procedure for eliciting reservation prices from utility maximisers.[3] Using procedures of this kind, experimental methods allow investigators to measure some of the parameters on which the predictions of a theory may depend, and which would be unobservable in non-experimental situations.

For example, the classical game theoretic models of bargaining which date from the work of Nash were unusually resistant to tests with field data because their predictions depend on difficult to observe elements of the bargainers' preferences. But laboratory experimentation presents the opportunity to measure or control these factors, and thus permits bargaining to be observed in environments for which the prediction of these theories can be known, and therefore tested. And when examined in this way, the evidence supports some of the qualitative predictions of these models, for example concerning the effect of risk aversion on the outcome of bargaining, while contradicting others, concerning, for example, what constitutes 'complete' information about a bargaining problem (see e.g. Roth, 1987). And a variety of unpredicted regularities have been brought to light and subsequently observed in a wide range of experimental environments. Some of these regularities have been the subject of vigorous investigation and productive exchange among experimenters with different intuitions about the way in which existing theory may need to be modified to account for them (see e.g. Guth *et al.*, 1982; Binmore *et al.*, 1985; Neelin *et al.*, 1988; and Ochs and Roth, 1989). Part of what allows this kind of exchange among experimenters to be so productive is that experimenters do not have to rely on one anothers' data, but can generate their own data from experimental environments well suited to testing their hypotheses precisely. And so series of experiments allow the experimental community to build upon and critique one anothers' work in ways that are not as readily available to economists using non-experimental methods.[4]

Experimental data can also provide insights into field data. A good example is the extended series of experiments that John Kagel and his colleagues have conducted on auction behaviour. Kagel's particular interest has been in a question that arose among oil companies involved in auctions for offshore oil

---

[3] And as alternative theories of individual choice have been developed, it has been noted that this procedure may not give the correct incentives to non-expected utility maximisers, and that alternative experimental procedures for eliciting reservation prices may be desirable for testing the predictions of these theories (see e.g. Safra *et al.*, 1990).

[4] I think that bargaining experiments have been particularly productive in this respect, with investigators showing an exemplary willingness to address each others positions. This is not yet uniformly the case in all areas of experimental economics, and in the nearest term, experimenters will have to learn more about how to conduct and report experiments so as to most efficiently conduct productive dialogues.

rights. In the trade journals people began talking about a phenomenon that has since been called the 'winner's curse'. The idea is that the winning bidder in an auction frequently finds out that he has bid too much, once he discovers how much oil is recoverable from the plot he has won the right to drill on. Now, (since oil prices do not hold still, and wells do not produce until years after the bidding) it has proved hard to judge from field data whether this is a real phenomenon, or just the self-interested talk of oil companies trying to convince each other not to bid too competitively. So this is the kind of phenomenon that naturally lends itself to experimental investigation. Kagel and his colleagues have shown in a series of experiments that, with inexperienced bidders, there is a clear winner's curse' that this tends to go away as they accumulate experience; but that the learning that they exhibit does not help them very much in adjusting to new environments, such as a different number of bidders.[5] And by observing in experimental environments that public information about the value of the object being auctioned effects the bid price in opposite directions depending on whether the winner's curse is present, Kagel and Levin (1986) suggest new ways to test for the winner's curse in field data, by comparing rates of return for wildcat tracts (on which no drilling data are available) and drainage tracts (for which drilling data from adjacent tracts are available).

(B) Field Studies

Field studies, as opposed to laboratory studies, are what economists traditionally do, but the field studies I want to draw attention to here are non-traditional in the sense that the economic importance of the particular markets being studied plays rather less than its usual role in motivating them. Rather, a primary motivation is the opportunity to make observations that will help economists formulate and test important theory.

A good example of what I have in mind is the study by Ehrenberg and Bognanno (1990) of the performance of professional golfers at different stages of tournaments. Tournaments have been proposed as models of executive compensation and promotion by large corporations, where, for example, many vice presidents may compete for promotion to president. These models have implications about the incentives for working hard in environments in which the outcome is determined by chance as well as by effort. But studies of executive career paths and compensation offer little hope of testing these predictions, both because of the difficulty of gathering appropriate data, and because of the many non-tournament features of corporate employment. Ehrenberg and Bognanno proposed instead to test the theory of tournaments per se on a domain to which it clearly applied, and on which unambiguous data was available on incentives (the prize distribution in each tournament) and on output (players' scores). Controlling for player quality and course difficulty, they were therefore able to examine tournament incentives much more directly than would have been possible using labour market data.

[5] And these conclusions hold for construction industry executives as well as for student subjects (Dyer et al., 1989).

Another set of field studies, in which I have been involved (in order to practice what I preach), is the study of various entry level labour markets. A large body of theory on two-sided matching markets has grown from Gale and Shapley's (1962) initial definition of *stability* for such markets, including a modern literature on the incentives and strategic choices facing agents in such markets (see Roth and Sotomayor, 1990). To initiate empirical tests of the theory, it has proved convenient to concentrate on markets which employ various kinds of centralised matching institutions, since in these markets the information about the 'rules of the game' required to test the theory is most readily available. For example, the market for new medical school graduates in the United States employs a centralised matching procedure which was developed in the early 1950s in response to a series of market failures in the decentralised markets that preceded it. In Roth (1984) it was shown that this centralised procedure yields stable outcomes. The performance of this procedure in the intervening years led to hypotheses about the role of stability in organising markets of this kind, and the role of instability in the earlier market failures and in recent difficulties caused by the growing number of two-doctor households in the market.

An opportunity to test these hypotheses arose in the United Kingdom, where similar centralised labour markets, inspired by similar market failures, were introduced in some regions of the National Health Service in the late 1960s and early 70s. Because different regions have used different procedures for organising the market, the United Kingdom presents a natural experiment that allows these procedures to be compared with each other. And because some of these centralised procedures have failed and been abandoned, whereas others have succeeded, this natural experiment also presents an opportunity to test the hypotheses about stability motivated by the U.S. market. (And the data supports the hypotheses, while suggesting some refinements. The stable market mechanisms – in Edinburgh and Cardiff – both perform comparably to the American market, while the mechanisms that have failed produced unstable outcomes (Roth, 1990 a, b)). And these hypotheses can be further tested on a different domain in the centralised 'markets' for new members run each year by sororities on American college campuses (Mongell and Roth, 1990).

My point about all these markets, from golf tournaments to physicians to sororities, is that their potential importance derives at least as much from the tests of theory they make possible as from their place in the world economy. And without direct tests of this sort, theorists are often forced to rely on indirect inferences from data which are ill suited for testing and refining theory, although they may concern very important parts of the economy.

SOME THOUGHTS ON THE NEAR AND INTERMEDIATE TERM

One of the most striking features of many of the experimental and field studies mentioned above is that the dynamics of economic processes when they are out of equilibrium appear to play a large role. (For example, agents had an incentive to circumvent the centralised matching procedures for new physicians in Birmingham and Newcastle, in ways that magnified this incentive for those who continued to follow the official rules. And, after a few years of operation, these procedures collapsed under the weight of the accelerating number of circumventers (Roth, 1990*b*).) So the development of useful theories of out-of-equilibrium adjustment seems likely to be a productive avenue of research. This is particularly so since, when multiple equilibria exist, out-of-equilibrium dynamics may play an important role in determining which one (if any) is reached, so that without a dynamic theory, current efforts at (static) equilibrium refinement may experience sharply diminishing returns.[6]

Another conclusion that is hard to escape after examining these experimental and field studies is that, even in situations designed or chosen to be particularly susceptible to game-theoretic analysis, it is hard to specify *precisely* what game is being played. In experiments this may be so because of uncontrolled aspects of the players' preferences or expectations, and in field studies it may be because no one knows the details of the game many moves off the equilibrium path. (For example, no one knows exactly what would happen if one year no graduating medical students sought employment in the Massachusetts General Hospital, one of the most prestigious in the United States. Since this has never happened, neither economists nor market participants can have any clear idea of the consequences if it should happen. Yet many kinds of game-theoretic analyses are sensitive to the modeller's specification of what would happen.) In general, when the rules of the game must be learned by observation, it may be impossible to know all of them, particularly when some formal rules turn out not to be binding while other, informal rules (e.g. social norms) may be decisive in some circumstances. So it will be productive to identify those aspects of strategic behaviour that are robust to changes in parts of the game that may not be observable. In this connection I anticipate that the distinction between 'cooperative' and 'non-cooperative' game theory will become much less important.[7]

TOWARDS A MICROECONOMIC ENGINEERING

In summary, I think the next step in the development of game theory as an integral part of economics, and a step we must take if game theory is to continue to thrive, is to bring to the fore the empirical questions associated with strategic environments. Accomplishing this will require some changes in the kinds of theory and empirical work we do, in order to regularly confront theory with evidence, and to use theory as a guide to what kinds of evidence we should collect.

[6] See Brandts and Holt (1990) for an experimental study that makes this point very forcefully. Some experimental studies of out of equilibrium dynamics which focus on coordination games are reported in Cooper *et al.* (1990), and Van Huyck *et al.* (1990), and some preliminary theoretical analyses of this process are contained in Crawford (1990) and Crawford and Haller (1990).

[7] A cynical observer might summarise the present situation by saying that the less detailed cooperative models, which try to represent a game without specifying all the rules, aspire to a spurious generality, while the non-cooperative, strategic models, which are analysed as if they represented *all* the potential moves in a game, offer a spurious specificity when the game in question is a model of some observable situation. It will be largely an empirical matter to determine which aspects of games need to be modelled in detail in order to confidently draw which kinds of conclusions.

I anticipate that experimental economics will play a growing role in this effort. There are many questions for which laboratory experimentation will be the most direct way to test theory, and to explore the effects of variables that are difficult to measure or control in any other way. This is not to say, of course, that experimentation in economics will come to play exactly the role it plays in any other science, or that there will not be many questions that are best addressed by field research, including new kinds of field research, which will pay particular attention to the details of economic environments, including both formal and informal 'rules of the game', and cultural and psychological constraints on individuals' actions.

In the long term, the real test of our success will be not merely how well we understand the general principles which govern economic interactions, but how well we can bring this knowledge to bear on practical questions of microeconomic engineering, to design appropriate mechanisms for price formation (as in different kinds of auction), dispute resolution, executive compensation, market organisation, etc. To do this we will need to learn more about the various kinds of frictions that enter economic environments as a function of size and complexity, about which properties of these environments are robust and which are fragile, and about which kinds of environments facilitate which kinds of learning.[8] Just as chemical engineers are called upon not merely to understand the principles which govern chemical plants, but to design them, and just as physicians aim not merely to understand the biological causes of disease, but its treatment and prevention, a measure of the success of microeconomics will be the extent to which it becomes the source of practical advice, solidly grounded in well tested theory, on designing the institutions through which we interact with one another.

University of Pittsburgh

REFERENCES

Allais, Maurice (1953). 'Le comportement de l'homme rationnel devant le risque: critique des postulats et axiomes de l'ecole americane.' *Econometrica*, vol. 21, pp. 503–46.
Aumann, Robert J. (1976). 'Agreeing to disagree.' *The Annals of Statistics*, vol. 4, pp. 1236–9.
Becker, Gordon M., DeGroot, Morris H. and Marschak, Jacob (1964). 'Measuring utility by a single-response sequential method.' *Behavioral Science*, vol. 9, pp. 226–32.
Binmore, Kenneth, Shaked, Avner and Sutton, John (1985). 'Testing noncooperative bargaining theory: a preliminary study.' *American Economic Review*, vol. 75, pp. 1178–80.
Brandts, Jordi and Holt, Charles A. (1990). 'An experimental test of equilibrium dominance in signaling games,' *American Economic Review*, forthcoming.
Cooper, Russell W., DeJong, Douglas V., Forsythe, Robert and Ross, Thomas W. (1990). 'Selection criteria in coordination games: some experimental results.' *American Economic Review*, vol. 80, pp. 218–33.
Crawford, Vincent P. (1990). 'An "evolutionary" explanation of van Huyck, Batallio, and Beil's experimental results on coordination.' *Games and Economic Behaviour*, forthcoming.
—— and Haller, Hans (1990). 'Learning how to cooperate: optimal play in repeated coordination games.' *Econometrica*, vol. 58, pp. 571–95.
Dyer, Douglas, Kagel, John H. and Levin, Dan (1989). 'A comparison of naive and experienced bidders in common value offer auctions: a laboratory analysis.' ECONOMIC JOURNAL, vol. 99, pp. 108–15.
Ehrenberg, Ronald G. and Bognanno, Michael L. (1990). 'The incentive effects of tournaments revisited: evidence from the European PGA tour.' *Industrial and Labor Relations Review*, vol. 43, pp. 74–88S.

---

[8] And while field studies will be central to this effort, laboratory studies will likely play a role here as well. See e.g. Plott (1987) for a discussion of some experimental studies carried out with a view to giving guidance to policy makers.

Gale, David and Shapley, Lloyd (1962). 'College admissions and the stability of marriage.' *American Mathematical Monthly*, vol. 69, pp. 9–15.

Guth, Werner, Schmittberger, R. and Schwarz, B. (1982). 'An experimental analysis of ultimatum bargaining.' *Journal of Economic Behavior and Organization*, vol. 3, pp. 367–88.

Harsanyi, John C. (1967–8). 'Games with incomplete information played by "Bayesian" Players.' *Management Science*, vol. 14, pp. 159–82, pp. 320–34, pp. 486–502.

Kalisch, Gerhard K., Milnor, J. W., Nash, John F. and Nering, E. D. (1954). 'Some experimental n-person games,' in (R. M. Thrall, C. H. Coombs and R. L. Davis, eds.), *Decision Processes*, New York: Wiley, pp. 301–27.

Kagel, John H. and Levin, Dan (1986). 'The winner's curse and public information in common value auctions.' *American Economic Review*, vol. 76, pp. 894–920.

Kreps, David M. and Wilson, Robert (1982). 'Sequential equilibria.' *Econometrica*, vol. 50, pp. 863–94.

Loomes, Graham and Sugden, Robert (1987). 'Testing for regret and disappointment in choice under uncertainty.' ECONOMIC JOURNAL, *Conference Papers*, vol. 97, pp. 118–29.

Maschler, Michael (1965). 'Playing on n-person game: an experiment.' Econometric Research Program Memorandum No. 73, Princeton University, reprinted in (H. Sauermann, ed.), *Coalition Forming Behavior*, Contributions to Experimental Economics vol. 8, 1978, pp. 283–328.

Mongell, Susan and Roth, Alvin E. (1990). 'Sorority rush as a two-sided matching mechanism.' *American Economic Review*, forthcoming.

Mosteller, F. and Nogee, P. (1951). 'An experimental measurement of utility.' *Journal of Political Economy*, vol. 59, pp. 371–404.

Myerson, Roger B. and Satterthwaite, Mark A. (1983). 'Efficient mechanisms for bilateral trading.' *Journal of Economic Theory*, vol. 29, pp. 265–81.

Neelin, Janet, Sonnenschein, Hugo and Spiegel, Matthew (1988). 'A further test of noncooperative bargaining theory.' *American Economic Review*, vol. 78, pp. 824–36.

Ochs, J. and Roth, A. E. (1989). 'An experimental study of sequential bargaining.' *American Economic Review*, vol. 79, pp. 355–84.

Plott, Charles R. (1987). 'Dimensions of parallelism: some policy applications of experimental methods.' In (ed. A. E. Roth), *Laboratory Experimentation in Economics: Six Points of View*, Cambridge: Cambridge University Press, pp. 193–219.

Roth, Alvin E. (1984). 'The evolution of the labor market for medical interns and residents: a case study in game theory.' *Journal of Political Economy*, vol. 92, pp. 991–1016.

—— (1987). 'Bargaining phenomena and bargaining theory.' In (ed. A. E. Roth), *Laboratory Experimentation in Economics: Six Points of View*, Cambridge: Cambridge University Press, pp. 14–41.

—— (1990a). 'New physicians: a natural experiment in market organization.' *Science*, forthcoming.

—— (1990b). 'A natural experiment in the organization of entry level labor markets: regional markets for new physicians and surgeons in the U.K.' *American Economic Review*, forthcoming.

—— and Sotomayor, Marilda (1990). *Two-Sided Matching: A Study in Game-Theoretic Modeling and Analysis*, Econometric Society Monograph Series, Cambridge University Press.

Safra, Zvi, Segal, Uzi and Spivak, Avia (1990). 'The Becker-DeGroot-Marschak mechanism and non-expected utility.' *Journal of Risk and Uncertainty*, vol. 3, pp. 177–90.

Sauermann, Heinz and Selten, Reinhard (1959). 'Ein Oligolpolexperiment.' *Zeitschrift für die Gesamte Staatswissenschaft*, vol. 115, pp. 427–71.

Schelling, Thomas C. (1957). 'Bargaining, communication, and limited war.' *Journal of Conflict Resolution*, vol. 1, pp. 19–36.

Shubik, Martin (1962). 'Some experimental non-zero-sum games with lack of information about the rules.' *Management Services*, vol. 8, pp. 215–34.

Van Huyck, John B., Battalio, Raymond C. and Beil, Richard O. (1990). 'Tacit coordination games, strategic uncertainty, and coordination failure.' *American Economic Review*, vol. 80, pp. 234–48.

CONTINUITY AND CHANGE IN THE ECONOMICS INDUSTRY

*Richard Schmalensee**

If asked to forecast long-term changes in the product mix of a manufacturing industry, most economists would consider likely trends in the industry's technology, the demand for outputs it might produce, and the supply of inputs it might use. This essay's examination of the long-term future of economics focuses on changes in three broadly analogous influences: the profession's internally-generated research agenda, the demands for answers that arise outside the profession, and the supply of tools and techniques available from outside economics. Unfortunately, these influences do not separate as clearly as their manufacturing-industry analogs, and the laws of motion that govern the evolution of intellectual activity are not well understood.

I. THE INTERNAL AGENDA

Economic research, like research in any scientific discipline, is driven in large part by an agenda that reflects the profession's shared sense of what problems are tractable and interesting at any time. In economics, as in other disciplines, most researchers spend most of their time on what Thomas Kuhn has called 'normal science'. They elaborate, extend, and apply existing tools and theories. The discipline's research agenda evolves more or less continuously in response to the results of these efforts. Discontinuous changes in the research agenda occur infrequently, when apparently intractable anomalies or problems are resolved through 'scientific revolutions'. Such revolutions involve what Kuhn has christened 'paradigm shifts', basic changes in the way the world is viewed that radically alter both the discipline and its agenda.

There is no doubt that economics has experienced revolutions in the last century; these include at least the emergence of macroeconomics as a core field and the methodological triumph of mathematical analysis as an 'engine of inquiry'. But it is easy for contemporaries to mistake important advances for revolutionary breaks with the past. It must be recognised that much contemporary economic research relies on refinements and elaborations of concepts of rational behaviour and competitive markets that would seem familiar to Marshall and perhaps even to Smith.

The durability of this core theoretical framework strongly suggests that many, if not most, of the problems on today's research agenda will be solved through 'normal science', just as many of the problems to which most late

---

* The views expressed in this essay are my own and are not necessarily those of the Council of Economic Advisers.

19th-century physicists devoted their attention did not require quantum theory or relativity for their solution. Thus I would expect that at least large portions of elementary texts and perhaps even non-specialist surveys written in 2090 could be readily understood by today's economists.

History also suggests, however, that some problems on today's research agenda and some that will emerge through its natural evolution will be solved only by 'paradigm shifts' and that these shifts will change both the tools economists use and the problems they study. Whatever the successes that will be achieved by natural extensions of current lines of research, these revolutions will dominate histories of 21st-century economic thought.

It is of course impossible to predict which items on the current research agenda will ultimately provoke revolutionary advances, but in the present context it is equally impossible to resist the temptation to try. Since 'normal science' in economics primarily involves deriving the testing implications of the assumption of rationality, it seems natural to yield to this temptation by looking for areas in which this approach may break down in some important way. Strategic behaviour may be one such area.

Recent research on game theory, pure and applied, has considerably clarified and deepened our understanding of the implications of rational behaviour in small-numbers situations, in which individual actors can directly affect each others' well-being. However, particularly in situations involving incomplete information, game-theoretic models seem often to have less than satisfactory predictive power. Multiple equilibria are common, and important features of equilibria often depend critically on apparently minor variations in assumptions. Game-theoretic research has thus tended to produce examples and possibilities rather than general predictions. Moreover, the actors in game-theoretic models must often possess a very high order of rationality indeed to compute their optimal strategies, and it appears difficult to argue that learning or natural selection will assure optimal behaviour in practice.

There are at least three views of how these problems will ultimately be resolved. First, the difficulties I have sketched may be only technical problems: 'normal science' may eventually produce game-theoretic models of strategic behaviour that have acceptable generality and predictive power. Second, game-theoretic research may have uncovered a basic limit to our ability to predict economic behaviour: the outcomes of some sorts of strategic interactions may in fact be essentially impossible to predict. Third, strategic behaviour may turn out to be predictable, but not with game-theoretic models of hyper-rational actors. If the first view is not proven correct in the near future, and I think there is a fair chance it will not be, I would expect economists and others to devote increasing attention to exploring the validity of the third view.

I would expect laboratory experiments to play an important role in such exploration. The experimental approach offers a way to circumvent serious limitations on the availability of micro-level data and seems particularly well-suited for testing the implications of models of strategic behaviour. Progress in computer hardware and software seems likely to reduce the cost of experiments. Unless future research reveals that laboratory experiments have fatal limitations, I would expect them to be used routinely in a number of fields of economics before much of the next century has passed.

Similarly, the invasion of other social sciences by economics may yield conceptual tools useful in exploring alternatives to current game-theoretic models. The success with which economists have applied rational actor models in the traditional domains of other disciplines suggests that this invasion will not end soon. And as economists work outside the traditional economic mainstream, they inevitably learn about the concepts and methods that have been generated by other social sciences. If the problem of strategic behaviour (or some other mainstream economic problem) begins to appear insoluble using 'normal' economic science, the temptation to use concepts and methods from other fields in the search for a solution will become stronger.

It is of course possible that economics will end its long intellectual isolation from the other social sciences by conquest, so that rational actor models will dominate sociology, anthropology, political science, and perhaps even psychology and marketing as thoroughly as they dominate economics. But occupying troops have a tendency to go native, so that it also seems possible, though by no means certain, that models embodying various empirically justified patterns of departure from full rationality may penetrate into mainstream economics from these other fields during the next century.

II. THE DEMAND FOR ANSWERS

Economists' research agendas have historically been responsive to questions posed in debates about public policy. As academic economists have come to think of themselves more as scientists and less as engineer-like practitioners of 'political arithmetic', the average academic's willingness to supply policy-relevant research has probably fallen. But the demand for such research has increased dramatically in recent decades and, for reasons I discuss below, I see no reason to expect a reversal of this trend. At least in Washington, economists may have almost realised Keynes' dream; we are sometimes perceived in at least some quarters to be almost as useful as plumbers.

Much of the demand for policy-relevant economic research is met by work done outside universities that does not appear in professional journals. But this work is a quantitatively important part of the profession's output. Moreover, much of it is read – and some of it is written – by those who do publish in leading journals. Thus public policy concerns, both those that will arise in the future and those visible today for which the economics is not settled, will have an important effect on developments in economics over the next century.

Similarly, while much of the theoretical research agenda in economics at any time does not reflect recent developments in real economies, applied research cannot completely ignore such developments. And theorists do eventually confront important problems posed by applied work. Thus recent and future changes in world economies, particularly those of the industrialised nations in which most economics is and will be done, will also shape the evolution of economics over the next century.

It is, of course, essentially impossible to forecast changes in policy agendas or real economies over anything like a century. But one can usefully point to a few current trends that seem likely to continue for some time, since changes in policy concerns and economic conditions seem to affect the profession's research agenda with a lag.

A century ago, government control (by regulation or direct ownership) of railroads, public utilities, and other enterprises was entering a period of rapid expansion, and U.S. antitrust policy was launched by the passage of the Sherman Act. These developments had an important impact on the economics research agenda. As a consequence of subsequent work, economists now enter policy debates in these areas armed with a powerful set of general concepts and results. The recent growth of 'social' regulation, dealing with externalities and information failures, may have a similar impact. A good deal of cost-benefit analysis has been done of particular regulatory programmes aimed at health, safety, environmental quality, and consumer protection. Some general principles of cost-effective regulatory design have been developed. But concepts applicable to social regulation with the normative power of natural monopoly, marginal cost pricing, or barriers to entry have yet to emerge. It is not obvious that such concepts will ever be uncovered, of course, but the demand for useful analysis of social regulation now is surely comparable to the demand for solution of 'the railroad problem' a century ago.

It has become clear that as natural and government-created barriers to flows of goods, services, and assets across national borders are reduced, policies that have hitherto generally been thought of as domestic emerge as sources of international friction. Comparative economic analysis of agricultural, environmental, industrial, regulatory, and other traditionally domestic policies can play an important role in what seems likely to be a prolonged policy harmonisation process. Such analysis also seems likely to enrich our understanding of the effects of those policies.

Similarly, the rise of potentially very long-lived concerns about trans-border pollution flows, global climate change, tropical deforestation, and ocean pollution suggests the importance of international harmonisation and perhaps even integration of energy and environmental policies. The current climate change debate both illustrates the difficulties involved in this process and raises economic issues that may take decades to resolve. Because of the long distributed lags with which greenhouse gas emissions may affect climate, for instance, variants of issues appearing in abstract form in the optimal growth literature may become important for policy formulation. Frictional effects of tax or price changes, informational imperfections, technology choice behaviour, and mechanisms of induced innovation may be critical determinants of the cost of reducing energy-related emissions. And long-term forecasts of both emissions levels and changes in adaptation costs associated with alternative levels of greenhouse gas buildup may be critical inputs to policy decisions.

Finally, no list of potentially long-lived economic policy concerns written in 1990 can exclude issues raised by recent events in the Soviet Union and Eastern Europe. While it now seems likely that these economies will have made the transition to various forms of capitalism well before the end of this JOURNAL's next century, it seems certain that the process of transition will not be quick or easy. I expect that economists will deepen knowledge of market-based economies by observing and, in some cases, participating in efforts to create them. One can hope that we will learn lessons that can be applied in the developing nations and, much more ambitiously, that economic development will be removed from the profession's list of hard problems before many more decades pass.

Turning to changes in the nature of economic activity, I expect the growing importance of service industries and technological competition in developed economies to cast long shadows on economic research. Service industries have received much less attention by economists than even their current importance would seem to warrant. Production theory is still dominated by stylised views of agriculture and manufacturing; little attention is paid to implications of queuing theory for capacity decisions in service sectors. Study of the regulation of financial institutions tends to fall in an intellectual crack between finance and regulatory economics. And economists have neglected the empirical study of distribution systems almost completely. It is difficult to believe that the profession will not devote more attention to services in the future than in the past, and roughly as difficult to believe that its tools and agenda will not be changed as a consequence.

In many modern markets, competition occurs largely, though not exclusively, through research and development decisions. Schumpeter saw this development a half-century ago, and his observations have proven seminal. But, despite a great deal of interesting research, I do not believe that we yet have adequate, useful models of the process of 'creative destruction' Schumpeter described. Patent race models describe episodes, at best, not processes, while cost reduction models cannot describe the search for new, typically differentiated products that consumes most industrial research and development spending. Not only do changes in the nature of competition call for better models of R & D competition, of course, so do heated public debates about patent policy, government support of research and development, and industrial policy.

III. THE SUPPLY OF TOOLS

Although economics has long been the most insular of the social sciences, it has imported tools and concepts on a large scale from mathematics and classical physics, and those inputs have affected its output mix. Mathematical techniques will no doubt continue to be imported on a fairly large scale, but it is harder to see modern physics having a major market share. If models in which actors are not fully rational become important in economics, imports from mathematical biology may take up the slack.

In some respects, economics' most important imports in recent decades have come from the computer industry and mathematical statistics. It is easy to predict a continued close and at times even synergistic relationship between econometrics and statistics for decades to come. The great advances in computer hardware and software that are universally predicted will lead to changes in the portfolio of available statistical and econometric techniques and will continue the trend toward employment of more computation-intensive methods in empirical research. One can also hope that reductions in the cost of data storage and processing will be exploited to increase the supply of disaggregated data, though it is difficult to predict that concerns for privacy and disclosure will soon cease to be a major barrier to such increases.

Advances in computation have made it much easier for economists to produce the quantitative estimates that are perhaps our most valued (if not always our most valuable) inputs into the policy process. Because the cost of quantitative analysis seems virtually certain to continue to fall, and it is hard to foresee policy-makers' losing interest in numbers, I think the place of economics in the policy process will remain secure for the foreseeable future, almost without regard to changes in the policy agenda. One can hope that economists' ability to make tied sales of numbers and principles will at least not diminish in coming decades.

Advances in computation are likely to affect economic theorists as well as applied researchers. Mathematicians already use computers to prove theorems, and earth scientists use massive simulation models to forecast long-term climate changes, while economic theorists still generally limit themselves to qualitative analysis using pencil and paper. Some qualitative economic analysis will surely be automated in the future, reducing the cost of routine analysis of algebraically complex models. I would also expect more fundamental changes to occur as economic theorists begin to exploit the power of computers to determine optima and equilibria numerically.

While this sort of simulation generally requires more or less arbitrary choice of functional forms, it permits relatively routine tests of robustness to such choices. Simulation can be used to make routine the search for counterexamples and thus for possible general relations. Chaos theory, which has become important in a wide variety of disciplines, will likely penetrate economics, if at all, only through the widespread acceptance of the computer as an engine of theoretical inquiry. Finally, the use of simulation to analyse theoretical models will tend to shift interest from general results of unknown quantitative importance to relations that are quantitatively important for plausible parameter values.

IV. SOME PERSPECTIVE

History suggests that long-term forecasts of almost anything are more likely to provide amusing quotes for future readers than examples of acute foresight. A. A. Michelson's famous 1894 assertion that 'The more important fundamental laws and facts of physical science have all been discovered...' suggests that long-term forecasts of scientific disciplines may be particularly risky, in part because the professional rewards for revolutionary scientific discoveries are so large.

Michelson's assertion reveals a good deal more about the mindset of physicists in 1894 than about ensuing developments in physics. It is a fair bet that the same will prove to be true of this essay and at least some of its companions. At any rate, I would like to think that somebody will find these speculations worth reading when the ECONOMIC JOURNAL prepares to begin its third century.

Council of Economic Advisers and Massachusetts Institute of Technology

THE DETERMINANTS OF GROWTH

*Nicholas Stern**

I. THE ISSUES

For the classical economists from Smith, and notably, Ricardo, Marx and Malthus, understanding the process of economic growth was central. And the question 'What determines the rate of growth?' has always constituted one focus of development economics, a subject which we may date from the Second World War. It has, however, been a popular topic for those involved in formal economic theory only for short periods, notably from the mid 1950s to the late 1960s. At the height of that period, now a quarter of a century ago, the ECONOMIC JOURNAL published what must be one of its most consulted papers, the estimable survey by Hahn and Matthews (1964). The loss of interest of the profession in the theory of growth for nearly twenty years, from the late sixties to the late eighties, was unfortunate.

The recent rekindling of that interest (see, for example, Romer, 1986 and 1990, and Lucas, 1988) is to be welcomed. It may be traced to a number of factors. These include, first, the progress in the microeconomic theories of industrial organisation, invention and innovation, and human capital, which have made the discussion of the advancement of knowledge and its relation to markets more coherent. Second, we now have 45 years of increasingly well-documented post-war experience from which a number of lessons can be gleaned. The time period is long enough to reveal accelerations and declines in rates of growth, to show that the growth experiences of different countries can differ in crucial respects, and to ask questions such as whether the incomes per capita of countries will converge. Central to this evidence is the fact that growth rates in different countries can differ, and differ for an extended period of time. This was indeed one of Kaldor's (1961) six stylised facts, to which he drew attention in the late 1950s, although at that time the post-war experience was only fifteen years old and the list of countries which could be included in that empirical analysis of experience was fairly narrow. It is perhaps appropriate, a quarter of a century since Hahn and Matthews (1964), a half-century since Harrod (1939), and with a half-century of extensive cross-country data, to make the determinants of growth a topic for the centenary of the ECONOMIC JOURNAL. Certainly many of the important contributions have been published here.

The first purpose of this paper is then to assess what we have learned from theory about the determinants of growth, and to examine where we should look

* I am very grateful for the helpful comments of Tony Atkinson, Robin Burgess, Peter Diamond, Francisco Ferreira, Gary Fields, Mervyn King and Amos Witztum and the support of the Suntory Toyota International Centre for Economics and Related Disciplines at the LSE.

for insights in the future. In doing this I shall be concerned particularly with advances since the Hahn–Matthews survey and with the lessons from developing countries. The study of growth is generally about the medium or long run. It is about the accumulation of physical capital, the progress of skills, ideas and innovation, the growth of population, how factors are used, combined, and managed and so on. It is therefore, principally, about the supply side.

Most of the theory of the fifties and sixties was positive, in the sense that it was concerned not with policy but with understanding what determines growth. The theory of optimal growth was indeed developed in the mid-1960s (notably Cass, 1965, Koopmans, 1965 and Mirrlees, 1967) but had a limited impact, and in retrospect its main contribution, which was an important one, should be seen in terms of understanding the logic of dynamic optimisation, rather than as an applied tool for solving real policy problems. Both in development economics and in economic theory there has been a resurgence of interest, over the last few years, in the role (beneficial and otherwise) of the state. Our second question is then 'How can, or should, the state influence the rate of growth?' This will be a minor theme for four reasons: first, theory and evidence on the determinants of growth are not yet sufficiently strong for confident assertions on policy for growth to be made; second, it raises difficult and important questions concerning what kind of growth we should be seeking in relation to standards of living and their distribution, to the environment and so on; third, I have recently set out my views on some relevant aspects of public policy and development elsewhere (Stern, 1991); and fourth, brevity has been enforced. We consider growth theory in Section II and growth experience in Section III. We conclude (Section IV) with some speculation and suggestions for future work.

It will be argued that the emphasis in the literature on the long run and on technical progress has, so far, led to only limited advancement in understanding. Further, whilst the questions raised are interesting, the emphasis has been excessive and basic medium-run questions of economic organisation and infrastructure have been missed. In drawing these conclusions I shall be particularly influenced by the experience of developing countries. There is every reason to expect fruitful empirical and theoretical research on the determinants of growth over the next few decades. Whilst not our main focus here, it should be stressed that the desire to understand the causes of growth should not lead us to think that the promotion of growth should be the first and over-riding aim of government policy. Experience has shown that there is no guarantee that growth will eliminate destitution and hunger (Drèze and Sen, 1990) or protect the environment (Kneese and Sweeney, 1988).

II. GROWTH THEORY

Harrod (1939) put the Keynesian savings-investment equilibrium in a dynamic context by observing that the level of investment, I, gives the growth, $\dot{K}$, in capital, K. On dividing the equilibrium condition that savings (S) are equal to investment by K, we obtain the Harrod–Domar condition,

$$\dot{K}/K = s/v, \tag{1a}$$

where $s = S/Y$ (Y is national income) and $v = K/Y$ (equilibrium in this context means that planned savings, given the level of income, are equal to actual savings; equivalently, it involves the clearing of the output market). An alternative version of (1a) is

$$\dot{Y}/Y = s/\nu, \tag{1b}$$

where ν is the incremental capital-output ratio (ICOR, equal to $\dot{K}/\dot{Y}$), the equality of the two growth rates being the same as the equality of v and ν.

This simple theory has been and remains very influential. Lewis (1954) saw the problem of raising the rate of growth as that of raising s, and saw this arising through the growth of an advanced sector which generated profits and thus, via a classical savings function, savings. Much discussion in planning, for example in India (see, for example, Gupta, 1989), has focused on the raising of savings rates and the control of ICORs. We must be careful not to be misled by the use of coefficients such as v and ν into thinking that factors are used efficiently subject to the technological constraints. We shall be emphasising this point, particularly for developing countries, in what follows. A discussion in terms of the reduction of the capital-output ratio is the beginnings of an examination of the role of efficiency in growth. Capital, of course, is not the only factor and a discussion of efficiency must extend to labour and intermediate goods. This takes us to the whole topic of social cost-benefit analysis, which is designed to identify the most productive investments, taking a broad view of social output and of social opportunity costs. Therefore that subject, properly viewed, is directly concerned with the intertemporal allocation of social consumption (see Drèze and Stern, 1987).

In the subsequent work on growth theory the realisation soon came that, whilst raising the rate of growth of capital could raise the rate of growth of output in the short or medium term, in the long run the rate of growth of the economy would be limited by the rate of growth of non-produced factors, notably labour. With constant returns to scale, no technical progress and an exogenous labour supply, we find that, in the long run, the rate of growth of output is determined by the rate of growth of the labour force, as demonstrated by Solow (1956). Raising s raises the rate of growth of output in the short run, but in the long run it merely increases v in the same proportion so that eventually s/v becomes equal to the rate of growth of labour (it follows from $\dot{K}/K = s/v > n = \dot{L}/L$ and constant returns to scale that $\dot{K}/K > \dot{Y}/Y$ so v rises). For developing countries (and probably developed too, see Atkinson, 1969) the focus on the long term is excessive, a point to which we shall return.

The concern to build models which allowed long-run growth in output per head led to a focus on technical progress which came to be seen as the main source of long-run growth. In its Harrod neutral or labour augmenting form this technical progress acts simply like an expansion of the labour force. For the most part, in the 1950s and 1960s, technical progress was seen as exogenous.

There were, however, notable examples (e.g., Kaldor, 1957, Arrow, 1962, Atkinson and Stiglitz, 1969), where experience was seen as the basis of learning. We shall return to the Arrow model shortly. There was also a group of papers in which the direction of technical progress was determined by economic choices (see, e.g., Kennedy, 1964, Ahmad, 1966, and Drandakis and Phelps, 1966 – all from the ECONOMIC JOURNAL). In these last cases, however, the frontier of choice for technical progress was unexplained and attention was focused on showing that the choice would tend in the limit to the Harrod-neutral form.

Solow (1957) showed how growth could be decomposed, using an aggregate production function, into contributions from different sources, namely the growth rates of factor inputs weighted by competitive factor shares (the 'contributions' of factors) plus a residual. This residual was often labelled technical progress, although it is perhaps best seen as what it is, i.e., the difference between the growth of output and a weighted sum of the growths of inputs or, by definition, the growth in total factor productivity. Formally, differentiating the production function $Y = F(X_1, X_2, \ldots, X_n, t)$ with respect to time where X_i is the quantity of input i we have

$$\dot{Y}/Y = \sum_i \alpha_i (\dot{X}_i/X_i) + F_t/Y, \tag{2}$$

where $\alpha_i \equiv (X_i \, \partial F/\partial X_i)/Y$.

Whilst this decomposition was suggestive it was unsatisfactory from the point of view of explaining growth since, apart from misgivings about the use of aggregate production functions for this purpose, it still left a major part of the sources of growth to be explained exogenously by 'technical progress'. Models followed in which the advance of the productivity of factors was endogenous, the most important example being that of Arrow (1962) incorporating learning by doing. Arrow chose to use a vintage model with technical progress available only for new investments. Kaldor (1957) (see also Kaldor and Mirrlees, 1962) used a technical progress function ($\dot{Y}/Y = g(\dot{K}/K)$) but had a view close in spirit to Arrow who, indeed, acknowledges his debt to Kaldor.

Analysis in vintage models becomes more complex since each piece of equipment must be identified using its date of construction. However, the central points of the Arrow approach can be neatly summarised in the non-vintage version provided by Sheshinski (1967). In the Sheshinski framework the production function of the representative firm (there are N firms) may be written

$$y = F(k, Al), \tag{3}$$

where l is labour in the firm, A is a factor denoting the level of knowledge and is taken to be K^γ where $K = Nk$ and $\gamma < 1$. Each firm learns not only from its own activities but also from those of other firms. The effectiveness of labour depends on total past investment with an elasticity of γ. There will be increasing returns at the level of the economy as a whole since a doubling of K and the labour force, L (equal to employment), would double output at constant A, but the increase of K, in addition to its direct effect on output, also increases A. There are, however, constant returns for the firm which acts as if A is fixed. It can, therefore, behave competitively. Putting $\dot{l}/l$ equal to n (the rate of growth of L) we find (if N is constant) that the Sheshinski model has a steady state with a constant capital-output ratio where output and capital both grow at the rate $n/(1-\gamma)$. This is the steady-state growth rate in Arrow (1962). Hence for Arrow and Sheshinski, notwithstanding endogenous technical progress, we have the conclusions that the long-run rate of growth cannot be positive unless n is positive and that this rate cannot be affected by policy.

From the early 1970s interest in models of growth subsided for over ten years. A central figure in the resurgence of interest has been Romer who provided (1986, 1989) a model which produces results sharply different from these last two conclusions. The approach is suggestive but we shall see that the difference between this model and that of Arrow–Sheshinski is essentially that γ is set at 1. To allow focus on economic growth without population growth l is assumed constant (normalised at unity). The crucial feature of the model is that with $\gamma = 1$ we now have constant returns (at the level of the whole economy) to K *taken alone* (doubling K doubles output). It must be emphasised that both Arrow and Romer retain the assumption of constant returns in the function $F( )$ with respect to the two arguments taken together, so that, with A viewed as fixed by the firm, perfect competition is sustainable. It is not obvious that we should rule out increasing returns in the firm-level production function, although this would involve a recasting of our microeconomic behavioural and aggregation stories. Kaldor (see Targetti and Thirlwall, 1989) emphasised, in the 1950s and 1960s, the possibility of both static and dynamic increasing returns but his pleas were largely ignored. With the improved ability of microeconomic theory to handle increasing returns (see e.g., Tirole, 1988) it is time to explore this possibility more deeply in the context of growth.

With a Cobb–Douglas form in (3) in the Romer framework, $Y = N^{1-\alpha}K$ and the marginal product of capital is $N^{1-\alpha}$. Intertemporal optimisation is by choice of consumption. A fully-informed government maximises the integral of an isoelastic utility function, $[c^{1-\sigma}/(1-\sigma)]e^{-\rho t}$, of consumption per head, c. It can be shown, straightforwardly (the basic optimality condition is that the marginal productivity of capital should be equal to the rate of fall of the marginal utility of consumption), to yield an optimal rate of growth of $(N^{1-\alpha}-\rho)/\sigma$ (we continue to assume N is constant). However, private firms see a marginal product of capital $\alpha N^{1-\alpha}$ (they think of A as constant in (3)) and if intertemporal optimisation occurred through private decisions by owner-consumers with the same utility function the growth rate would be lower at $(\alpha N^{1-\alpha}-\rho)/\sigma$. If, further, capital income were to be taxed at rate τ then the growth rate would be still lower at $[\alpha(1-\tau) N^{1-\alpha}-\rho]/\sigma$. Hence we have long-run growth without population growth and without exogenous technical progress. Further, government action, by change of τ, could influence the long-run rate of growth.

We noted, however, that the difference was essentially that Romer's model was a boundary case of Arrow–Sheshinski, with $\gamma = 1$. That such important conclusions turn on such a fine distinction (which is unlikely to be settled empirically) should make us uneasy about relying on the Romer (1986, 1989) model as a basis for explaining the role of policy in determining the rate of growth. Notice that if $\gamma > 1$ we can have growth rates which increase without bound.

There is a different class of models which can explain endogenously the long-run rate of growth following in the tradition of Uzawa (1965), and Shell (1973), and more recently, Romer (1990) and Lucas (1988). Technical advance comes from a sector which produces productivity enhancing ideas. The crucial endogenous variable is then the amount of resources which are allocated to that sector. Ideas produced by that sector may be used at zero cost in resources by firms in the other sector, which produces outputs of a good which may be consumed or invested. The resources allocated to the ideas sector may be determined in an optimal plan derived from a model for the optimal intertemporal allocation of consumption or from the equilibrium of a market economy. Without intervention the market outcome will not be optimal because ideas will be generated privately only if their dissemination is limited (by, e.g., patents) thus allowing those who generate them to sell them for a positive price. Without restrictions such as patents no-one would pay for an idea which was freely available to everybody. In these circumstances there is scope for state intervention to increase the flow of ideas. This could take place, for example, through government funding of research.

There are problems with this approach, however, if we try to tell empirical stories. It is extremely difficult to identify anything approximating to a knowledge-producing sector in real economies. R & D activity, for example, is poorly defined, difficult to interpret and in many cases in practice probably contains little real research in the sense of the 'ideas' in the model (see e.g. Griliches, 1984).

Have these newer theories provided advances which take us considerably beyond the position of the late 1960s? In my judgement, given the difficulties we have described, we have not yet advanced very far. We really do not know which, if any, of the many stories which might 'explain' the 'residual' or 'growth in total factor productivity' together or separately get to the heart of what is going on. We are faced by an identification problem of major proportions. But some of the right kinds of questions are being asked. We know that markets are not always very good at dealing with knowledge (see, e.g., Spence, 1984) and it is surely sensible to ask about the implications of this observation for growth. It seems plausible to see human capital as a major part of the story. In neither the Arrow–Romer nor the Uzawa–Lucas approaches should we expect the market economy to deliver efficient growth. The externalities of learning and the publicness of ideas provide important scope for policy and in some models such policy can have the effect of increasing the rate of growth.

As far as further research goes I think we shall need both approaches. I confess, however, to finding the Arrow–Romer route more promising, both since R & D is so hard to define and identify and because I do not see knowledge as arising only where it is deliberately sought through the application of resources to that sole end. Both Scott (1989) and King and

Robson (1989) have argued persuasively that it is the act of investment itself that generates the ideas and this indeed is the notion Arrow and Kaldor were seeking to capture in their earlier models. Kaldor's route invoked the technical progress function $(\dot{Y}/Y = F(\dot{K}/K))$. It was common in the 1960s to criticise him for basing his models (1957 and 1962) on something which was not clearly related to a familiar production function. However, we should look at this concept again (as King and Robson, 1989, and Scott, 1989, have done).

How does this very brief review of theory leave us as regards the agenda for understanding the determinants of growth in output per head and how they might be influenced? The growth theories have emphasised three (related) determinants: (i) capital accumulation, (ii) human capital (including learning), and (iii) research, development and innovation. We may associate all three determinants with the augmentation of input, notwithstanding that central in that story are inputs called skills and knowledge. From this perspective we should go beyond the standard theory and add (iv) management and organisation, which may provide better output from given inputs. It may not be unreasonable to apply all four of these ideas at an aggregate level.

If we go beyond the aggregate, however, there are two further crucial issues which arise: (v) infrastructure, and (vi) the allocation of output across directly productive sectors (discussed below). The deficiencies of infrastructure, together with the weakness of management and economic organisation, are likely to account for a substantial part of low factor productivity in developing countries. It is very hard to run factories and businesses effectively when the electricity and water supplies are unreliable, the telephone and the mail services are weak, and transport is slow, costly and hazardous. We may also include as a part of infrastructure what we might term social infrastructure. By this I mean the way in which business is done, rather than human capital (in terms of literacy, knowledge and so on). A system in which individuals behave dishonestly or where bureaucracy is obstructive, or where property rights are unclear may lead to a very wasteful allocation of resources in insuring against dishonesty, circumventing bureaucracy or enforcing property rights. The costs involved and the distortion of incentives may constitute serious impediments to growth (see, e.g. Platteau, 1990, Reynolds, 1983, Thomas, 1991).

These weaknesses of management, organisation and infrastructure may explain why scarce capital can be unproductive and why countries, such as India in the 1960s and 1970s, which have succeeded in raising their savings rates have not seen a higher growth rate (and measured rates of growth of total factor productivity have been negative; see Ahluwalia, 1985, and Bruton, 1989). It is interesting that in the last five years India has seen growth rates of GDP per capita around 3%, compared with an average of 1% or so in earlier periods and this appears to have coincided with increased capacity utilisation (UNIDO, 1990) – one index of the efficiency with which resources are used (see Bautista et al. 1981, Betancourt and Clague, 1981, and Phan-Thuy, 1981). These growth rates seem to have been associated with a high level of domestic demand and an interesting research programme could be constructed on the relation between demand and growth – whilst growth and productivity have improved in India, macroeconomic imbalances (in terms of inflation and trade deficits) are becoming severe.

Different sectors in developing countries may have very different institutional arrangements and there may be a number of distortions preventing the allocation of resources in such a way that social marginal products in different sectors are equalised. In this context the shift of resources from one sector to another may have an important effect on the overall level of output (and Chenery, 1979, and Chenery *et al.*, 1986, found some evidence in support of this view). Thus close study of the institutional and other impediments to the movement of resources from one sector to another could have a substantial pay-off (in addition to the arrangements within the sector which we include under management and organisation).

I would argue, therefore, that whilst growth theory has both contributed to our understanding of how growth is determined and how it might be influenced, it has in many ways missed some of the crucial issues for developing countries. It may well be possible to model these productively, and I am sure that careful applied study of the role of management and organisation, the improvement of infrastructure, and sectoral transfer in developing economies could make a real contribution to our understanding of the determinants of growth and to the design of policy. They are not directly concerned with the long-run rate of growth in the sense of the steady-states in the models we have been discussing, but are none the less important for a medium term of some considerable duration. In this sense the focus on the long run in the theories may have been, at least in part, diversionary.

III. GROWTH EXPERIENCE

The theory of growth has been stimulated by and has stimulated the documentation and analysis of the empirical growth process by economic historians and statisticians, the notable pioneer being Kuznets (1955, 1961, 1963, 1966, 1971). Important subsequent contributions have come from Chenery and Syrquin (1975), Chenery *et al.* (1986), Morris and Adelman (1988), and Reynolds (1983). A particularly valuable set of data, which has provided recomputations of national income on the basis of purchasing power parity, has been made available recently (Summers and Heston, 1988). The combination of the availability of these data and the newer theories has provided a further stimulus to cross-section work, particularly by Barro (1989 a, b). We provide a very brief review.

The work of Chenery and his collaborators (see, e.g., Chenery *et al.*, 1986) has constituted a substantial and important attempt to analyse the sources of growth in different countries. This builds on the growth accounting approaches pioneered by Solow (1957) and Denison (1967). Reviewing work on the period 1960–73, Chenery (1983) found that the 'contribution' to growth of the unexplained residual was substantial. For developed countries the residual constituted generally more than one-half of the growth rate. However, for middle-income developing countries the proportion of growth explained by factor input was generally above three-quarters, with the residual explaining less than one-quarter. The explained proportion for developing countries becomes higher still if we take into account sectoral transfer from less productive to more productive sectors, whereas an attempt to use this type of idea to explain some of the residual for developed countries has been less successful (Chenery *et al.*, 1986).

In the studies cited, Chenery and collaborators, Morris and Adelman, and Reynolds have also tried to examine the circumstances under which different government policies and competitive environments have stimulated or inhibited growth. Some have argued, for example Krueger (1978), that those countries where government intervention has been lower, particularly in trade, have exhibited higher growth rates, with influential examples being the four tigers: Hong Kong, Singapore, South Korea, Taiwan. In all four countries, except Hong Kong, government intervention was, however, more extensive than is often portrayed (see, for example, Amsden, 1989). Other authors have been more cautious (see Chenery and Syrquin, 1975, Chenery *et al.*, 1986, and Morris and Adelman, 1988).

The importance of competition in promoting growth has been a common theme from Marx through Schumpeter, and more recently the neo-Austrians (see, e.g., Kirzner, 1987) and the management analysts (Porter, 1990). When Marx wrote 'Accumulate, accumulate! That is the Moses and the prophets!' (1974, p. 558) he saw, according to Kaldor's interpretation in his lectures which I attended in 1968, capitalists being obliged, by the forces of competition and increasing returns to scale, to invest the maximum possible in order to survive (although re-reading that section of Volume 1 of Kapital suggests that Kaldor may have been attributing his own ideas to Marx). Schumpeter's 'creative gale of destruction' (see, e.g., 1954) pictured inter-temporal competition with inventions and innovations creating short-term monopolies which were later eroded by further competitive inventions and innovations. This picture was endorsed by Hicks (1973) in his Nobel lecture with its emphasis on the 'impulse'. Porter (1990) in his study of Japan and other countries, has emphasised the role of competition between Japanese firms (rather than the role of the government, e.g., through MITI) in generating rapid technical advance. The experience of privatisation in the United Kingdom appears to confirm the importance of competition, relative to private ownership, in improving industrial performance (Vickers and Yarrow, 1988). A number of studies, however, have pointed to the importance in long-term growth of the establishment of an industrial base and technical skills (see, e.g., Chenery *et al.*, 1986, p. 358), and here the government may have a major role to play.

The recent work of Barro (1989 *a*, *b*) is stimulated by the newer theories and based on the Summers–Heston data. It attempts to treat the problems of simultaneous causation, although at the level of aggregation involved (growth rates of GDP per capita, investment and so on being key variables, and the unit of observation being the country) these are probably insuperable. The results can nevertheless be suggestive and examples are (for the period 1960–85 and a sample of 98 countries) that growth in GDP per capita is positively related to initial human capital and to investment (although the public/private breakdown seems unimportant) and negatively related to GDP per capita (suggesting some 'convergence'), 'political instability' and 'price distortions'. These relationships are based on significant coefficients of variables in an equation for the growth rate of GDP per capita in the simultaneous system.

The study of the experience of growth provides some confirmation of the importance of the six factors described in the preceding section and has pointed to both the role of competition and the potential for government action through, for example, the provision of education and infrastructure, both physical and social, in stimulating the growth process. There is less in theory or experience, however, that tells us that public ownership of the means of production is a necessary or indeed a helpful element.

IV. THE FUTURE

We have seen that the application of theory and a systematic accumulation of data and their analysis have taken us some way in the understanding of growth. At the same time growth theories, be they of the 1960s or the 1980s, leave much to be desired in their explanation of growth experience. The theories have shown an excessive concern with the long-run growth of total factor productivity and have made only a limited contribution to explaining it. We seem to have too many theories claiming 'property rights' in the unexplained 'residual', and have no reassurance that any of them, separately or together, really capture what is going on. Just as worrying is that they omit many issues which are probably crucial to growth in the medium run, including economic organisation and the social and physical infrastructure. We still have a great deal to learn about the six factors which we have identified as contributing to growth and about the role of the state in improving their contribution. Just as it has been a major concern over the last 100 years, I would expect research on these fundamental problems to continue. We will be greatly advantaged by longer runs of data on different countries and by the more sophisticated microeconomic theories of competition, information and technical progress which we have begun to see in the past 20 or 30 years.

We shall have to take much greater account of the closer integration of national economies through world markets and the role of trade in technological advance (see, for example, Grossman and Helpman, 1990). A concern with the understanding of the process of growth should also include an analysis of the role of the distribution of income in that process. This was a theme central to Smith, Ricardo and Marx, and one which, whilst perhaps less prominent in very recent growth theories was a focus of the discussion in development economics in the fifties and sixties (see, for example, Lewis, 1954 and 1955). It was critical to the work of Kalecki, who left a substantial tradition, including his influence on Kaldor (see, for example, Targetti and Thirlwall, 1989). On this and other topics, I would expect a resurgence of interest in the work of Kaldor, including his emphasis on both static and dynamic increasing returns. So far only a limited aspect of what Kaldor had in mind has been captured by the new growth theories.

There will also be a much broader view of advancement or development than consumption or income as conventionally measured. The perspective of standard of living will include health, education, political liberties and the environment. These should be of central concern for their own sakes, as well as through any contribution they might make to the production of consumer goods in the long run. The positive analysis of the determinants of the standard of living, and its improvement, of individuals in society will go hand-in-hand with an appraisal of what governments can do to protect individuals through social programmes, and in other ways. We now have enough experience of economic development to know that growth in aggregate income cannot, by itself, be guaranteed to eliminate deprivation.

London School of Economics

REFERENCES

Ahluwalia, I. J. (1985). *Industrial Growth in India*, Delhi: Oxford University Press.
Ahmad, S. (1966). 'On the theory of induced invention.' ECONOMIC JOURNAL, vol. 76, pp. 344–57.
Amsden, A. E. (1989). *Asia's Next Giant: South Korea and Late Industrialisation*, Oxford: Oxford University Press.
Arrow, K. J. (1962). 'The economic implications of learning by doing.' *Review of Economic Studies*, vol. 29, pp. 155–73.
Atkinson, A. B. (1969). 'The time-scale of economic models: how long is the long run?' *Review of Economic Studies*, vol. 36, pp. 137–52.
—— and Stiglitz, J. E. (1969). 'A new view of technological change.' ECONOMIC JOURNAL, vol. 79, pp. 573–8.
Barro, R. J. (1989a). 'A cross-country study of growth, saving and government', National Bureau of Economic Research Working Paper No. 2855, February.
—— (1989b). 'Economic growth in a cross-section of countries', National Bureau of Economic Research Working Paper No. 3120, September.
Bautista, R. *et al.* (1981). *Capital Utilisation in Manufacturing*, Washington: The World Bank.
Betancourt, R. and Clague, C. (1981). *Capital Utilisation*, New York: Cambridge University Press.
Bruton, H. (1989). 'Import substitution', Chapter 30 in (H. Chenery and T. N. Srinivasan eds.), *Handbook of Development Economics*, Volume 2, Amsterdam: North Holland.
Cass, D. (1965). 'Optimum economic growth in an aggregative model of capital accumulation.' *Review of Economic Studies*, vol. 32, pp. 233–40.
Chenery, H. B. (1979). *Structural Change and Development Policy*, New York: Oxford University Press.
—— (1983). 'Interaction between theory and observation in development.' *World Development*, vol. 11, pp. 853–61.
——, Robinson, S. and Syrquin, M. (1986). *Industrialisation and Growth: A Comparative Study*, Washington: World Bank.
—— and Syrquin, M. (1975). *Patterns of Development, 1950–1970*, London: Oxford University Press.
Denison, E. F. (1967). *Why Growth Rates Differ: Post-War Experience in Nine Western Countries*, Washington: Brookings Institution.
Drandakis, E. M. and Phelps, E. S. (1966). 'A model of induced invention, growth and distribution.' ECONOMIC JOURNAL, vol. 74, pp. 541–7.
Drèze, J. P. and Sen, A. K. (1990). *Hunger and Public Action*, Oxford: Oxford University Press.
—— and Stern, N. H. (1987). 'The theory of cost-benefit analysis.' In *Handbook of Public Economics* (eds A. Auerbach and M. Feldstein). North Holland: Elsevier Science Publishers BV.
Griliches, Z. (ed.) (1984). *R and D, Patents and Productivity*, Chicago: University of Chicago Press.
Grossman, G. M. and Helpman, E. (1990). 'Product development and international trade.' *Journal of Political Economy*. Forthcoming.
Gupta, S. P. (1989). *Planning and Development in India*, New Delhi: Allied.
Hahn, F. H. and Matthews, R. C. O. (1964). 'The theory of economic growth.' ECONOMIC JOURNAL, vol. 74, pp. 779–902, reprinted Macmillan, 1967.
Harrod, R. F. (1939). 'An essay in dynamic theory.' ECONOMIC JOURNAL, vol. 49, pp. 14–33.
Hicks, J. R. (1973). 'The mainspring of economic growth.' *Swedish Journal of Economics*, vol. 75, pp. 336–48.
Kaldor, N. (1957). 'A model of economic growth.' ECONOMIC JOURNAL, vol. 67, pp. 591–624.
—— (1961). 'Capital accumulation and growth.' In *The Theory of Capital* (eds F. A. Lutz and D. C. Hague). London: Macmillan.
—— and Mirrlees, J. A. (1962). 'A new model of economic growth'. *Review of Economic Studies*, vol. 29, pp. 174–90.

Kennedy, C. (1964). 'Induced bias in innovation and the theory of distribution.' ECONOMIC JOURNAL, vol. 74, pp. 541–7.

King, M. A. and Robson, M. (1989). 'Endogenous growth and the role of history.' LSE Financial Markets Group Discussion Paper No. 63, October.

Kirzner, I. (1987). 'Austrian school of economics.' In The New Palgrave: a Dictionary of Economics (Eatwell, J., Milgate, M. and Newman, P. eds.), London: Macmillan.

Koopmans, T. C. (1965). 'On the concept of optimal growth.' Pontificia Academia Scientiarum, pp. 225–88, Vatican City.

Kneese, A. V. and Sweeney, J. L. (eds.) (1988). Handbook of Natural Resources and Energy Economics, Amsterdam: North Holland.

Krueger, A. O. (1978). Liberalization Attempts and Consequences, New York: National Bureau of Economic Research.

Kuznets, S. (1955). 'Economic growth and income inequality.' American Economic Review, vol. 65, pp. 1–29.

—— (1961). 'Quantitative aspects of the economic growth of nations: IV. Long-term trends in capital formation proportions.' Economic Development and Cultural Change, vol. 9, pp. 1–124.

—— (1963). 'Quantitative aspects of economic growth of nations: VIII Distribution of income by size.' Economic Development and Cultural Change, vol. 11 (2), pp. 1–80.

—— (1966). Modern Economic Growth, New Haven: Yale University Press.

—— (1971). Economic Growth of Nations: Total Output and Production Structure, Cambridge, Mass: Harvard University Press.

Lewis, W. A. (1954). 'Economic development with unlimited supplies of labour.' Manchester School, vol. 22, pp. 139–91.

—— (1955). The Theory of Economic Growth, Homewood, Ill.: Irwin.

Lucas, R. E. (1988). 'On the mechanics of economic development.' Journal of Monetary Economics, vol. 22, pp. 3–42.

Marx, K. (1867). Das Kapital: Volume 1, English Edition (1974), London: Lawrence and Wishart.

Mirrlees, J. A. (1967). 'Optimum growth when technology is changing.' Review of Economic Studies, vol. 34, pp. 95–124.

Morris, C. and Adelman, I. (1988). Comparative Patterns of Economic Development 1850–1914, Maryland: John Hopkins University Press.

Phan-Thuy, N. (1981). Industrial Capacity and Employment, Westmead: International Labour Organisation.

Platteau, J. Ph. (1990). 'Land reform and structural adjustment in sub Saharan Africa: controversies and guidelines.' Report prepared for the Food and Agricultural Organisation, August.

Porter, M. E. (1990). The Comparative Advantage of Nations, London: Macmillan.

Reynolds, J. (1983). 'The spread of economic growth to the third world: 1850–1980.' Journal of Economic Literature, vol. 21, pp. 941–80.

Romer, P. M. (1986). 'Increasing returns and long-run growth.' Journal of Political Economy, vol. 94, pp. 1002–37.

—— (1989). 'Capital accumulation in the theory of long-run growth.' In Modern Macroeconomics (ed. R. Barro), Cambridge, Mass.: Harvard University Press.

—— (1990). 'Endogenous technical change.' Journal of Political Economy (forthcoming).

Schumpeter, J. A. (1954). Capitalism, Socialism, and Democracy, 4th edition, London: Allen and Unwin.

Scott, M. F-G. (1989). A New View of Economic Growth, Oxford: Oxford University Press.

Shell, K. (1973). 'Inventive activity, industrial organisation and economic growth.' In Models of Economic Growth, (J. A. Mirrlees and N. H. Stern eds.), London: Macmillan.

Sheshinski, E. (1967). 'Optimal accumulation with learning by doing.' In Essays on the Theory of Optimal Growth, (K. Shell eds.), Cambridge, Mass.: MIT Press.

Solow, R. (1956). 'A contribution to the theory of economic growth.' Quarterly Journal of Economics, vol. 70, pp. 65–94.

—— (1957). 'Technical change and the aggregate production function.' Review of Economics and Statistics, vol. 39, pp. 312–20.

Spence, A. M. (1984). 'Cost reduction, competition and industry performance.' Econometrica, vol. 52, pp. 101–21.

Stern, N. H. (1989). 'The economics of development: a survey.' ECONOMIC JOURNAL, vol. 99, pp. 597–685.

—— (1991). 'Public policy and the economics of development.' European Economic Review (forthcoming).

Summers, R. and Heston, A. (1988). 'A new set of international comparisons of real product and price levels estimates for 130 countries, 1950–1985.' Review of Income and Wealth, pp. 1–25.

Targetti, F. and Thirlwall, A. P. (eds.) (1989). The Essential Kaldor, London: Duckworth.

Thomas, J. (1991). Informal Economic Activity, Deddington, Philip Allan, forthcoming.

Tirole, J. (1988). The Theory of Industrial Organisation, Cambridge: MIT Press.

UNIDO (1990). India: New Dimensions of Industrial Growth, Oxford: Basil Blackwell.

Uzawa, H. (1965). 'Optimum technical change in an aggregative model of economic growth.' International Economic Review, vol. 6, pp. 18–31.

Vickers, J. and Yarrow, G. (1988). Privatization: An Economic Analysis, Cambridge: MIT Press.

ANOTHER CENTURY OF ECONOMIC SCIENCE*

Joseph E. Stiglitz

I. METHODOLOGICAL INNOVATION: THE TRIUMPHS OF TWENTIETH-CENTURY ECONOMICS

There is a widespread consensus that during the past century, economic science has come of age. It has developed powerful statistical tools to analyse economic data, to make forecasts, and to test alternative hypotheses, and it has employed sophisticated mathematical techniques to articulate its theories and to prove basic theorems characterising the economy. Samuelson (1947) encapsulated the mid-century enthusiasm for the scientific method in his classic *Foundations of Economic Analysis,* arguing that economics should be based on observable behaviour and testable hypotheses, and, with his theory of revealed preference, showing how this could be done with the theory of consumers' behaviour.[1]

II. METHODOLOGY OVER SUBSTANCE? OR IDEOLOGY OVER SCIENCE?

Yet, in spite of these methodological triumphs, the subject does not bear all the hallmarks of some of the other sciences. Most strikingly, while economists of many persuasions may agree about the tools to be employed, there is no agreement about the basic economic model for describing the economy: while in many circles, the competitive model, with perfectly informed agents, rational consumers and value maximising firms, is believed to provide the foundations for understanding both the aggregative behaviour of the economy and its components, in other circles, that model is viewed with some circumspection. Evidently, the tools are not strong enough to discriminate among fundamentally different hypotheses, or at least not strong enough to overcome differences in prior beliefs, beliefs which are often influenced by ideological concerns.

III. TWENTY-FIRST CENTURY ECONOMICS: CLOSER TO A TRUE SCIENCE?

My hope – and belief – is that the next century will be marked by a greater confluence of ideas, a greater degree of agreement on the underlying descriptions of the economy, not just on the tools used to analyse it. To be sure, economists will continue to differ in the detailed interpretation of events, and in the appropriateness of a particular model to a particular situation.

* Financial support from the National Science Foundation and the Hoover Institution are gratefully acknowledged.
[1] The irony that the logical foundations of Logical Positivism had already been severely attacked by the time that Samuelson tried to import it into economics need not detain us here.

IV. A GENERAL ECONOMIC THEORY, SYNTHESISING MACROECONOMICS AND MICROECONOMICS

The disparity in how different economists view the economy is perhaps most apparent if we reflect on the two great achievements of the past century: the development of the neoclassical–Walrasian paradigm, including the proofs of the fundamental theorems of welfare economics, the formal articulation of Adam Smith's invisible hand conjecture on the efficiency of market economies; and the development of Keynesian economics, with its argument that capitalist economies may be characterised by unemployment equilibria. The view of capitalism reflected in these two achievements seem diametrically opposed, and not even Samuelson's assertion of the neoclassical synthesis – that the economy, once the problems of unemployment were corrected, was well described by the neoclassical model – could smooth over the obvious schizophrenia in the profession. As I have written elsewhere (Greenwald and Stiglitz, 1987), there were two obvious remedies: making macroeconomics like neoclassical microeconomics (the new classical and real business cycle theories); and trying to develop a microeconomics which yielded aggregative implications which were more consistent with the observed behaviour. As the memories of the Great Depression and the multitude of other, earlier episodes of mass unemployment receded, the former school enjoyed a brief moment in the sun – maybe the Great Depression was not that bad, after all! But events have an uncanny way of interfering with such euphoria about the market economy, and the extended periods of high unemployment in Europe have placed new emphasis on research attempting to provide the micro-foundations of unemployment and business fluctuations. During the next century, I am confident that we will construct a unified theory, based on the recognition of the importance of information costs and other imperfections in labour, capital, and product markets.[2]

V. THE DEMISE OF EARLY TWENTIETH-CENTURY NEOCLASSICAL ECONOMICS[3]

One of the great achievements of the neoclassical economics of the past half century is the formulation of testable hypotheses. Some of the most interesting – such as the Modigliani–Miller theorem, showing that firm financial structure did not matter, and its correlate implication, that investment and other aspects

[2] As, for example, sketched out in my 1987 paper with Bruce Greenwald which discusses both information problems in the labour market (efficiency wage theories) and in the capital market, and in subsequent work. Other strands of ongoing research, such as those stressing the role of increasing returns and complementaries, will undoubtedly play a part in the unified theory which will ultimately be developed.

[3] There seems no agreed-upon definition of neoclassical economics; by some, the term neoclassical is synonymous with 'good'; thus recent work in transactions costs and information economics is embraced as part of neoclassical economics. I am using the term here (with the qualifier 'early twentieth century,' lest there be any confusion) to represent the perfect competition, perfect market model in all of its representations, including Samuelson's *Foundations*, Arrow–Debreu, and Modigliani–Miller.

of firm behaviour did not depend on firm balance sheet and cash flow variables – have been tested and rejected, both on the basis of casual empiricism and detailed econometric studies. While debates remain about which of the assumptions underlying the analysis is *most* faulty, e.g. the absence of bankruptcy, the assumption of perfect information, the hypothesis that firm income in each state of nature is fixed (unaffected by firm behaviour, which in turn might be affected by financial structure), the absence of transactions costs, it is clear that dropping any one of these assumptions leads to markedly different results.

The economists of the twentieth century, by pushing the neoclassical model to its logical conclusions, and thereby illuminating the absurdities of the world which they had created, have made an invaluable contribution to the economics of the coming century: they have set the agenda, work on which has already begun. We have already seen how the information theoretic paradigm can explain behaviour in the capital market (such as credit rationing and red-lining), product market (such as price dispersion and a variety of arrangements, such as non-linear pricing, intended to price discriminate in an environment in which informational imperfections limit perfect price discrimination), and labour market (with wages set at levels above market clearing).

VI. THE NEW INSTITUTIONAL ECONOMICS

Not only does this strand of literature offer the hope of providing the micro-foundations required to explain observed aggregative behaviour of the economy, but it also provides an explanation of many of the central institutional features of the economy. In the earlier part of the century there were major conflicts between institutional economists, who saw the particular arrange-ments by which particular economies conducted their economic affairs as essential, and neoclassical economists, who sought to see through these inessential details to the underlying fundamental forces – the forces of demand and supply. By the middle of the century, the triumph of neoclassical economics was – almost – complete, certainly in America and England, and by 1980, even in Germany. Yet, before the death-knell had been sounded, a New Institutional Economics had arisen, attempting to use the new insights to explain the institutions and to examine their consequences. For instance, Cheung (1969) argued that transactions costs could explain the institution of sharecropping, while Stiglitz (1974) developed a theory of sharecropping based on the costs of monitoring workers' effort. While both theories provided explanations of the persistence and pervasiveness of this institution, and even provided suggestions of the conditions under which one might expect it to become relatively less important, they had markedly different implications for, for instance, the consequences of a land reform. I expect that during the next century, this New Institutional economics will flourish, providing insights into more and more of the detailed arrangements through which economic affairs are conducted, and in some cases, provide bases for altering those arrangments in ways which will enhance economic efficiency.

VII. ORGANISATIONAL ECONOMICS AND COMPARATIVE ECONOMIC SYSTEMS

The major *economic* event of the latter part of the twentieth century has undoubtedly been the demise of socialism. While the desirability of socialism was a central subject of discussion in debates (e.g. between Hayek and Von Mises, on the one hand, and Lange-Lerner-Taylor on the other) during the first half of the century, it was not until the development of information economics during the past fifteen years that the nature of the information problem stressed by Hayek in his classic (1945) paper has been better understood.[4] We have begun to understand, for instance, *which* of the many information problems facing an economy prices really adequately address. As the former socialist economies think about the kind of economic system they would like to adopt – is there, for instance, a 'third way'? – their discussions have focused attention on such central issues as the role of property and the role of competition. The exploration of these questions, and an enhanced understanding of the merits of alternative economic systems, is likely to be another major achievement of economics of the next century.[5, 6]

One aspect of this analysis will focus on the economics of organisations. Most economic activity occurs within organisations, within which only limited use is made of the price system. It has frequently been observed that General Motors is larger than many economies. The success of the economy depends not just on how well markets work, but how well these organisations work. We have only just begun the exploration of how organisations function, what are the consequences of alternative ways of organising decision making, and what are the interactions between organisational design and incentives. (See, for example, Sah and Stiglitz (1985).) We know, for instance, that rent-seeking behaviour may be important within private organisations, just as it is in the public sphere.[7] While I predict major advances in this area, which until recently has remained on the periphery of mainstream economics, I see one major obstacle that will limit the success of this research endeavour: the interactions within organisations, particularly small organisations, are governed not just by the narrow 'rational' concerns upon which economics has traditionally focused. (See Simon and March (1955).)

VIII. BROADENING THE 'RATIONAL ECONOMIC MODEL'

The deficiencies in the 'rational actor' model have long been recognised, but economists have defended their pursuit of the rational actor model on the grounds that it was the best game in town: it gave well-defined (refutable, and,

---

[4] For a fuller discussion of these issues, see Stiglitz (1990).

[5] Whether the recent literature on mechanism design will contribute significantly to these discussions remains a moot question. So far, it has not.

[6] Already, these discussions have made clear the central importance of certain 'institutional' features (including laws regulating competition and bankruptcy) which were ignored in traditional neoclassical economics, though focused upon in the imperfect information–imperfect markets paradigm.

[7] See Hannaway (1989) or Milgrom and Roberts (1990).

unfortunately, refuted) predictions, while the alternative was a Pandora's box – there was an infinity of possible irrational behaviours.

Just as one of the great contributions of twentieth-century neoclassical economics was to make clear why considerations which they had excluded from their analyses – such as information and transactions costs – simply *had* to be brought into the analysis, so too one of the central contributions of game theory has been to make it clear that the 'rational' actor model is not only descriptively inaccurate (as earlier economists had charged), but internally incomplete and/or inconsistent (see Binmore (1987, 1988) and Reny (1985)). The hope of game theory that some simple version of rationality could lead to well-defined, let alone reasonable, predictions of behaviour has been dashed. Game theorists have increasingly relied in their analyses on 'small' degrees of irrationality, while at the same time showing that the exact nature of the equilibrium depends precisely on the nature of these small irrationalities (see Fudenberg and Maskin (1990)). This research makes it clear (if it was not already so) that economists must study how individuals actually behave, whether that conforms to some economists' preconception of rationality or not.

Fortunately, advances in sociology and psychology (see, for example, the work of Tversky) have shown that there may be systematic patterns to individual behaviour, even when they are irrational. Economic science is concerned with exploring predictable behaviour; the fact that behaviour is not rational, in some sense, does not mean that is not predictable. Akerlof, in a variety of papers, has shown that these concerns can be incorporated into economic models. I anticipate that over the next century major advances in this direction will occur. At the same time, different people behave differently in different situations. It is not clear that there will emerge out of this work a general theory – a theory of the generality of the 'rational actor' model.

IX. THE ROLE OF GOVERNMENT

Deciding on the appropriate role for government has long been one of the central concerns of economics. This, too, is one of the questions which the former socialist economies are now asking themselves. As the century draws to a close, many of the achievements of twentieth-century economics in this regard are being called into question.

First, the Fundamental Theorems of Welfare Economics provided not only the formal articulation of Adam Smith's invisible hand conjecture, they also provided the framework for the market failures approach to the role of government. Yet, more recently, Greenwald and Stiglitz (1986, 1988) have shown that whenever markets are incomplete and information is imperfect – that is, essentially, always – the economy is almost never constrained Pareto efficient; there are, in principle, government interventions, consistent with the limitations on markets and information, which can make some individuals better off without making anyone else worse off.

The market failures approach itself was attacked by the Public Choice economists, who emphasised that one had to analyse the behaviour of the government in terms of rational behaviour of voters, bureaucrats, and special interest groups. But while these theories share with stock market analysts the ability to provide ready interpretations of whatever occurs, their success in predicting these political forces is much more limited. How do we explain why alleged rent-seeking behaviour interferes with economic efficiency in Pakistan, but has much more limited deleterious effects in Korea; why corruption in Korea was a problem in some periods and not in others; why agriculture is subsidised in those countries where it is small and taxed where it is large; why the same pattern does not exist for other commodities; why was there 'regulatory capture' in some states, in some industries and not in others? If economists really believed these models, why devote so much effort to changing the Common Agriculture policy? Surely the words of a few economists cannot change the economic realities?

Yet the centrality of the issues will ensure that these issues will continue to be a primary focus of research in the coming century. I envisaged considerable advances in defining the ways in which government is different from other economic institutions,[8] understanding the circumstances under which markets are not constrained Pareto efficient and devising institutional arrangements which will enable the government to effect Pareto improvements, and in enhancing our understanding of public failures, both the circumstances in which they occur and the reasons for them. These advances, I suspect, will make use of the insights into organisations and the broader perspectives on economic behaviour described in the preceding two subsections.

X. DYNAMICS

The formal achievements in dynamic economics of the past century are indeed impressive; these include developments in linear and nonlinear business cycles, chaos, turnpike theory, and neoclassical growth theory. We have come to recognise the central role of expectations, and the kind of dichotomy common in the earlier part of the century, where ad hoc dynamics are adjoined to sophisticated equilibrium behaviour, is now eschewed by the profession at large. Yet, when all is said and done, while our mathematical tools for analysing dynamics are greatly improved, I am not sure that we have learned a great deal about either the short- or long-run dynamics of the economy. Short-run dynamic models have ignored the central role that credit constraints, partly based on information asymmetries, play.

In the long run, technological change is central, as Schumpter emphasised and as the neoclassical growth models of the 1960s helped to quantify. We now have a *better* understanding of the microeconomics of technological change, and work has begun on the construction of macroeconomic models based on those microeconomic foundations, models which reflect some of Schumpeter's views concerning the role of credit constraints and imperfect competition. These models incorporate both learning by doing and R & D expenditures.

Though over the years, economists have played a certain amount of lip-service to evolutionary processes and the role of natural selection, there has

[8] I have attempted a beginning of this line of enquiry in Stiglitz (1989).

been relatively little formal modelling of this evolutionary process,[9] of the role that bankruptcy laws and competition policy play in that process, and indeed, no evaluation of the efficiency with which that process works, and upon what that depends.

These failures have increasingly been recognised, and the work that has recently begun trying to remedy these deficiencies at least holds out the hope that over the coming decades, significant progress will be made.

XI. THE FAILURES OF TWENTY-FIRST-CENTURY ECONOMICS

I have dwelt extensively on what I see as the most important achievements of economics over the next century: the development of a general economic theory, unifying macroeconomics and microeconomics, able both to explain its aggregative behaviour and the details of some of its more important institutions.

I have forecast partial success in three other dimensions: an understanding of the economic behaviour of organisations, within which so much economic activity occurs; a development which in turn will be based on an incorporation into economics of systematic findings of other social sciences, notably psychology and sociology; and an enhanced understanding of the economic role of the government, and the development of a theory of public failure to parallel our analysis of market failure. Within the more developed countries, these enhanced understandings will, I am confident, lead to better public economic policies and greater economic efficiency, both within the public and private sectors, contributing a modicum to an enhanced standard of living.

There is one important area in which I am less sanguine about the future success of our profession. I began the study of economics with the (admittedly naive) hope that the study of economics would somehow enable something to be done about the plight of the three-quarters of mankind living in desperate poverty, particularly within the Third World. In the ensuing quarter of a century, we have seen remarkable growth in several countries, some of which have moved out of the ranks of the less developed. In each case, we can, with the vision of hindsight, tell stories about what led to success. But we have no prescription, no formula with which to go to those who remain among the poor, which gives them even a reasonable hope of success. Indeed, we can only imperfectly guess which among the LDCs will be successful, or even which of the more developed countries will fail to grow. Who in the middle of the nineteenth century, could have forecast the fortunes of England and Argentina? In the ensuing century, several of the less developed countries will undoubtedly join the ranks of the middle and upper income countries. If we are lucky, our studies of developing countries will enable a few more countries to escape the mire of poverty within which they have lived for centuries. We can only try.

Stanford University

REFERENCES

Akerlof, George A. (1982). 'Labor contracts as partial gift exchange.' *Quarterly Journal of Economics*, vol. 97, November, pp. 543–69.

[9] There are, of course, exceptions; see, for example, Nelson and Winter (1982).

Arrow, Kenneth (1964). 'The role of securities in the optimal allocation of risk bearing.' *Review of Economic Studies*, vol. 31, pp. 91–6.

Binmore, K. (1987 and 1988). 'Modelling rational players I and II.' *Economics and Philosophy*, 3 and 4, pp. 179–214 and pp. 9–55.

Cheung, Steven (1969). 'Transactions costs, risk aversion, and the choice of contractual arrangements.' *Journal of Law and Economics*, vol. 12, pp. 23–42.

Debreu, G. (1959). *The Theory of Value*. New York: Wiley.

Fudenberg, D. and Maskin, E. (1990). 'Evolution and cooperation in noisy repeated games.' *American Economic Review Papers and Proceedings*, vol. 80, no. 2, pp. 274–9.

Greenwald, Bruce and Stiglitz, J. E. (1986). 'Externalities in economies with imperfect information and incomplete markets.' *Quarterly Journal of Economics*, May, pp. 229–64.

—— and —— (1987). 'Keynesian, New Keynesian and New Classical Economics.' *Oxford Economic Papers*, vol. 39, pp. 119–33, subsequently reprinted in (ed. P. J. N. Sinclair), *Price, Quantities and Expectations*, pp. 119–33. Oxford: Oxford University Press.

—— and —— (1988). 'Pareto inefficiency of market economies: search and efficiency wage models.' *American Economic Association Papers and Proceedings*, vol. 78, no. 2.

Hannaway, Jane, (1989). *Managing Managers*. Oxford: Oxford University Press.

Hayek, F. A. (1945). 'The use of knowledge in society.' *American Economic Review*, vol. 35, September, pp. 519–30.

March, James G. and Simon, Herbert A. (1958). *Organizations*. New York: Wiley.

Milgrom, Paul and Roberts, John, (1990). 'Bargaining and influence costs and organization of economic activity.' *American Economic Review*, vol. 80, no. 3, pp. 511–29.

Miller, M. H. and Modigliani, Franco (1958). 'The cost of capital, corporate finance and the theory of investment.' *American Economic Review*, vol. 48, June, pp. 261–97.

Nelson, Richard R. and Winter, Signey G. (1982). *An Evolutionary Theory of Economic Change*. Cambridge, MA: Belknap Press of Harvard University Press.

Reny, P. (1985). 'Rationality, common knowledge, and the theory of games.' Princeton University Department of Economics mimeo.

Sah, Raaj and Stiglitz, J. E. (1985). 'Human fallibility and economic organization.' *American Economic Review Papers and Proceedings*, vol. 75, May, pp. 292–7.

Samuelson, Paul (1947). *Foundations of Economic Analysis*. Cambridge, MA: Harvard University Press.

Stiglitz, J. E. (1974). 'Incentives and risk sharing in sharecropping.' *Review of Economic Studies*, vol. 41, April, pp. 219–55.

—— (1989). 'On the economic role of the state.' In *The Economic Role of the State* (ed. A. Heertje). Amsterdam: Bank Insinger de Beaufort NV.

—— (1990). 'Whither socialism? perspectives from the economics of information.' Wicksell Lectures, presented at Stockholm, May.

THE NEXT HUNDRED YEARS

Stephen J. Turnovsky

Given the difficulties of making predictions in social sciences, to forecast the development of economics over the next hundred years is a daunting task. It represents almost 50 % of the modern history of the discipline as measured say from the publication of Adam Smith's *Wealth of Nations* in 1776. One way to get some idea of what kinds of changes a time period of this length is likely to entail is to look at how the discipline has evolved over the past hundred years. For this purpose one can view the ECONOMIC JOURNAL as being representative of the profession and I have used this opportunity to take a quick look at the evolution of the JOURNAL over the past century.

In comparing early issues of the JOURNAL with current issues, the following observations are immediately apparent. First, the early issues were much more general, and by today's standards, more applied. There was a heavy concentration of papers dealing with various issues in labour economics, including strike activity. Many papers discussed issues pertaining to agricultural topics, as well as the value of land, rent, and the role of railways. Several papers dealt with different aspects of economic conditions in various parts of the British Commonwealth. But at the same time, the early issues included subjects which continue to be topical today. for example, Vol. 1 included a paper entitled 'The Alleged Difference in the Wages Paid to Men and Women for Similar Work'. Vol. 2 contained a paper entitled, 'A Fixed Value of Bullion Standard – A Proposal for Preventing General Fluctuations of Trade', covering another topic which continues to be widely discussed today. As a third example, Vol. 2 also includes a paper entitled 'Influence of Opinion on Markets'. The same topic today is being discussed under the heading of the theory of expectations and the role of information. There are many other examples of issues which are being actively studied today, the origins of which appear in early volumes of the JOURNAL. In this respect, the subject has exhibited a certain stability over the past century.

The methods of analysis were, of course, very different. Early articles were almost entirely literary with a few statistical tables occasionally being included to provide quantitative support for the arguments. One notable exception to this was the sophisticated mathematical and geometric treatment of the theory of utility by Edgeworth in Volume 4, although this was a restatement of a literary treatment presented in an earlier article.

The evolution of the discipline as reflected in the ECONOMIC JOURNAL did not proceed at an even rate. Volume 50, published in 1940, looks much more like the early volumes than the more recent ones, both in content and in terms of the analytical methods employed. To that time, the use of mathematics and statistical methods was rare. Indeed, it is only in the last 30 years or so that mathematics and econometrics have been used as an integral part of economic analysis.

As one looks through the ECONOMIC JOURNAL and other journals, it is clear that the use of increasingly sophisticated analytical methods is associated with increased specialisation of the profession. Over the first 75 years of the last century, most articles would have been of interest to a large fraction of the economists of the time and certainly accessible to them. During the past 25 years this has clearly changed. Economists are now typically pigeon-holed into one category or another. They are either microeconomists, macroeconomists, labour economists, international economists, public finance economists, resource economists, econometricians etc., frequently having an interest in only their subarea of expertise and ignoring, and being happy to ignore, other areas of the discipline. Even within an area such as macroeconomics, they may be further classified according to whether they belong to the MIT School, the Chicago School, the Minnesota School etc., depending upon their style of training. This increased compartmentalisation of the profession is exacerbated by two developments. The first is the growth in the last 20 years or so of specialist journals, although perhaps one can argue that this is a response rather than a cause. Also, for marketing purposes, especially in the United States, it is important for a job candidate to be firmly identified with a particular subarea of the discipline. Anyone claiming to have a broad expertise is treated with suspicion.

While one might find the increased segmentation of the discipline to be unfortunate, it is perhaps an inevitable consequence of the maturing of our subject. As progress is made into understanding the various branches and processes of economics, more detailed knowledge and expertise is required. This involves investment on the part of the individual in certain analytical techniques, necessitating his specialisation to that subarea. This process of specialisation characterises much older disciplines such as mathematics and physics, so it is not too surprising that it should come to characterise economies as well.

There are several aspects of economics as it is currently practised which I find to be troubling and which I hope will be reversed over the next several years. First, economics, particularly in the United States, is very much subject to fads. Certain topics become hot for a period, consuming a lot of research effort, only to become obsolete in a relatively short period of time and to be superseded by something else. In this process, sometimes something of lasting value remains, but very often, the time spent is insufficient to make real progress on the problem.

For example, the theory of economic growth was in vogue for about 15 years around 1955–70. During that period many elegant variants of the neoclassical growth model were developed. While undoubtedly several aspects of the process of economic growth and capital accumulation became better understood, our knowledge of this fundamental process was certainly less than complete by 1970. Moreover, the research of that period tended to look at growth from a fairly narrow perspective and devote little attention to integrating it into the broader process of macroeconomic development. Yet since 1970, when attention turned to issues such as inflation, unemployment, and oil shocks, there has been relatively little interest in economic growth, though there is some evidence that interest in that subject is now reviving. But when considered within the time frame of 100 years, the decade or so when growth theory occupied centre stage really is not very long. It is hoped that in the future fundamental problems like this will receive more continued attention, even when for short periods of time they appear to be dominated by other current events.

Another example of a fad is certain aspects of the rational expectations hypothesis. I do not refer to the basic notion or methodology, as I regard its basic insight, namely stressing the importance of forward-looking behaviour, to be of fundamental importance. Rather, I refer to the association of rational expectations with the ineffectiveness of anticipated government policy. For a time some years ago, the profession seemed to be obsessed with trying to establish conclusively how rational expectations implied that policy rules were ineffective. Models in which policy rules were effective were sometimes ridiculed as being silly (irrational). It is now generally recognised that the so-called policy neutrality propositions associated with rational expectations are not robust. Under plausible conditions policy can still be effective with rational expectations, and in some circumstances, very effective indeed. In my opinion the value added of much of this debate, as opposed to the introduction and development of the rational expectations methodology itself, was dubious.

Secondly, I am concerned about certain methodological procedures which currently seem to be in fashion. It is becoming increasingly widespread in the development of macroeconomic theory, for example, to motivate a model, by coming up with some observed empirical regularities and show how these predictions are consistent with the model. It is not clear to me what this accomplishes. It would seem to me that we have a serious identification problem. Most observed patterns of behaviour can be reconciled with a range of models and frequently with many different patterns and types of disturbances within the same model. Unless one has complete information on all exogenous disturbances there does not seem to be any way of knowing precisely what the observed pattern of behaviour is reflecting. I contrast this with the practice of starting with the development of some model, presumably as rich, relevant, and interesting as is necessary and feasible and using this framework to enrich our understanding of the transmission of policy shocks and other disturbances on the behaviour of the economy. This approach was more characteristic of macroeconomics of the 1960s and 1970s and seems to have been less fashionable recently.

I think that it is important to return more to this procedure in the future. Economists generally enjoy at best a mixed press insofar as their ability to give policy advice is concerned. We are often ridiculed for the contradictory nature of the advice that we, as a profession give, or sometimes its equivocating nature. (On the one hand, ..., on the other hand, ...). But the fact is that the real world is a complicated place and that any policy change that is undertaken will impact on the economy through a variety of channels, giving rise to many influences, some of which invariably offset others. The contradictory advice which is often given may, in many cases, reflect different economists' views of the relative importance of different channels. This may be largely an empirical matter, on which there is little concrete evidence, and on which people may reasonably differ. I think that it is important that we continue to develop macroeconomic models which may throw insight on policy and help us understand the channels through which policies impact on the performance of the economy, both in the short run and over time.

For many years economics, and in particular macroeconomics, has been split by ideology. People have often talked about the Monetarist approach to a problem or a Keynesian approach to the problem and have often had to declare themselves as belonging to one camp or another. I have never found this labelling of approaches to be particularly useful. The absurdity of this was highlighted in an article published by Frankel, Glyfason and Helliwell in this JOURNAL in 1980, entitled 'A Synthesis of Monetary and Keynesian Approaches to Short-Run Balance of Payments Theory.' Using a very simple model, the authors show very clearly how the two alternatives are simply partial approaches and that a complete analysis incorporates both. I have always felt that is the right direction to go. If one is interested in studying a particular phenomenon, whether it be the balance of payments, supply shocks, or whatever, one should get on with the business of developing the best model one can to help our understanding of that problem, using whatever parts of theory we feel are appropriate. That may very well involve a synthesis as in the example just noted. I am pleased to see some breakdown of this type of ideology over the past decade or so and hope that this will continue.

What guide is all of this for the future of the discipline? In terms of methodology, the past 25 years have seen the establishment of the use of mathematics and statistics (econometrics) as integral parts of economic analysis. During this time, the development of dynamic and stochastic economic models has become firmly established. This process will presumably continue over the foreseeable future and one would hope and expect to see the refinement of these technical approaches.

Few would disagree that our analytical treatment of uncertainty is pretty primitive. Typically, it is represented by probability distributions, the relevant characteristics of which (means, variances, etc.) are assumed to be known to the agents in the economy. By any standard this is a restrictive representation of the issue. Moreover, in macroeconomics, where uncertainty is perhaps at its greatest, the analytical treatment is even more restrictive, in that the standard procedure is to introduce these known probability distributions in what is sometimes referred to as a 'certainty-equivalent' way. The focus is very much on the mean behaviour of relevant agents under uncertainty. Yet the interaction of mean behaviour with higher monuments, such as variances, is important, particularly if the insights of the theory of finance, with its emphasis on the tradeoffs between risk and return, are going to be integrated into a more general macroeconomic framework. Some work at a more generalised introduction of uncertainty in a macroeconomic framework along these lines is currently being pursued at both a theoretical and an empirical level. Hopefully this will continue throughout the near future. In the longer term one would like to see less restrictive representations of uncertainty incorporated into economics. But this is a very difficult task.

By the same token, the conventional analysis of economic dynamics is also highly restrictive. For the most part, formal dynamic analysis is usually carried out for linear systems or by taking linear approximations to more general systems. In important respects linear analysis is highly misleading and it is important to see the further application and development of nonlinear dynamic analysis. By its nature, a linear dynamic system will either ultimately converge to a specific equilibrium point, if stable, or will ultimately explode, if unstable. It is incapable of generating recurring cyclical behaviour. Yet this is the type of behaviour which best characterises many economic time series. This observation is not new and was well known to pioneers of nonlinear business cycle models such as Michal Kalecki and Richard Goodwin around 40 years ago. I suspect the problems of intractability they encountered at the time caused the theory of nonlinear business cycles to go into abeyance for a substantial period of time. Recently, there has been a revival of nonlinear dynamics in the form of chaotic behaviour, strange attractors etc., which may prove to be promising in economics. The use of these methods is heavy in computation, but the recent revolution in computation techniques indicates that the intractability encountered by the earlier authors is no longer a serious problem.

To pursue this a little further, consider, for example, an economic model which can be represented by a system of quadratic differential equations having the property that the linear part of the system is unstable, while the quadratic part exerts a stabilising influence. Such models can be constructed quite naturally, with the quadratic term arising as revenues (price times quantity). Research on models of this type (in other disciplines) shows that while the system is not stable in the sense of converging to a specific equilibrium point, it need not explode either. Rather it may remain within some bounded region. There is in effect a conflict between the unstable linear component, which drives it away from a stationary point, and the stable quadratic element, which attracts it back, when it gets too far away. This kind of framework can generate continuing cyclical economic behaviour and yields a kind of stability which is probably more relevant for ongoing dynamic economic systems. To my mind it represents an exciting approach to economic dynamics, which I hope will be pursued further in the coming years.

As noted, these methods of nonlinear dynamics are heavily numerical though with the rapid improvement in computational techniques over the recent past, this does not pose any particular problem. More generally, with the improved computational techniques one would expect a greater reliance on numerical methods in all branches of economics. This has already been happening and I would expect it to continue. The method of the numerical calibration of models and sensitivity analysis can be a very effective way of getting insight into the analytical properties of a particular economic system. At the same time, I find it puzzling that the recent revolution in computational facilities has not been accompanied by a proliferation of large computer-oriented econometric models. On the contrary, interest in the large mega models such as the Brookings model of the 1960s seems to be at a low ebb. Perhaps technical issues such as problems in identification, the likely non-stationarity of the underlying parameters, and the non-linearity of the system, may all help to provide an explanation of this.

The developments I have been discussing so far can largely be characterised as being 'incremental'. That is, they represent the evolution of existing analytical methods. An important question, to which I have no real answer, is whether at any time over the next one hundred years some quantum change in how the subject is studied will occur. By that I mean, will there be some event which causes a fundamental rethinking of the economic system? Obviously such events occur only infrequently. The *Wealth of Nations* and Keynes' *General Theory* are two such examples. Perhaps the Lucas Critique, developed in 1976, which caused fundamental rethinking of the theory of policy and the application of econometrics to macroeconomic systems, also falls into this category. While obviously one cannot predict the probability that such an event will occur, the increased specialisation of the subject, the increased formalisation, which tends to put much of economic theory into a strait-jacket, would seem to make such an event an unlikely occurrence. It is more likely to emerge from a looser structure than currently prevails. It is also probably the case that big breakthroughs are likely to occur at the early stages of a discipline, rather than as it matures.

What issues are likely to occupy the attention of economists over the next century? No doubt, to some extent, many of the present ones will continue. As noted earlier, glancing at the first few volumes of this JOURNAL indicated a certain continuity of issues and presumably the same will apply one hundred years hence. Unless inflation, unemployment, and oil shocks are eradicated, which seems unlikely, they presumably will be studied, at least intermittently, over the next century. Of course just as financial institutions have evolved, and national economic systems are currently changing at great rates, it is difficult to speculate what the national economy will look like in one hundred years. The unification of Europe in 1992 may be just the start of one big global economy. International economics may become obsolete, and macroeconomics of the closed economy, as it was taught for so long in the United States, may once again prevail!

Economics will undoubtedly branch out into other areas. One issue which occurs to me is the importance of spatial considerations. I have been stressing the role of time and risk as representing two dimensions of the economic process and I believe that space could become an equally important third dimension over the long term. To this point, it would seem to have played a peripheral role in economics. The development of urban economics and that of resource economics are regarded largely as specialised applied fields and are not at this time incorporated into the main body of basic economic theory. Yet it would seem that as the world gets more crowded, and the allocation of land to various alternative uses becomes more critical, one would expect that the spatial aspects of production and consumption will become more centrally integrated into the general body of economics.

In many respects, economics has made considerable progress over the last century. The analytical tools and models employed are often quite sophisticated. But the growth in specialisation which has been occurring has meant that the typical economist has brought these increasingly sophisticated tools to bear on increasingly narrower issues. The integration of the economic system into the broader political and social systems has been all but ignored. The welfare criterion of the typical economic model, namely the utility of consumption, is a narrow view of what is desirable. The political constraints facing policy-makers are generally ignored, or at best represented in some crude way such as by some kind of cost function. One of the challenges for economists for the next hundred years is to bring the more sophisticated tools to bear on a broader range of issues. I believe that the profession is well placed to meet that challenge.

University of Washington, Seattle

THE BLACK BOX

Jack Wiseman

I must begin with a justification, if not an apology.

I have long preached that mainstream economics is fundamentally flawed, not least by its inability or unwillingness to come to terms with the reality that the future is unknowable. How then can I accept an invitation to express a view about the state of economics a century from now?

There is a pragmatic reason. The position I espouse is uncomfortable for the dominant paradigm, and is consequently apt to be ignored, or dismissed as 'extreme' or 'destructive'. Although the heretics grow in numbers, and I become increasingly confident that they will be tomorrow's priests, that tomorrow will lie beyond my own lifetime, and the opportunity for a heretic to give his ideas an airing in this JOURNAL now is not lightly to be ignored.

The second reason is more respectable; or at least more scholarly. While I assert that the future is unknowable. I do not suggest that it is beyond conjecture. People's plans have unanticipated outcomes. This does not surprise them; but neither does it persuade them that purposive behaviour is pointless. We cannot know what the world will be like in a hundred years' time. But we can make conjectures, particularly about what is *not* likely. There is no guarantee that even the broadest of scenarios will not be wildly wrong; what will economists be doing if, for example, communities exercise their growing power to destroy one another? But it is by the use of imagination in the evolution of such scenarios that people decide how to act. Given the scope for error, it is questionable whether speculations about the state of the world a century from now are of much importance to people's decisions about how to act now. The benefit from focussing different minds on such a question is likely to relate less to our confidence in our ability to foresee what the distant future will actually be like, than to mutual learning from the nature of the insights and perceptions of others. At most, we may see a little through the glass, darkly. But it may not be without interest to learn what others think that they can see.

We can distinguish two aspects of our perception of the future; those concerned with the kind of intellectual constructs which people calling themselves economists will be using, and those, within this, which attempt to identify the nature of the actual problems with which such people will be preoccupied. Our ability to say anything about either is severely constrained. But we can perhaps be more confident that there will be a new perspective, and about the (very general) ways in which it will differ from the present, than we can about the particular issues that will command attention.

For example, the market may have become less dominant a particular topic, not just because of recognition of its inescapable embodiment in a broader set of social processes, but also because changing technology has caused other, not-yet-invented social arrangements to become preferable substitutes for the market process as we now know it. On the other hand, it is equally imaginable that the process of change will embody inventions which widen the scope and sophistication of markets, and in so doing radically alter the nature, scale and problems of non-market (government, etc.) arrangements and institutions. Within my inescapable ignorance, I feel less comfortable in speculating about this kind of detailed issue, than in reflecting upon how economists will be thinking (the general nature of their paradigm).

Accordingly, the most useful place to begin is with the way economists think now: with the dominant paradigm and its limitations. This will open the way for speculation about whether and how that situation might change, and what broad form the emergent new ideas might take. This in turn will support some reflections – I can put it no higher – as to what 'economics' might be 'about' in 2090, and what might by then have happened to the teaching of what passes for economics now.

THE STATE OF THE ART

It is tempting, but unduly optimistic, to see economics as in process of a paradigm change. There is need for a new paradigm, but the form it might take is as yet incompletely articulated. The subject is diversifying, but the theoretical coherence required of an alternative paradigm still lies in the future.

Certainly, the accepted wisdom (what might be labelled neoclassical positivism) is increasingly being questioned, and the need for a new paradigm is coming to be more generally accepted. But while it is possible to observe a growing consensus about the nature of the problems which the new paradigm will need to resolve, there has not evolved the kind of consensus between the dissidents which is requisite for the displacement of received doctrine.

There consequently exists a classic situation, in which the dominant paradigm can sustain its position through such means as (e.g.) control of established outlets (the 'recognised journals'); encouragement of conformity through control of power structures; mutual citation; and so on. At the same time, the absence of a well-articulated and agreed alternative can be used to reject specific criticism, or treat it as irrelevant or trivial. Galileo defeated the Church, it is argued, not by preaching but by 'science'; he had a demonstrably better theory. Failing a better theory, preaching is irrelevant. But this is a simplistic interpretation of the nature of intellectual change. To produce a new theory, Galileo had first to become aware that there was something which needed to be explained; observations which fitted uneasily within the received wisdom. Such observations have become important in economics. Those who ignore them because they are not accompanied by a fully-articulated theoretical construct capable of embracing them, simply impose the burden of search for such a construct upon others. They may in this way delay the process of paradigm change. They are unlikely to prevent it.

The growing dissatisfaction with the dominant neo-classical orthodoxy manifests itself in several ways. The major one is the emergence of more-or-less-fundamentally competitive schools of thought. Notable examples are the Austrian School, the New Institutionalists (particularly in relation to microeconomics and the theory of the firm), evolutionary economics, public choice, constitutional economics, behavioural economics, and the radical subjectivists personified by Shackle. Such dissident groups differ considerably, however, in the extent to which their intellectual position can be regarded (or would be regarded by themselves) as implying outright rejection of the neoclassical model rather than requiring its embellishment or modification. The now numerous adherents to 'the' Austrian School in the United States, for example, may belong to any one of several sub-groups, which all to different but usually significant degrees regard themselves as custodians of the 'true' neoclassical paradigm, in contrast with what they see as its perversion by mainstream (Chicago-positivist mathematical-econometric) economics. Equally, there is an important body of public choice literature which is essentially an extension of the neoclassical logic of choice, in contrast with 'political economy' public choice (now evolving into constitutional economics), which demands a much more radical shift in intellectual perspective. Other groups are even less conciliatory. The evolutionary economists, for example, dismiss the behavioural assumptions of neoclassical economics as destructively simplistic. The 'radical subjectivist' group is even more identified by dissent, insisting upon a specification of human choice as the use of imagination to adapt to an unknowable future. Such a specification of the nature of the human decision-process is simply incompatible with the intellectual constraints imposed by the neoclassical paradigm.

Another, related manifestation is the proliferation of new journals and periodicals in recent years. This no doubt owes something to the discovery by commercial publishers that journal publication can produce a steady flow of bread-and-butter income. But there is little doubt that it has also been encouraged by the perceived need for new outlets for heterodox views which do not readily find sufficient space in the established organs. A superficial scan of new titles supports this view. At least a dozen new journals/periodicals providing a forum for dissident (as distinct from simply specialised) views have been established within the last decade.

The dissident groups differ from each other as well as from neoclassical orthodoxy. The interesting question for the future concerns the extent to which they can be recognised to share significant common insights, of a kind that suggest that they could in time become part of a new common body of thought. It is my belief that two fundamental insights are widely shared. These concern, respectively, the possible nature and extent of our 'knowledge' of the future; and the need for a broader interpretation of the behaviour of man-as-a-choosing-animal. In these two respects, the world as defined by neoclassical economics cannot embrace important aspects of the actual world of human decision. The problem is not one of adaptation but of fundamental reappraisal; we need a different, more embracing paradigm.

UNDERSTANDING UNKNOWLEDGE

Human plans and decisions concern the future. In adapting to the future, people have available to them incomplete information about the past and partial information about the continuous present (the moving point of actual decision). They can have no 'information' about the future. Since it has yet to happen, there can be only opinion about it. In Shackle's graphic term, the future is characterised by 'unknowledge'. People will of course hold some opinions with more confidence than others. For example, their confidence that particular physical relationships (such as the sun rising) will continue to hold will be strong enough to render the difference between subjective and objective probability meaningless in respect of them. But in general the future is not of that kind: we expect it to contain events which we did not foresee. For it is of the essence of unknowledge that the future is unbounded. The problem is not simply that we do not know which of a possible set of futures will be the actual future; it is that we do not know the content of the possible set. In these circumstances, people will behave 'probabilistically' only insofar as they conceive this to be an efficient way of coping with unknowability, in which case a satisfactory explanation of their decision behaviour must explain not only the attachment of probabilities to conceived outcomes, but also the selection process by which the unknowable future is reduced by decision-makers to those finite 'relevant' outcomes.

Unknowledge presently poses two problems for economists. The first concerns acceptance of its implications and importance. There would appear to be two related obstacles. There is no doubt that neoclassical economics has been instrumental in greatly improving human understanding of the characteristics of scarcity, and there is reluctance to accept that an intellectual construct which has been so successful in the past will not, with appropriate modification, continue to be so in the future, particularly in the light of the increasing technical sophistication of the subject. But the technical sophistication has not seriously addressed the issue of unknowledge, and there is arguably little relation between our improved understanding of the real world and the growing sophistication of our models, while the more extreme manifestations of mathematical economics bear – and indeed would often claim to bear – only the most tenuous relation with the real world of actual decisions. At the same time, acceptance of the fundamental implications of an unknowable future has consequences for the obsolescence of the intellectual capital of economists which many are naturally reluctant to bear.

Nevertheless, as I have already argued, there is evidence of a growing recognition of the need to come to terms with this problem. The second problem however remains unresolved: what to do about it? How are we to evolve a theoretical framework which will preserve what is valuable in the neoclassical construct, yet provide the means to study purposive behaviour in the context of an unknowable future?

The observation that human decisions are not 'objective' but are acts of choice between futures conceived by individuals to be possible, is very damaging to the accepted paradigm, and is of itself enough to render many of the propositions deriving from it untrustworthy. But the creation of a superior alternative still lies before us. The necessary first step: a satisfactory specification of the nature of the decision-problem, is in my view now on the way to resolution. I can offer only the barest summary. People take decisions on the basis of historical information, embracing information about the actual outcome of past plans, and 'opinion' about possible futures. Through time, the input to the planning (decision) process is modified by emergent information, both from the ongoing outcomes of plans and from other sources. This 'learning process' modifies human decisions (influences the choice-process). But learning does not make the future more 'knowable'. There is no known nexus between the past, the continuous present and the future, and the bearing of new learning on adaptation to the emergent unknowable future is thus itself uncertain. Further, 'the future' is not something which exists independently of human action. The plans which emerge from human imagination and inventiveness themselves create the future, though not simply in the ways expected by the decision-takers.

If we postulate a 'black box' of 'unknowledge', which consists of 'things not conceived of' in human plans, we can envisage the (unknowable) content of that box as changing through time. It is being emptied from one side by human learning (the recent San Francisco earthquake demonstrated that earthquakes have become a component of the plans of people in that area, though at an earlier time such things clearly belonged in the 'black box'), but replenished from the other both by 'nature' and by the unforeseen consequences of human action. (It would be my own guess that it is the importance of 'future-creating' human activity that chiefly distinguishes our choice-behaviour from that of other animals: but that is perhaps by the way.)

Within this 'black box' context, it is possible to construct a taxonomy of decisions, of a kind that might be illustrated by a simple decision concerning the journey from home to office along a single route (the only opportunity-cost problem concerning whether to make the journey), through a simple choice between two possible routes, through the increasing complexities associated with variable traffic patterns (permitting serial decision-making), accidents, earthquakes, and the 'black box'. None of the decision-situations is to be envisaged as 'free from unknowability'. Their purpose is simply to provide a structured mode of thought about it.

What I am offering here is no more than a thumbnail description of a possible taxonomy. Its translation into more sophisticated models will be a major task: we are concerned not just with a logic of random events, which produces difficulties enough, but with the explanation of purposive behaviour which embraces the expectation of plan (decision) failure (in the sense of unanticipated outcomes). But the problem is beginning to attract increasing interest, among 'outsiders' as well as among economists. (Two interesting recent contributions, chosen for illustration, would be Allen (1988) and Holland (1988).) There is a long way to go; but I begin to believe that a hundred years from now, the dominant paradigm will embrace unknowledge as a central feature of the economic problem. As a corollary, I would expect current econometric techniques to have disappeared or become marginalised, being displaced by the much more general use of experimental methods.

THE DOMAIN OF CHOICE

Apart from its conceptual shortcomings in the treatment of subjectivity and unknowability, the treatment of choice in mainstream economics is also deficient in its interpretation of the relevant domain of choice-behaviour. Analysis is preoccupied with choice-through-markets, to the neglect of other significant choice-situations which are complementary to or potentially substitutable for market choice. When particular problems are seen to demand it, efforts are of course made to extend the core model. For example, special models of group behaviour have been developed as economists became aware that particular aspects of market behaviour could not be satisfactorily understood without them. Such models have two interesting characteristics. They develop as 'special studies' (of the behaviour of firms, trade unions, charities, or whatever), although it has become increasingly clear that they are part of a common extended logic of choice; and they became increasingly frustrated by the constraints of the original general model, and begin to break away from it. (An interesting example is the development of the theory of the firm through ever more sophisticated concepts of property and contracting towards integration with the 'breakaway' concepts of evolutionary economics.)

More generally, the theory of public choice attempts to extend the scope of the logic of choice to non-market situations. The literature, now extensive, began from dissatisfaction with an intellectual construct which supported policy recommendations derived from study of choice through the institutions of the market, while treating the institutions responsible for implementing those policies (the government and its agencies) as lying outwith the analysis. Development since then has followed two main lines. One of these considers alternative systems of choosing (such as voter behaviour) in contexts that need not formally require outright rejection of the constraints of the neoclassical model, so that 'public choice' becomes simply an additional dimension of the mainstream model. For the most part, this has the self-defeating consequence of emasculating the kind of direct study of the behaviour of government which the original insight might have been expected to promote. (The popular median voter model, for example, treats the government, once elected, as the passive agent of the wishes of that voter). The other line of development, followed notably by Buchanan (e.g. Buchanan, 1959), is concerned explicitly with the behaviour of government and its agencies, and uses a Wicksellian (right of veto) interpretation of efficient choice in place of the neoclassical welfare notion. At present, this 'new political economy' (whose most recent manifestation is the development of constitutional economics) is best described as existing in uneasy cohabitation with the dominant paradigm, in that its mentors are as yet reluctant simply to abandon the analytical aids furnished by neoclassical economics. But there are manifest and destructive inconsistencies between the two, and I am myself in no doubt either that the 'new political economy' offers the most fruitful potential for the future development of public choice, or that in course of time the new paradigm to which this development will contribute will require the assimilation of 'market choice' as an integral part of this broader choice-construct.

ECONOMICS IN 2090

The developments I have described suggest how economics might look (or perhaps I should say only: how I hope it will look), a hundred years from now. Economists will be working within a paradigm which accepts that human plans are characterised by unknowledge, and will study human behaviour in this environment using a logic of choice wide enough to embrace all aspects of choice-in-society. I would expect the study of market choice to continue to be of major importance, but in the context of a wider framework of choice which gave due weight to the interrelationships and dependencies between market and other institutional-choice arrangements.

In the unlikely event that this prediction proved accurate, it would have interesting implications for 'the profession' – the broad academic discipline now taught under the name of economics. Two related strands of development would be stimulated: the study of the wider logic of choice through the growing integration of present-day economics, political science, and significant areas of philosophy, as a 'new' discipline of political economy; and the development out of the present dissident groups of an integrated discipline of (broadly-defined) 'market-related' behaviour (which might well on the way displace the (non-training) disciplines of present-day business schools). Experimental and computer-related laboratory-based research will have largely replaced present-day econometrics. Insofar as this latter kind of activity, and the more esoteric branches of mathematical economics, continue to exist at all, they will occupy the kind of academic niche currently enjoyed by endowed Chairs of Divinity.

A final thought, which the Editor is welcome to excise should he think my piece too long: Since I expect scarcity still to be an endemic problem, I would predict that this JOURNAL will still exist in 2090. If its officers continue to show the capacity for using learning which has characterised them in the past, it will still enjoy its present prestige, though its content will be very different. There are other prestigious journals about which I would be less hopeful.

University of York

REFERENCES

Allen, P. M. (1988). 'Evolution, innovation, and economics.' In *Technical Change and Economic Theory* (Dosi, G., *et al.*, eds.). London: Pinter.
Buchanan, J. M. (1959). 'Positive economics, welfare economics, and political economy.' *Journal of Law and Economics*, vol. 11, pp. 124–38.
Holland, J. H. (1988). 'The global economy as an adaptive process.' In *The Economy as an Evolving Complex System* (Anderson, P. W. *et al.*, eds.). New York: Addison-Wesley.

INDEX

Note: Contributions to this book are shown in bold type.

THE ROYAL ECONOMIC SOCIETY

The Royal Economic Society was founded in 1890 as the British Economic Association and incorporated by Royal Charter in 1902, to promote the general advancement of economic knowledge. It is one of the oldest associations of economists in the world, with an international membership among professional economists in business, government service and higher education as well as individuals with an active interest in economic questions.

Among the advantages of membership are:

1 Free subscription to the *Economic Journal*, including the annual volume of Conference Papers for all members.

2 Members can submit articles and notes to the *Economic Journal* free of charge. Every two years the Royal Economic Society awards a prize of £1000 to the author(s) of the best paper published during that period.

3 Members can attend the Royal Economic Society conferences, including the new annual Easter Conference, at greatly reduced rates.

4 Members receive free copies of the Royal Economic Society quarterly Newsletter which contains a register of scholars visiting the UK, a diary of forthcoming events, plus other information about appointments and scholarships. From 1990 the Newsletter has doubled in size, to allow the speedy publication of reactions to the issues raised in the Policy Forum section of the *Journal*. David Greenaway is responsible for editing the new enlarged Newsletter.

5 Members are offered discounted copies of Royal Economic Society publications and some Blackwell Publishers' books.

6 Members can apply through the Society for permission to use the Reading Room of the British Library of Political Economic Science

Membership Rates for 1992:

£35 per annum (US $65). There is a reduced rate of £16 (US $28.50) for applicants under 30, members who have retired and members who reside in Third World Countries (with per capita incomes below US $500).

Applications for membership should be addressed to: Membership Secretary, Royal Economic Society, University of York, Heslington, York YO1 5DD, UK.

The *Economic Journal* is published six times a year in January, March, May, July, September and November, for the Royal Economic Society, by Blackwell Publishers.